Enjoy Your Symptom!

"Žižek's interest in pop culture, combined with his clear, conventional writing style, makes his books more accessible than most critical theory, perhaps to the greatest degree since Foucault."

San Francisco Bay Guardian

"A startling critic of great daring, who doesn't watch his back or observe the pieties as he swerves and swoops through the age of globalised images and fabricated realities."

Times Literary Supplement

"The most formidably brilliant exponent of psychoanalysis, indeed of cultural theory in general, to have emerged from Europe for some decades."

Terry Eagleton

Routledge Classics contains the very best of Routledge publishing over the past century or so, books that have, by popular consent, become established as classics in their field. Drawing on a fantastic heritage of innovative writing published by Routledge and its associated imprints, this series makes available in attractive, affordable form some of the most important works of modern times.

For a complete list of titles visit
www.routledge.com/classics

Slavoj

Žižek

Enjoy Your Symptom!

Jacques Lacan in Hollywood and Out

With a new preface by the author

Routledge
Taylor & Francis Group
NEW YORK AND LONDON

First published 1992 by Routledge

Second edition published 2001 by Routledge

First published in the Routledge Classics 2008
by Routledge
711 Third Avenue, New York, NY 10017

Simultaneously published in the UK
by Routledge
2 Park Square, Milton Park, Abingdon, Oxfordshire OX14 4RN

First issued in hardback 2015

Routledge is an imprint of the Taylor & Francis Group, an informa business

Typeset in Joanna by RefineCatch Limited, Bungay, Suffolk

British Library Cataloguing in Publication Data
A catalogue record for this book is available from the British Library

Library of Congress Cataloging in Publication Data
Žižek, Slavoj.
Enjoy your symptom! : Jacques Lacan in Hollywood and out /
Slavoj Zizek ; with a new preface by the author.
p. cm.
Includes bibliographical references and index.
1. Motion pictures – Psychological aspects. 2. Lacan, Jacques,
1901–1981. I. Title.
PN1995.Z65 2007
150.19′5–dc22 2007022948

ISBN 13: 978-1-138-12788-3 (hbk)
ISBN 13: 978-0-415-77259-4 (pbk)

Contents

Preface to the Routledge Classics Edition

Enjoy Your Symptom—or Your Fetish?

1

There are two ways to understand the thesis that we live in a post-ideological world: either we take it in a naive post-political sense (finally liberated from the burden of great ideological narratives and causes, we can dedicate ourselves to solving pragmatically real problems), or, in a more critical way, as a sign of today's predominant cynicism (today's power no longer needs a consistent ideological edifice to legitimize its rule; it can afford to state directly the obvious truth—search for profits, brutal imposition of economic interests). According to the second reading, there is no longer a need for refined procedure of *Ideologiekritik*, for a "symptomal reading" that detects the faults in an ideological edifice: such a procedure knocks on an open door, since the thoroughly cynical power-discourse concedes all this in advance, like today's analysant who calmly accepts the analyst's suggestions about his innermost obscene desire, no longer being shocked by anything.

Is this, however, effectively the case? If it is, then *Ideologiekritik* and psychoanalysis are today ultimately of no use, since the wager of their interpretive procedure is that the subject CANNOT openly admit and really assume the truth about what s/he is doing. However, psychoanalysis opens up a way to unmask this apparent proof of its uselessness, by way of detecting, beneath the deceiving openness of post-ideological cynicism, the contours of fetishism, and thus to oppose the *fetishist* mode of ideology, which predominates in our allegedly "post-ideological" era, to its traditional *symptomal* mode, in which the ideological lie which structures our perception of reality is threatened by symptoms, *qua* "returns of the repressed," cracks in the fabric of the ideological lie. Fetish is effectively a kind of *envers* of the symptom. That is to say, symptom is the exception which disturbs the surface of the false appearance, the point at which the repressed Other Scene erupts, while fetish is the embodiment of the Lie which enables us to sustain the unbearable truth. Let us take the case of the death of a beloved person: in the case of a symptom, I "repress" this death, I try not to think about it, but the repressed trauma returns in the symptom; in the case of a fetish, on the contrary, I "rationally" fully accept this death, and yet I cling to the fetish, to some feature that embodies for me the disavowal of this death. In this sense, a fetish can play a very constructive role of allowing us to cope with the harsh reality: fetishists are not dreamers lost in their private worlds, they are thoroughly "realists," able to accept the way things effectively are—since they have their fetish to which they can cling in order to cancel the full impact of reality. There is a wonderful early short story by Patricia Highsmith, "Button," about a middle-class New Yorker who lives with a mongoloid nine-year-old son who babbles meaningless sounds all the time and smiles, while saliva is running out of his open mouth; one late evening, unable to endure the situation, he decides to take a walk on the lone Manhattan streets where he stumbles upon a destitute homeless beggar who pleadingly extends his hand towards him; in an act of inexplicable fury, the hero beats the beggar to death and tears off from his jacket a button. Afterwards, he returns home a changed man, enduring his family nightmare without any traumas, capable of even a kind smile towards his mongoloid son; he keeps this button all the time in the pocket of his trousers—a perfect fetish, the embodied disavowal of his miserable reality, the constant remainder that, once at least, he did strike back against his miserable destiny.

In psychiatric circles, there is a story told about a man whose wife was diagnosed with acute breast cancer and died three months afterwards; the husband survived her death unscathed, being able to talk coolly about his traumatic last moments with her—how? Was he a cold distanced monster with no feelings? Soon, his friends noticed that, while talking about his deceased wife, he always held in his hands a hamster, her pet object: his fetish, the embodied disavowal of her death. No wonder that, when, a couple of months later, the hamster died, the guy broke down and had to be hospitalized for a long period, treated for acute depression. So, when we are bombarded by claims that in our post-ideological cynical era nobody believes in the proclaimed ideals, when we encounter a person who claims he is cured of any beliefs, accepting social reality the way it really is, one should always counter such claims with the question: OK, but *where is your hamster—the fetish which enables you to (pretend to) accept reality "the way it is"?*

2

The way I proceed to analyze this impregnation of our daily lives by ideology is through the reference to numerous examples—so a note about my (often criticized) use of examples is, perhaps, appropriate here.

The difference between the idealist and the materialist use of examples is that, in the Platonic-idealist approach, examples are always imperfect, they never perfectly render what they are supposed to exemplify, so that we should take care not to take them too literally, while, for a materialist, there is always more in the example than in what it exemplifies, i.e., an example always threatens to undermine what it is supposed to exemplify since it gives body to what the exemplified notion itself represses, is unable to cope with. (Therein resides Hegel's materialist procedure in his *Phenomenology*: each "figure of consciousness" is first staged-exemplified and then undermined through its own example.) This is why the idealist approach always demands a multitude of examples—since no single example is fully fitting, one has to enumerate them to indicate the transcendent wealth of the Idea they exemplify, the Idea being the fixed point of reference of the floating examples. A materialist, on the contrary, tends to repeat one and the same example, to return to it obsessively: it is the particular example which remains the same in all symbolic universes, while the universal notion it is supposed to exemplify continually changes its shape, so that we get a multitude of universal notions circulating, like flies around the light, around a single example. Is this not what Lacan is doing, returning to the same exemplary cases (the guessing-game with five hats, the dream of Irma's injection), each time providing a new interpretation? Such an example is the *universal Singular*: a singular entity which persists as the universal in the multitude of its interpretations.

In a recent conversation, Hanif Kureishi was telling me about his new novel, whose narrative is different from what he wrote hitherto; I ironically asked him: "But the hero is nonetheless an immigrant with a Pakistani father who is a failed writer . . ." He replied: "What's the problem? Do we not all have Pakistani fathers who are failed writers?" He was right—and this is what Hegel meant by singularity elevated into universality: the pathological twist that Hanif Kureishi experienced in his father is part of EVERY father, there is no normal father, everybody's father is a figure who failed to live up to his mandate and thus left to his son the task to settle his symbolic debts. In this sense, again, Kureishi's Pakistani failed writer is a universal singular, a singular standing in for the universality.

This is what hegemony is about, this short-circuit between the universal and its paradigmatic case (in the precise Kuhnian sense of the term): it is not enough to say that Kureishi's own case is one in the series of the cases exemplifying the universal fact that father is yet another "impossible profession"—one should make a step further and claim that, precisely, we all have Pakistani fathers who are failed writers. In other words, let us imagine being-a-father as a universal ideal which all empirical fathers endeavor to approach and ultimately fail to do: what this means is that the true universality is not that of the ideal being-a-father, but that of failure itself.

Therein resides today's true impasse of paternal authority: in the (biological) father's growing reluctance to accept the symbolic mandate "father"—this impasse is the secret motif that runs through Steven Spielberg's films. All his key films—*ET*, *Empire of the Sun*, *Jurassic Park*, *Schindler's List*—are variations on this motif. One should remember that the family to whose small boy ET appears was deserted by the father (as we learn in the very beginning), so that ET is ultimately a kind of "vanishing mediator" who provides a new father (the good scientist who, in the film's last shot, is already seen embracing the mother)—when the new father is here, ET can leave and "go home." *Empire of the Sun* focuses on a boy deserted by his family in the war-torn China and surviving through the help of an ersatz-father (played by John Malkovich). In the very first scene of *Jurassic Park*, we see the paternal figure (played by Sam Neill) jokingly threatening the two kids with a dinosaur bone—this bone is clearly the tiny object-stain which, later, explodes into gigantic dinosaurs, so that one can risk the hypothesis that, within the film's fantasmatic universe, the dinosaurs' destructive fury merely materializes the rage of the paternal superego. A barely perceptible detail that occurs later, in the middle of the film, confirms this reading. The pursued group of Neill with two kids take refuge from the murderous carnivorous dinosaurs in a gigantic tree, where, dead tired, they fall asleep; on the tree, Neill loses the dinosaur bone that was stuck in his belt, and it is as if this accidental loss has a magic effect—before they fall asleep, Neill is reconciled with the children, displaying warm affection and care for them. Significantly, the dinosaurs who approach the tree next morning and awaken the sleeping party, turn out to be of the benevolent herbivorous kind. *Schindler's List* is, at the most basic level, a remake of *Jurassic Park* (and, if anything, worse than the original), with the Nazis as the dinosaur monsters, Schindler as (at the film's beginning) the cynical-profiteering and opportunistic parental figure, and the ghetto Jews as threatened children (their infantilization in the film is eye-striking)—the story the film tells is about Schindler's gradual rediscovery of his paternal duty towards the Jews, and his transformation into a caring and responsible father. And is *The War of the Worlds* not the last installment of this saga? Tom Cruise plays a divorced working-class father who neglects his two children; the invasion of the aliens reawakens in him the proper paternal instincts, and he rediscovers himself as a caring father—no wonder that, in the last scene, he finally gets the recognition from his son who, throughout the film, despised him. In the mode of the eighteenth-century stories, the film could thus also have been subtitled "A story of how a working father finally gets reconciled with his son." One can effectively imagine the film WITHOUT the blood-thirsty aliens: what remains is in a way "what the film really is about," the story of a divorced working-class father who strives to regain the respect of his two children. (And one can easily repeat this mental experiment apropos Spielberg's other films: *Jurassic Park* as a film about a father on a trip to wild nature with the two children where they resolve their tensions; ET as a film about a frustrated boy in a family abandoned by the father, etc. Of course, one can argue that such a reading is too naively Freudian in the way it reduces the foreign element (aliens, dinosaurs) to a *metaphor* for family tensions, ignoring the *metonymic* level of monsters as immanent prolongation of humans, not only their metaphor—however, the answer to this reproach is that such a Freudian reduction is a feature of films themselves, its immanent ideology.) Therein resides the film's ideology: with regard to the two levels of the story (the Oedipal level of the lost and regained paternal authority; the spectacular level of the conflict with the invading aliens), there is a clear dissymmetry, since the Oedipal level is what the story is "really about," while the external spectacular is merely its metaphoric extension. There is a nice detail in the film's soundtrack which makes clear the predominance of this Oedipal dimension: the aliens' attacks are accompanied by a terrifying one-note low-trombone sound weirdly resembling the low bass and trumpet sound of the Tibetan Buddhist chant, the voice of the suffering-dying evil father (in clear contrast to the "beautiful" five-tones melodic fragment that identifies the "good" aliens in Spielberg's *Encounters of the Third Kind*).

3

But is the ultimate goal of the analysis of ideology not practical: to enable us to intervene and change our reality? Does my jumping from one to another example not contradict this professed goal, condemning us to narcissistic pleasure in theory and thus effectively sabotaging the urgency of practical engagement?

A fake sense of urgency pervades the Left-liberal humanitarian discourse—recall rhetorical figures such as "a woman is raped every six seconds in this country," or "in the time it takes you to read this paragraph, ten children will die of hunger." Underlying all this is a sentiment of moral outrage. This pseudo-urgency was exploited by Starbucks a couple of years ago, when, at the entrance, posters greeted customers pointing out that half or so of their profits went to the health care of the children of Guatemala (from where their coffee originates), so that, with every cup you drank, you so to speak, saved a child's life. There is a fundamental anti-theoretical edge to it—the underlying point is here: no time to reflect on all of it, we have to ACT NOW. (See, against this, Marx's wonderful letter to Engels from 1870, when, for a brief moment, it seemed that a European revolution was again at the gates: in this letter, he conveys his sheer panic—can't the revolutionaries wait for a couple of years, since he, Marx, had not yet finished his *Capital*?). Through this fake sense of urgency, the post-industrial rich, living in their secluded virtual world, not only do not deny or ignore the harsh reality outside their area, they actively refer to it all the time. As Bill Gates recently put it: "What do computers matter when millions are still unnecessarily dying of diarrhea?"

Nothing demonstrates better the fake nature of this sense of urgency than the reverberations of the cover story of the *Time* magazine in the Summer of 2006, reporting that around four million people died there as the result of political violence in the last decade, and no usual humanitarian uproar followed—as if some kind of filtering mechanism blocks these news from achieving their full impact on our symbolic space. The Congo is today effectively re-emerging as a Conradian "heart of darkness" that no one dares fully to confront. Do we need more proofs that the humanitarian sense of urgency is mediated/overdetermined by clear political considerations—which considerations? To answer this question, we need precisely to step back and take a look.

When, in a critical analysis of the present global constellation, one offers no clear solution, no "practical" advice on what to do, when one paints no light at the end of the tunnel (well aware that this light might belong to a train crashing towards us), one is usually reproached: "So what should we do, nothing? Just sit and wait?" One should gather the courage to answer: YES, precisely that! There are situations where the only truly "practical" thing to do is to resist the temptation to engage immediately, and to "wait and see" by means of a patient critical analysis. Engagement seems to exert its pressure on us from all directions. In a well-known passage from his *Existentialism is Humanism*, Sartre deployed the dilemma of a young man in France in 1942, torn between the duty to help his lone, ill mother and the duty to enter

Resistance and fight the Germans; Sartre's point is, of course, that there is no *a priori* answer to this dilemma—the young man should make a decision grounded only in his own abyssal freedom, assuming full responsibility for it. An obscene third way out of this dilemma would have been to advise the young man to tell his mother that he will join the Resistance, and to tell his Resistance friends that he will take care of his mother, while, in reality, withdrawing to a secluded place and studying. There is more than cheap cynicism in this advice—it brings to mind a well-known Soviet joke about Lenin. Under Socialism, Lenin's words to young people, his answer to what they should do, "Learn, learn, and learn," were evoked all the time, displayed on all school walls. So here is how the joke goes: Marx, Engels and Lenin are asked what would they prefer to have: a wife or a mistress. As expected, Marx, rather conservative in private matters, answers "A wife!", while Engels, more of a *bon vivant*, opts for a mistress; however, to everyone's surprise, Lenin says: "I would like to have both of them!" Why? Is there a hidden strike of decadent *jouisseur* to his austere revolutionary image? No—he explains: "So that I can tell my wife that I am going to my mistress, and my mistress that I have to be with my wife." "And then, what do you do?" "I go to a lone place to learn, learn, and learn!" Is this not exactly what Lenin did after the catastrophy of 1914? He withdrew to a lone place in Switzerland, where he "learned, learned, and learned," reading Hegel's logic. And, perhaps, this is what we should do today.

Introduction to the New Revised Edition

From Desire to Drive . . . and Back

The present book was first published in 1992, as an attempt to introduce the doctrine of Jacques Lacan to the American public via Hollywood cinema. How are we to judge the receptivity of American academia to Lacan now, almost ten years later? One of the stories that snobbish French Lacanians like to quote against translating *jouissance* as "enjoyment"—with, of course, an undertone of French arrogance and a patronizing stance toward the American scene—is that Lacan, on his first visit to the United States, watched in Baltimore a TV commercial with the motto "Enjoy Coke!" and, dismayed at its vulgarity, emphatically claimed that his *jouir* is NOT this "enjoy." Against this argument, one should claim that "enjoy" in the unfortunate "Enjoy Coke!" precisely is the *jouir* in its superego imbecility, what better example of Lacan's thesis that superego is an injunction to enjoy than "Enjoy Coke"? Is there, then, a hope for the breakthrough of Lacanian theory in the United States?

Whatever the vicissitudes and deformations of Lacan in cultural studies, one should focus on what happens with children in their early age, following the wise Jesuit motto, "Give me a child till he is seven, and afterward you can do with him whatever you want." So I am tempted to claim that there is hope for us Lacanians as long as American children are massively exposed to Shel Silverstein's two classic books, *The Missing Piece* and *The Missing Piece Meets the Big O*; one is almost embarrassed by the direct way these two books render in naked form the basic matrix of the Lacanian opposition of desire and drive. The first book tells of the adventures of an it, a circle with a point for an eye and a triangular gap for a mouth, a subject in search of a missing piece that would fill in the gap and thus change it into a complete circle, somewhat like the perfect spheric human being preceding sexual difference from Plato's *Symposium*: "It was missing a piece. And it was not happy. So it set off in search of its missing piece. And as it rolled it sang this song: 'Oh I'm lookin' for my missin' piece/I'm lookin' for my missin' piece/Hi-dee-ho, here I go,/Lookin' for my missin' piece.' "[1] So after a long journey full of adventurous encounters, one day it finds a triangular missing piece that will fill its void; however, the piece tells him, "Wait a minute! I am not your missing piece. I am nobody's piece. I am my own piece. And even if I was somebody's missing piece I don't think I'd be yours!" So it sadly rolls on, finds another piece that is too small, another that is too big, another too sharp, another too square, another that it doesn't hold tightly enough and thus loses, another that it holds too tightly and thus breaks. Finally it encounters a triangular piece that seems to be just right and asks, " 'Are you anybody else's missing piece?' " The piece answers, " 'Not that I know of.' " " 'Well, maybe you want to be your own piece?' " " 'I can be someone's and still be my own.' " So they get together and they fit perfectly, forming a perfect sphere. Because it is now complete, it rolls faster and faster, but, for that reason, it cannot smell a flower or talk to a worm. Could it still sing? It began to sing: " 'I've frown my nizzin' geez/Uf vroun my mitzin' brees.' " Now that it was complete, it could not sing at all! So it stopped rolling, set the piece down gently, rolled away and started to sing softly " 'Oh I'm lookin' for my missin' piece/I'm lookin' for my missin' piece.' " It is the paradox of *desire* at its purest: in order to sustain itself as desire, to articulate itself (in a song), a piece must be missing. Do we not have here the matrix of Robert Schumann's tragedy? His fate was the opposite of a standard lover caught in an unhappy love affair and dreaming about happy unification with his beloved—his deadlock was that his wishes *were* realized—life *spared* him the disappointment of unhappy love—so that his position was that of a lover united forever with his beloved and dreaming about some new obstacle that would make the beloved distant. It is no wonder that the outcome was a psychotic breakdown: " 'Things were far more beautiful when one imagined them breaking,' Schumann would say to himself. Was not the mere idea of a possible setback more agreeable than the certainty of familiar things?"[2]

The trajectory of Freud's and Lacan's theory goes from desire to drive. It is no surprise, then, that *The Missing Piece*, which narrates the myth of how the it (the Lacanian lamella) constitutes itself as desiring subject through a lack, was followed six years later by *The Missing Piece Meets the Big O*, which tells the story as it were from the opposite end: not from the standpoint of the desiring subject looking for its missing piece, but from the standpoint of the missing piece itself. This piece is not the Freudian partial object satisfied to remain its own piece, like the first piece encountered by the it in the first book, but the piece that is sitting alone, waiting for someone to take it. Here, of course, problems emerge: some who come along fit but cannot roll, others can roll but do not fit; some are too delicate; some put the piece on a pedestal and leave it there; some have too many pieces missing; some have "too many pieces, period"; some look too closely at the piece, while others roll by without even noticing it. The piece tries to make itself more attractive, but it doesn't help; it tries being flashy, but this just frightens away the shy ones. At last one it comes along that fits just right, looking like the it from the first book, so, as in the first book, they form a perfect sphere and start to roll happily. However, once inserted into the it, the missing piece begins to grow and grow, the it drops the piece out and goes away, complaining " 'I'm lookin' for my missin' piece, one that that won't increase.' " Then, one day, an it comes along that looks different: a perfect circle in itself. The piece, a good Lacanian partial object, asks the it the obvious *Che vuoi?* question: "What do you want of me?" ' " 'Nothing' " is the answer. " 'What do you need from me?' " asks the piece, putting its bets on the distinction between demand and need. Again, " 'Nothing.' " " 'Who are you?' " 'I am the big O,' " in short, the primordial, noncastrated big Other who, as such, wants nothing. " 'Maybe I am your missing piece?' " asks the piece, to which the big O answers,: " 'But I am not missing a piece. There is no place you would fit.' 'That is too bad,' " says the missing piece. " 'I was hoping that perhaps I could roll with you . . .' 'You cannot roll with me,' " says the big O, " 'but perhaps you can roll by yourself.' 'By myself? A missing piece cannot roll by itself.' 'Have you ever tried?' 'But I am not shaped for rolling.' 'Corners wear off and shapes change,' " says the big O, and rolls away. Alone again, the missing piece lifts itself, flops over, and slowly learns to roll; its edges begin to wear off, and soon it goes on carelessly rolling instead of bouncing, rejoining the big O, accompanying it, attached to it as a small sphere on the border of the large sphere, the small other clinging, like a parasite, to the big Other, the two together forming a perfect example of the "inner eight," the matrix of the self-perpetuating repetitious circulation of the drive.

Apart from some minor corrections of typographical errors, the big difference between the first and this edition of the book is a new substantial final chapter, focusing on the fantasmatic support of the notion of reality. Since my standard book formula is for a length of six chapters, and since the book had in its first edition only five chapters, it is only now, after the delay of eight years, that *Enjoy your symptom!* effectively became my book.

NOTES

1 See Shel Silverstein, *The Missing Piece* (New York: HarperCollins 1975), and Shel Silverstein, *The Missing Piece Meets the Big O* (New York: Harper-Collins 1981).

2 Dominique Druhen, notes to the Siegfried Jerusalem/Elena Bashkirova recording of *Dichterliebe and Liederkreis* (Erato 1992), p. 8–9.

Introduction

I have always found extremely replusive the common practice of sharing the main dishes in a Chinese restaurant. So when, recently, I gave expression to this replusion and insisted on finishing my plate alone, I became the victim of an ironic "wild psychoanalysis" on the part of my table neighbor: is not this replusion of mine, this resistance to sharing a meal, a symbolic form of the fear of *sharing a partner*, i.e., of sexual promiscuity? The first answer that came to my mind, of course, was a variation on de Quincey's caution against the "art of murder"—the true horror is not sexual promiscuity but sharing a Chinese dish: "How many people have entered the way of perdition with some innocent gangbang, which at the time was of no great importance to them, and ended by sharing the main dishes in a Chinese restaurant!"

Such a shift of accent (an exemplary case of what Freud called "displacement") underlies the comical effect of *understatement*, allegedly characteristic of the English sense of humor and so much admired by Hitchcock. Yet we are here far from indulging in affected wisecracking: the point is rather that this de Quniceyian "displacement" enables us to discern the logic of a split which, as a kind of fatal flaw, is at work in the Englightenment from its very beginning. That is to say, when, in his programmatic text *What Is Enlightenment?*, Immanuel Kant provides the famous definition of Enlightenment as "man's release from his selfincurred tutelage," i.e., his courage to make use of his understanding without direction from another, he supplements the motto "Argue freely!" by "Argue as much as you will, and about what you will, but obey!" This and not "Do not obey but argue!" is, according to Kant, the Enlightenment's answer to the demand of traditional authority, "Do not argue but obey!" We must be careful here not to miss what Kant is aiming at—he is not simply restating the common motto of conformism, "In private, think whatever you want, but in public, obey the authorities!" but rather its opposite: in public, "as a scholar before the reading public," use your reason freely, yet in private (at your post, in your family, i.e., as a cog in the social machine) obey authority! This split underlies the famous Kantian "conflict of the faculties" between the faculty of philosophy (free to indulge in arguing about what it will, yet for that reason cut off from social power—the performative force of its discourse being so to speak suspended) and the faculties of law and theology (which articulate the principles of ideological and political power and are therefore devoid of the freedom to argue). The same split occurs already in Descrates who, prior to entering the way of universal doubt, established a "provisional morality," a set of rules regulating his everyday existence for the time of his philosophical journey: the very first rule emphasizes the need to obey the customs and laws of the country into which he was born without questioning their authority . . . In short, I am free to entertain doubts about anything, about the very existence of the universe, yet for all that I am compelled to obey the Master—or, as the de Quinceyian version of it would run: "How many people have entered the way of perdition with some innocent doubt about the existence of the world around them, which at the time was of no great importance to them, and ended by treating their superiors with insufficient respect!"

The ideological attitude opened up by this split, of course, is that of cynicism, of cynical distance which pertains to the very notion of Enlightenment and which today seems to have reached its apogee: although officially undermined, devalorized, authority returns through the sidedoor—"we know there is no truth in authority, yet we continue to play its game and to obey it in order not to disturb the usual run of things . . ." Truth is suspended in the name of efficiency: the ultimate legitimization of the system is that it works. In Eastern

Europe's now-defunct "really existing socialism," the split was that between a public ritual of obedience and private cynical distance, whereas in the West, the cynicism is in a way redoubled: we publicly pretend to be free, whereas privately we obey. In both cases, we are victims of authority precisely when we think we have duped it: the cynical distance is empty, our true place is in the ritual of obeying—or, as Kurt Vonnegut put it in his *Mother Night*: "We are what we pretend to be, so we must be careful about what we pretend to be."

In contrast to what the media desperately endeavor to convince us, *the enemy today is not the fundamentalist" but the cynic*—even a certain form of "deconstructionism" partakes in the universal cynicism by proposing a more sophisticated version of the Cartesian "provisional morality": "In theory (in the academic practice of writing) deconstruct as much as you will and whatever you will, but in your everyday life, play the predominant social game!" The present book was written with a view to bringing to public notice the nullity of cynical distance. Its subtitle is not to be taken ironically: it simply refers to the two divisions of each chapter. As it is indicated by their didactic titles ("Why . . ."), the aim of each of the five chapters is to elucidate some fundamental Lacanian notion or theoretical complex (*letter, woman, repetition, phallus, father*). In the first division of each chapter, Lacan is "in Hollywood," i.e., the notion or complex in question is explained by way of examples from Hollywood or popular culture in general; in the second division, we are "out of Hollywood," i.e., the same notion is elaborated as it is "in itself," in its inherent content. Or, to put it in Hegelese: Hollywood is conceived as a "phenomenology" of the Lacanian Spirit, its appearing for the common consciousness, whereas the second division is closer to the "logic" *qua* articulation of the notional content in and for itself.

1

WHY DOES A *LETTER* ALWAYS ARRIVE AT ITS DESTINATION?

1.1 DEATH AND SUBLIMATION: THE FINAL SCENE OF *CITY LIGHTS*

The trauma of the voice

It may seem peculiar, even absurd, to set Chaplin under the sign of "death and sublimation": is not the universe of Chaplin's films, a universe bursting with nonsublime vitality, vulgarity even, the very opposite of a damp romantic obsession with death and sublimation? This may be so, but things get complicated at a particular point: the point of the intrusion of the *voice*. It is the voice which corrupts the innocence of the silent burlesque, of this pre-Oedipal, oral-anal paradise of unbridled devouring and destroying, ignorant of death and guilt: "Neither death nor crime exist in the polymorphous world of the burlesque where everybody gives and receives blows at will, where cream cakes fly and where, in the midst of the general laughter, buildings fall down. In this world of pure gesticularity, which is also the world of cartoons (a substitute for lost slapstick), the protagonists are generally immortal . . . violence is universal and without consequences, there is no guilt."[1]

The voice introduces a fissure into this pre-Oedipal universe of immortal continuity: it functions as a strange body which smears the innocent surface of the picture, a ghost-like apparition which can never be pinned to a definite visual object; and this changes the whole economy of desire, the innocent vulgar vitality of the silent movie is lost, we enter the realm of double sense, hidden meaning, repressed desire—the very presence of the voice changes the visual surface into something delusive, into a lure: "Film was joyous, innocent and dirty. It will become obsessive, fetishistic and ice-cold."[2] In other words: film was Chaplinesque, it will become Hitchcockian.

It is therefore no accident that the advent of the voice, of the talking film, introduces a certain duality into Chaplin's universe: an uncanny split of the figure of the tramp. Remember the three great Chaplin talking films: *The Great Dictator, Monsieur Verdoux, Limelight*, distinguished by the same melancholic, painful humor. All of them turn on the same structural problem: that of an indefinable line of demarcation, of a certain feature, difficult to specify at the level of positive properties, the presence or the absence of which changes radically the symbolic status of the object:

> Between the small Jewish barber and the dictator, the difference is as negligible as that between their respective moustaches. Yet it results in two situations as infinitely remote, as far opposed as those of victim and executioner. Likewise, in *Monsieur Verdoux*, the difference between the two aspects or demeanours of the same man, the lady-assassin and the loving husband of a paralysed wife, is so thin that all his wife's intuition is required for the premonition that somehow he "changed." . . . the burning question of *Limelight* is: what is that "nothing," that sign of age, that small difference of triteness, on account of which the funny clown's number changes into a tedious spectacle?[3]

This differential feature which cannot be pinned to some positive quality is what Lacan calls *le trait unaire*, the unary feature: a point of symbolic identification to which clings the real of the subject. As long as the subject is attached to this feature, we are faced with a charismatic, fascinating figure; as soon as this attachment is broken, all that remains is dreary remnants. The crucial point, however, not to be missed is how this split is conditioned by the arrival of the voice, i.e., by the very fact that the figure of the tramp is forced to *speak*: in *The Great Dictator*, Hinkel speaks, while the Jewish barber remains closer to the mute tramp; in the *Limelight*, the clown on the stage is mute, while the resigned old man behind the stage speaks . . .

Chaplin's well-known aversion to sound is thus not to be dismissed as a simple nostalgic commitment to a silent paradise; it reveals a far deeper than usual knowledge (or at least presentiment) of the disruptive power of the voice, of the fact that the voice functions as a foreign body, as a kind of parasite introducing a radical split: the advent of the Word throws the human animal off balance and makes of him a ridiculous, impotent figure, gesticulating and striving desperately for a lost balance. Nowhere is this disruptive force of the voice made clearer than in *City Lights*, in this paradox of a silent movie with a sound track: a sound track without words, just music and a few typified noises of the objects. It is precisely here that death and the sublime erupt with full force.

The tramp's interposition

In the whole history of cinema, *City Lights* is perhaps the purest case of a film which, so to speak, stakes everything on its final scene—the entire film serves ultimately only to prepare for the final, concluding moment, and when this moment arrives, when (to use the final phrase of Lacan's "Seminar On 'The Purloined Letter' ") "the letter arrives at its destination,"[4] the film can end at once. The film is thus structured in a strictly "teleological" manner, all its elements point toward the final moment, the long-awaited culmination; which is why we could also use it to question the usual procedure of the deconstruction of teleology: perhaps it announces a kind of movement toward the final denouement which escapes the teleological economy as depicted (one is even tempted to say: reconstructed) in deconstructionist readings.[5]

City Lights is a story about a tramp's love for a blind girl selling flowers on a busy street who mistakes him for a rich man. Through a series of adventures with an eccentric millionaire who, when drunk, treats the tramp extremely kindly, but when sober fails even to recognize him (was it here that Brecht found the idea for his *Puntilla and his*

Servant Matti?), the tramp gets his hands on the money needed for an operation to restore the poor girl's sight; whereupon he is arrested for theft and sentenced to prison. After he has done his time, he wanders around the city, alone and desolate; suddenly, he comes across a florist's shop where he sees the girl. The operation was successful and she now runs a thriving business, but still awaits the Prince Charming of her dreams, whose chivalrous gift enabled her sight to be restored. Every time a handsome young customer enters her shop, she is filled with hope; and time and again disappointed on hearing the voice. The tramp immediately recognizes her, whereas she doesn't recognize him, because all she knows of him is his voice and the touch of his hand: all she sees through the window (separating them like a screen) is the ridiculous figure of a tramp, a social outcast. Upon seeing him lose his rose (a souvenir of her), she nevertheless takes pity on him, his passionate and desperate gaze stirs her compassion; so, not knowing who or what awaits her, still in a cheerful and ironic mood (she comments to her mother in the store: "I've made a conquest!"), she steps out on the pavement, gives him a new rose and presses a coin into his hand. At this precise moment, as their hands meet, she finally recognizes him by his touch. She is immediately sobered and asks him: "You?" The tramp nods and, pointing to her eyes, asks her: "You can see now?" The girl answers: "Yes, I can see now"; the film then cuts to a medium close-up of the tramp, his eyes filled with dread and hope, smiling shyly, uncertain what the girl's reaction will be, satisfied and at the same time insecure at being so totally exposed to her—and this is the end of the movie.

On the most elementary level, the poetic effect of this scene is based on the double meaning of the final exchange: "I can see now" refers to the restored physical sight as well as to the fact that the girl sees now her Prince Charming for what he really is, a miserable tramp.[6] This second meaning sets us at the very heart of the Lacanian problem: it concerns the relation between symbolic identification and the leftover, the remainder, the object-excrement that escapes it. We could say that the film stages what Lacan, in his *Four Fundamental Concepts of Psychoanalysis*, calls "separation," namely the separation between I and *a*, between the Ego Ideal, the subject's symbolic identification, and the object: the falling out, the segregation of the object from the symbolic order.[7]

As Michel Chion pointed out in his brilliant interpretation of *City Lights*,[8] the fundamental feature of the figure of the tramp is his *interposition*: he is always interposed between a gaze and its "proper" object, fixating upon himself a gaze destined for another, ideal point or object—a stain which disturbs "direct" communication between the gaze and its "proper" object, leading the straight gaze astray, changing it into a kind of squint. Chaplin's comic strategy consists in variations of this fundamental motif: the tramp accidentally occupies a place which is not his own, which is not destined for him—he is mistaken for a rich man or for a distinguished guest; on the run from his pursuers, he finds himself on a stage, all of a sudden the center of the attention of numerous gazes . . . In Chaplin's films, we even find a kind of wild theory of the origins of comedy from the blindness of the audience, i.e., from such a split caused by the mistaken gaze: in *The Circus*, for example, the tramp, on the run from the police, finds himself on a rope at the top of the circus tent; he starts to gesticulate wildly, trying to keep his balance, while the audience laughs and applauds, mistaking his desperate struggle for survival for a comedian's virtuosity—the origin of comedy is to be sought precisely in such cruel blindness, unawareness of the tragic reality of a situation.[9]

In the very first scene of *City Lights*, the tramp assumes such a role of stain in the picture: in front of a large audience, the mayor of the city unveils a new monument; when he pulls off the white cover, the surprised audience discovers the tramp, sleeping calmly in the lap of the gigantic statue; awakened by the noise, aware that he is the unexpected focus of attention of thousands of eyes, the tramp attempts to descend the statue as quickly as possible, his bumbling efforts triggering bursts of laughter . . . The tramp is thus an object of a gaze aimed at something or somebody else: he is mistaken for somebody else and accepted as such, or else—as soon as the audience becomes aware of the mistake—he turns into a disturbing stain one tries to get rid of as quickly as possible. His basic aspiration (which serves as a clue also for the final scene of *City Lights*) is thus finally to be accepted as "himself," not as another's substitute—and, as we shall see, the moment when the tramp exposes himself to the gaze of the other, offering himself without any support in ideal identification, reduced to his bare existence of objectal remainder, is far more ambiguous and risky than it may appear.

The accident in *City Lights* that triggers the mistaken identification occurs shortly after the beginning. Running from the police, the tramp crosses the street by passing through cars that are blocking it in a traffic jam; when he steps out of the last car and slams its rear door, the girl automatically associates this sound—the slam—with him; this and the rich payment—his last coins—that the tramp gives to her for a rose, generate in her the image of a benevolent and rich owner of a luxury car. Here, a homology with the no-less-famous initial misunderstanding in Hitchcock's *North by Northwest* offers itself automatically, i.e., the scene where, because of a contingent coincidence, Roger O. Thornhill is mistakenly identified as the mysterious American agent George Kaplan (he makes a gesture toward the hotel clerk exactly as the clerk enters the saloon and cries out: "Phone call for Mr. Kaplan!"): here also, the subject accidentally finds himself occupying a certain place in the symbolic network. However, the parallel goes even further: as is well known, the basic paradox of the plot in *North by Northwest* is that Thornhill is not simply mistaken for another person; he is mistaken for *somebody who doesn't exist at all*, for a fictitious agent concocted by the CIA to divert attention from its real agent; in other words, Thornhill finds himself occupying, filling out, a certain empty place in the structure. And this was also the problem which caused so many delays when Chaplin was shooting the scene of the mistaken identification: the shooting dragged on for months and months. The result didn't satisfy Chaplin's demands as long as Chaplin insisted on depicting the rich man for whom the tramp is mistaken as a "real person," as another subject in the film's diegetic reality; the solution came about when Chaplin realized, in a sudden insight, that the rich man didn't have to exist at all, that it was enough for him to be the poor girl's fantasy formation, i.e., that in reality, one person (the tramp) was enough. This is also one of the elementary insights of psychoanalysis. In the network of intersubjective relations, every one of us is identified with, pinned down to, a certain fantasy place in the other's symbolic structure. Psychoanalysis sustains here the exact opposite of the usual, commonsense opinion according to which fantasy figures are nothing but distorted, combined, or otherwise concocted figures of their "real" models, of people of flesh and blood that we've met in our experience. We can relate to these "people of flesh and blood" only insofar as we are able to identify them with a certain place in our symbolic fantasy space, or, to put it in a more pathetic way, only insofar as they fill out a place preestablished in our dream—we fall in love with a woman insofar as her features coincide with our fantasy figure of a Woman, the "real father" is a miserable individual obliged to sustain the burden of the Name of the Father, never fully adequate to his symbolic mandate, and so forth.[10]

The function of the tramp is thus literally that of an intercessor, middleman, purveyor: a kind of go-between, love messenger, intermediary between himself (i.e., his own ideal figure: the fantasy figure of the rich Prince Charming in the girl's imagination) and the girl. Or, insofar as this rich man is ironically embodied in the eccentric millionaire, the tramp mediates between him and the girl—his function is ultimately to transfer the money from the millionaire to the girl (which is why it is necessary, from the point of view of the structure, that the millionaire and the girl never meet). As Chion showed, this intermediary function of the tramp can be detected through the metaphoric interconnection between two consecutive scenes which have nothing in common on the diegetic level. The first takes place in the restaurant where the tramp is treated by the millionaire: he eats spaghetti in his own way, and when a coil of confetti falls on his plate, he mistakes it for spaghetti and swallows it continuously, rising up, standing on his toes (the confetti hangs from the ceiling like a kind of heavenly manna), until the millionaire cuts it off; an elementary Oedipal scenario is thus staged—the confetti band is a metaphorical umbilical cord linking the tramp to the maternal body, and the millionaire acts as a substitute father, cutting his links with the mother. In the next scene, we see the tramp at the girl's place, where she asks him to hold the wool for her to coil into a ball; in her blindness, she accidently grabs the tip of his woollen underwear which projects from his jacket and starts to unfold it by pulling the thread and rolling it up. The connection between the two scenes is thus clear: what he received from the millionaire, the swallowed food, the endless spaghetti band, he now secrets from his belly and gives to the girl.

And—herein consists our thesis—for that reason, in *City Lights*, the letter twice arrives at its destination, or, to put it another way, the postman rings twice: first, when the tramp succeeds in handing over to the girl the rich man's money, i.e., when he successfully accomplishes his mission as the go-between; and second, when the girl recognizes in his ridiculous figure the benefactor who rendered possible her operation. The letter definitely arrives at its destination when we are no longer able to legitimize ourselves as mere mediators, purveyors of the messages of the big Other, when we cease to fill out the place of the Ego Ideal in the other's fantasy space, when a separation is achieved between the point of ideal identification and the massive weight of our presence outside symbolic representation, when we cease to act like placeholders of the Ideal for the other's gaze—in short, when the other is confronted with the remainder left over after we have lost our symbolic support. The letter arrives at its destination when we are no longer "fillers" of the empty places in another's fantasy structure, i.e., when the other finally "opens his eyes" and realizes that the real letter is not the message we are supposed to carry but our being itself, the object in us that resists symbolization. And it is precisely this separation that takes place in the final scene of *City Lights*.

The separation

Up to the end of the film, the tramp is confined to the role of mediator, circulating between the two figures who, put together, would form an ideal couple (the rich man and the poor girl) and thus enabling communication between them but at the same time being an obstacle to their immediate communication, the stain preventing their immediate contact, the intruder who is never in his own place. With the final scene, however, this game is over: the tramp finally exposes himself in his presence, here he is, representing nothing, holding the place of nobody, we must accept him or refuse him. And the genius of Chaplin is attested by the fact that he decided to end the movie in such a brusque, unexpected way, at the very moment of the tramp's exposure: the film does *not* answer the question "Will the girl accept him or not?"—The idea that she will and that the two of them will live happily ever after has no foundation whatsoever in the film. That is to say, for the usual happy ending, we would need an additional countershot to that of the tramp looking with hope and tremor at the girl: a shot of the girl returning a sign of acceptance, for example, and then, perhaps, a shot of the two of them embracing. We find nothing of the sort in the film: it is over at the moment of absolute uncertainty and openness when the girl—and, together with her, we the spectators—is confronted directly with the question of the "love for her neighbor". Is this ridiculous, clumsy creature whose massive presence strikes us all of a sudden with an almost unbearable proximity really worthy of her love? Will she be able to accept, to take upon herself this social outcast that she has got in answer to her ardent desire? And—as was pointed out by William Rothman[11]—the same question has to be asked also in the opposite direction: not only "is there a place in her dreams for this ragged creature?" but also "is there still a place in *his* dreams for her, who is now a normal, healthy girl running a successful business?"—in other words, didn't the tramp feel such a compassionate love for her precisely because she was blind, poor, and utterly helpless, needing his protective care? Will he still be prepared to accept her *now* when she has every reason to patronize *him*? When in his *L'éthique de la psychanalyse,*[12] Lacan emphasizes Freud's restraint toward the Christian "love for one's neighbor," he has in mind precisely such embarrassing dilemmas: it is easy to love the idealized figure of a poor, helpless neighbor, the starving African or Indian, for example; in other words, it is easy to love one's neighbor as long as he stays far enough from us, as long as there is a proper distance separating us. The problem arises at the moment when he comes too near us, when we start to feel his suffocating proximity—at this moment when the neighbor exposes himself to us too much, love can suddenly turn into hatred.[13]

City Lights ends at the very moment of this absolute undecidability when, confronted with the other's proximity as an object, we are forced to answer the question "Is he worthy of our love?" or, to use the Lacanian formulation, "Is there in him something more than himself, *objet petit a*, a hidden treasure?" We can see here how far we are, at this moment when "the letter arrives at its destination," from the usual notion of teleology: far from realizing a predestined telos, this moment marks the intrusion of a radical openness in which every ideal support of our existence is suspended. This moment is the moment of death and sublimation: when the subject's presence is exposed outside the symbolic support, he "dies" as a member of the symbolic community, his being is no longer determined by a place in the symbolic network, it materializes the pure Nothingness of the hole, the void in the Other (the symbolic order), the void designated, in Lacan, by the German word *das Ding*, the Thing, the pure substance of enjoyment resisting symbolization. The Lacanian definition of the sublime object is precisely "an object elevated to the dignity of the Thing."[14]

When the letter arrives at its destination, the stain spoiling the picture is not abolished, effaced: what we are forced to grasp is, on the contrary, the fact that the real "message," the real letter awaiting us is the stain itself. We should perhaps reread Lacan's "Seminar on 'The Purloined Letter' " from this aspect: is not the letter itself ultimately such a stain—not a signifier but rather an object resisting symbolization, a surplus, a material leftover circulating among the subjects and staining its momentary possessor?

Now, to conclude, we can return to the introductory scene of *City Lights* where the tramp figures as the spot disturbing the picture, as a kind of blot on the white marble surface of the statue: in the Lacanian perspective, the subject is strictly correlative to this stain on the picture. The only proof we have that the picture we are looking at is subjectified is not meaningful signs in it but rather the presence of some meaningless stain disturbing its harmony. Let us recall what is a kind of counterpart to the first scene of *City Lights*, the final scene of Chaplin's *Limelight*, another scene in which Chaplin's body is covered by a white cloth. This scene is unique insofar as it marks the point at which Chaplin and Hitchcock, two authors whose artistic universes appear wholly incompatible at the level of both form and content, finally meet. That is to say, it seems as if Chaplin in *Limelight* finally discovered the Hitchcockian tracking shot: the very first shot of the film is a long tracking shot progressing from the establishing shot of an idyllic London street to a closed apartment door which leaks deadly gas (signaling the attempted suicide of the young girl who lives in the apartment), whereas the last scene of the film contains a magnificent backward tracking shot from the close-up of the dead clown Calvero behind the stage to the establishing shot of the entire stage where the same young girl, now a successful ballerina and his great love, is performing. Just before this scene, the dying Calvero expresses to the attending doctor his desire to see his love dancing; the doctor taps him gently on the shoulders and comforts him: "You shall see her!" Thereupon Calvero dies, his body is covered by a white sheet, and the camera withdraws so that it embraces the dancing girl on the stage, while Calvero is reduced to a tiny, barely visible white stain in the background. What is here of special significance is the way the ballerina enters the frame: from behind the camera, like the birds in the famous "God's-view" shot of Bodega Bay in Hitchcock's *Birds*—yet another white stain which materializes out of the mysterious intermediate space separating the spectator from the diegetic reality on the screen . . . We encounter here the function of the gaze *qua* object-stain at its purest: the doctor's forecast is fulfilled, presisely insofar as he is dead, i.e., insofar as he cannot *see* her anymore, Calvero *looks at her*. For that reason, the logic of this backward tracking shot is thoroughly Hitchcockian: by way of it, a piece of reality is transformed into an amorphous stain (a white blot in the background), yet a stain around which the entire field of vision turns, a stain which "smears over" the entire field (as in the backward tracking shot in *Frenzy*)—the ballerina is dancing for it, for that stain.[15]

1.2 IMAGINARY, SYMBOLIC, REAL

So why *does* the letter always arrive at its destination? Why could it not—sometimes, at least—also *fail* to reach it?[16] Far from attesting to a refined theoretical sensitivity, this Derridean reaction to the famous closing statement of Lacan's "Seminar on 'The Purloined Letter' "[17] rather exhibits what we could call a primordial response of common sense: what if a letter does *not* reach its destination? Isn't it always possible for a letter to go astray?[18] If, however, the Lacanian theory insists categorically that a letter *does* always arrive at its destination, it is not because of an unshakable belief in teleology, in the power of a message to reach its preordained goal: Lacan's exposition of the way a letter arrives at its destination *lays bare the very mechanism of teleological illusion*. In other words, the very reproach that "a letter can also miss its destination" misses its own destination: it misreads the Lacanian thesis, reducing it to the traditional teleological circular movement, i.e., to what is precisely called in question and subverted by Lacan. A letter always arrives at its destination—especially when we have the limit case of a letter *without* addressee, of what is called in German *Flaschenpost*, a message in a bottle thrown into the sea from an island after shipwreck.

This case displays at its purest and clearest how a letter reaches its true destination the moment it is delivered, thrown into the water—its true addressee is namely not the empirical other which may receive it or not, but the big Other, the symbolic order itself, which receives it *the moment the letter is put into circulation*, i.e., the moment the sender "externalizes" his message, delivers it to the Other, the moment the Other takes cognizance of the letter and thus disburdens the sender of responsibility for it.[19] How, then, *specifically*, does a letter arrive at its destination? How should we conceive this thesis of Lacan which usually serves as the crowning evidence for his alleged "logocentrism"? The proposition "a letter always arrives at its destination" is far from being univocal: it offers itself to a series of possible readings[20] which could be ordered by means of reference to the triad Imaginary, Symbolic, Real.

Imaginary (mis)recognition

In a first approach, a letter which "always arrives at its destination" points to the logic of recognition/misrecognition (*reconnaissance/méconnaissance*) elaborated in detail by Louis Althusser and his followers (Michel Pêcheux):[21] the logic by means of which one (mis)recognizes oneself as the addressee of ideological interpellation. This illusion constitutive of the ideological order could be succintly rendered by paraphrasing a formula of Barbara Johnson:[22] "A letter always arrives at its destination *since its destination is wherever it arrives.*" Its underlying mechanism was elaborated by Pêcheux apropos of jokes of the type: "Daddy was born in Manchester, Mummy in Bristol and I in London: strange that the three of us should have met!"[23] In short, if we look at the process backward, from its (contingent) result, the fact that "events took precisely this turn" couldn't but appear as uncanny, concealing some fateful meaning—as if some mysterious hand had taken care that "the letter arrived at its destination," i.e., that my father and my mother met . . . What we have here is, however, more than a shallow joke, as is attested by contemporary physics, where we encounter precisely the same mechanism under the name of the "anthropocentric principle": life emerged on Earth due to numerous contingencies which created the appropriate conditions (if, for example, in Earth's primeval time the composition of soil and air had differed by a small percentage, no life would have been possible); so, when physicists endeavor to reconstruct the process culminating in the appearance of intelligent living beings on Earth, they either presuppose that universe was created in order to render possible the formation of intelligent beings (the "strong," overtly teleological anthropocentric principle) or accept a "circular" methodological rule requiring us to always posit such hypotheses about the primeval state of universe as to enable us to deduce its further development toward the conditions for the emergence of life (the "weak" version).

The same logic is also at work in the well-known accident from the *Arabian Nights*: the hero, lost in the desert, quite by chance enters a cave; there he finds three old wise men, awoken by his entry, who say to him: "Finally, you have arrived! We have been waiting for you for the last three hundred years," as if, behind the contingencies of his life, there was a hidden hand of fate which directed him toward the cave in the desert. This illusion is produced by a kind of "short circuit" between a place in the symbolic network and the contingent element which occupies it: *whosoever* finds himself at this place is the addressee since the addressee is not defined by his positive qualities but by the very contingent fact of finding himself at this place. Although the religious idea of *predestination* seems to be the very exemplar of the delusive "short circuit", it simultaneously intimates a foreboding of radical contingency: if God has decided in advance who will be saved and who will be damned, then my salvation or perdition do not depend on my determinate qualities and acts but on the place in which—*independently of my qualities, that is to say: totally by chance, in so far as I'm concerned*—I find myself within the network of God's plan. This contingency manifests itself in a paradoxical inversion: I'm not damned because I act sinfully, trespassing His Commandments, I act sinfully because I'm damned . . . So, we can easily imagine God easing His mind when some big sinner commits his crime: "Finally, you did it! I have been waiting for it for the whole of your miserable life!" And to convince oneself of how this problematic bears on psychoanalysis, one has only to remember the crucial role of contingent encounters in triggering a traumatic crackup of our psychic balance: overhearing a passing remark by a friend, witnessing a small unpleasant scene, and so forth, can awaken long-forgotten memories and shatter our daily life—as Lacan put it, the unconscious trauma repeats itself *by means of* some small, contingent bit of reality. "Fate" in psychoanalysis always asserts itself through such contingent encounters, giving rise to the question: "What if I had missed that remark? What if I had taken another route and avoided that scene?" Such questioning is, of course, deceitful since "a letter *always* arrives at its destination": it waits for its moment with patience—if not this, then another contingent little bit of reality will sooner or later find itself at this place that awaits it and fire off the trauma. This is, ultimately, what Lacan called "the arbitrariness of the signifier."[24]

To refer to the terms of speech-act theory, the illusion proper to the process of interpellation consists in the overlooking of its *performative* dimension: when I recognize myself as the addressee of the call of the ideological big Other (Nation, Democracy, Party, God, and so forth), when this call "arrives at its destination" in me, I automatically misrecognize that it is this very act of recognition which *makes me* what I have recognized myself as—I don't recognize myself in it because I'm its addressee, I become its addressee the moment I recognize myself in it. *This* is the reason why a letter always reaches its addressee: because one becomes its addressee when one is reached. The Derridean reproach that a letter can also miss its addressee is therefore simply beside the point: it makes sense only insofar as I presuppose that I can be its addressee *before* the letter reaches me—in other words, it presupposes the traditional teleological trajectory with a preordained goal. Translated into the terms of the joke about my father from Manchester, my mother from Bristol, and me from London, the Derridean proposition that a letter can also go astray and miss its destination discloses a typical obsessional apprehension of what would happen if my father and mother had *not* come across each other—all would have gone wrong, I would not exist . . . So, far from implying any kind of teleological circle, "a letter always arrives at its destination" exposes the very mechanism which brings about the amazement of "Why me? Why was I chosen?" and thus sets in motion the search for a hidden fate that regulates my path.

Symbolic circuit I: "There is no metalanguage"

On a symbolic level, "a letter always arrives at its destination" condenses an entire chain (a "family" in the Wittgensteinian sense) of propositions: "the sender always receives from the receiver his own message in reverse form," "the repressed always returns," "the frame itself is always being framed by part of its content," "we cannot escape the symbolic debt, it always has to be settled," which are all ultimately variations on the same basic premise that "there is no metalanguage." So let us begin by explaining the impossibility of metalanguage apropos of the Hegelian figure of the "Beautiful Soul," deploring the wicked ways of the world from the position of an innocent, impassive victim. The "Beautiful Soul" pretends to speak a pure metalanguage, exempted from the corruption of the world, thereby concealing the way its own moans and groans *partake actively* in the corruption it denounces. In his "Intervention on Transference,"[25] Lacan relies on the dialectic of the "Beautiful Soul" to designate the falsity of the hysterical subjective position: "Dora," Freud's famous analysand, complains of being reduced to a pure object in a play of intersubjective exchanges (her father is allegedly offering her to Mister K. as if in compensation for his own flirtation with Miss K.), i.e., she presents this exchange as an objective state of things in the face of which she is utterly helpless; Freud's answer is that the function of this stance of passive victimization by cruel circumstances is just to conceal her complicity and collusion—the square of intersubjective exchanges can only sustain itself insofar as Dora *assumes actively* her role of victim, of an object of exchange, in other words, insofar as she finds libidinal satisfaction in it, insofar as this very renunciation procures for her a kind of perverse surplus enjoyment. A hysteric continually complains of how he cannot adapt himself to the reality of cruel manipulation, and the psychoanalytic answer to it is not "give up your empty dreams, life is cruel, accept it as it is" but quite the contrary "your moans and groans are false since, by means of them, you are *only too well adapted* to the reality of manipulation and exploitation:" by playing the role of helpless victim, the hysteric assumes the subjective position which enables him to "blackmail emotionally his environs," as we would put it in today's jargon.[26]

This answer, in which the "Beautiful Soul" is confronted with how it actually partakes of the wicked ways of the world, closes the circuit of communication: in it, the subject/sender receives from the addressee his own message in its true form, i.e., the true meaning of his moans and groans. In other words, in it, the letter that the subject put into circulation "arrives at its destination," which was from the very beginning the sender himself: the letter arrives at its destination when the subject is finally forced to assume the true consequences of his activity. This is how Lacan, in the early 1950s, interpreted the Hegelian *dictum* about the rationality of the real ("What is rational is actual and what is actual is rational"):[27] the true meaning of the subject's words or deeds—their *reason*—is disclosed by their actual consequences, so the subject has no right to shrink back from them and say "But I didn't mean it!" In this sense, we may say that Hitchcock's *Rope* is an inherently Hegelian film: the homosexual couple strangles their best friend to win recognition from professor Caddell, their teacher who preaches the right of Supermen to dispose of the useless and weak; when Caddell is confronted with the verbatim realization of his doctrine—when, in other words, he gets back from the other his own message in its inverted, true form, i.e., when the true dimension of his own "letter" (teaching) reaches its proper addressee, namely himself—he is shaken and shrinks back from the consequence of his words, unprepared to recognize in them his own truth. Lacan defines "hero" as the subject who (unlike Caddell and like Oedipus, for example) fully assumes the consequences of his act, that is to say, who does not step aside when the arrow that he shot makes its full circle and flies back at him—unlike the rest of us who endeavor to realize our desire without paying the price for it: revolutionaries who want Revolution without revolution (its bloody reverse). Hitchcock's benevolent-sadistic playing with the spectator takes into account precisely this halfway nature of our desiring: he makes the spectator shrink back by confronting him with the full consequence of the realization of his desire ("you want this evil person killed? OK, you will have it—with all the nauseating details you wanted to pass over in silence . . ."). In short, Hitchcock's "sadism" corresponds exactly to the superego's "malevolent neutrality:" he is nothing but a neutral "purveyor of truth," giving us only what we wanted, but including in the package the part of it that we prefer to ignore.

This reverse of the subject's message is its *repressed*; so it is not difficult to see how the impossibility of metalanguage is linked to the return of the repressed. "There is no metalanguage" insofar as the speaking subject is always already spoken, i.e., insofar as he cannot master the effects of what he is saying: he always says more than he "intended to say," and this surplus of what is effectively said over the intended meaning puts into words the repressed content—in it, "the repressed returns."[28] What are symptoms *qua* "returns of the repressed" if not such slips of the tongue by means of which "the letter arrives at its destination," i.e., by means of which the big Other returns to the subject his own message in its true form? If, instead of saying "Thereby I proclaim the session open," I say "Thereby I proclaim the session closed," do I not get, in the most literal sense, my own message back in its true, inverted form? So what could, at this level, the Derridean notion that a letter can also *miss* its destination mean? That the repressed can also *not* return—yet by claiming this, we entangle ourselves in a naive substantialist notion of the unconscious as a positive entity ontologically preceding its "returns," i.e., symptoms *qua* compromise formations, a notion competently called in question by Derrida himself.[29] Here, we cannot but repeat after Lacan: there is no repression previous to the return of the repressed; the repressed content does not precede its return in symptoms, there is no way to conceive it in its purity undistorted by "compromises" that characterize the formation of the symptoms.[30]

This brings us to the third variation, that of the frame always being framed by part of its content; this formula[31] is crucial insofar as it enables us to oppose the "logic of the signifier" to hermeneutics. The aim of the hermeneutical endeavor is to render visible the contours of a "frame," a "horizon" that, precisely by staying invisible, by eluding the subject's grasp, in advance determines its field of vision: what we can see, as well as what we cannot see, is always given to us through a historically mediated frame of preconceits. There is of course nothing pejorative in the use of the term "preconceit" here: its status is transcendental, i.e., it organizes our experience into a meaningful totality. True, it involves an irreducible limitation of our vision, but this finitude is in itself ontologically constitutive: the world is open to us only within radical finitude. At this level, the impossibility of metalanguage equals the impossibility of a neutral point of view enabling us to see things "objectively," "impartially": there is no view that is not framed by a historically determined horizon of "preunderstanding". Today, for example, we can ruthlessly exploit nature only because nature itself is disclosed to us within a horizon that gives it to be seen as raw material at our disposal, in contrast to the Greek or medieval notion of nature. The Lacanian "logic of the signifier" supplements this hermeneutical thesis with an unheard-of inversion: the "horizon of meaning" is always linked, as if by a kind of umbilical cord, to a point *within* the field disclosed by it; the frame of our view is always already framed (re-marked) by a part of its content. We can easily recognize here the topology of the Moebius band where, as in a kind of abyssal inversion, the envelope itself is encased by its interior.[32]

The best way to exemplify this inversion is via the dialectic of view and gaze: in what I see, in what is open to my view, there is always a point where "I see nothing," a point which "makes no sense," i.e., which functions as the picture's stain—this is the point from which the very picture returns the gaze, looks back at me. "A letter arrives at its destination" precisely in this point of the picture: here I encounter myself, my own objective correlative—here I am, so to speak, inscribed in the picture; this ontic "umbilical cord" of the ontological horizon is what is unthinkable for the entire philosophical tradition, Heidegger included. Therein lies the reason of the uncanny power of psychoanalytical interpretation: the subject pursues his everyday life within its closed horizon of meaning, safe in his distance with respect to the world of objects, assured of their meaning (or their insignificance), when, all of a sudden, the psychoanalyst pinpoints some tiny detail of no significance whatsoever to the subject, a stain in which the subject "sees nothing"—a small, compulsive gesture or tic, a slip of the tongue or something of that order—and says: "You see, this detail is a knot which condenses all you had to forget so that you can swim in your everyday certainty, it enframes the very frame which confers meaning on your life, it structures the horizon within which things make sense to you; if we unknot it, you will lose the ground from under your very feet!" It is an experience not unlike that rendered in the old Oriental formula: "Thou art that!"—"Your entire fate is decided in this idiotic detail!" Or, if we keep ourselves to a more formal level of the set theory: among the elements of a given set, there is always One which overdetermines the specific weight and color of the set as such; among the species of a genus, there is always One which overdetermines the very universality of the genus. Apropos of the relationship of different kinds of production within its articulated totality, Marx wrote:

> In all forms of society there is one specific kind of production which predominates over the rest, whose relations thus assign rank and influence to the others. It is a general illumination which bathes all the other colours and modifies their particularity. It is a particular ether which determines the specific gravity of every being which has materialized within it.[33]

Do not these propositions amount to the fact that the very frame of production (its totality) is always enframed by a part of its content (by one specific kind of production)?

Symbolic circuit II: Fate and repetition

The encounter with "Thou art that!" is of course experienced as an encounter with the knot which condenses one's fate; this brings us to the last variation on the theme "a letter always arrives at its destination": one can never escape one's fate, or, to replace this rather obscurantist formulation with a more appropriate psychoanalytic one, the symbolic debt has to be repaid. The letter which "arrives at its destination" is also a letter of request for outstanding debts; what propels a letter on its symbolic circuit is always some outstanding debt. This dimension of fate is at work in the very formal structure of Poe's "The Purloined Letter": isn't there something distinctly "fateful" in the way the self-experience of the main character in Poe's story is determined by the simple "mechanical" shift of their positions within the intersubjective triad of the three glances (the first which sees nothing; the second which sees that the first sees nothing and deludes itself as to the secrecy of what it hides; the third which sees that the two first glances leave what should be hidden exposed to whomever would seize it)? In the way, for example, the minister's fate is sealed not because of his personal miscalculation or oversight but because the simple shift of his position from the third to the second glance in the repetition of the initial triad causes his structural blindness? Here, we encounter again the mechanism of imaginary (mis)recognition: the participants in the play automatically perceive their fate as something that pertains to the letter as such in its immediate materiality ("This letter is damned, whosoever comes into possesion of it is brought to ruin!")—what they misrecognize is that the "curse" is not in the letter as such but in the intersubjective network organized around it. However, to avoid repeating the played-out analysis of Poe's story, let us address a formally similar case, the classical Bette Davis melodrama *Now, Voyager*, the story of Charlotte Vale, a frustrated spinster, the "ugly duckling" of the family, who is pushed into a nervous breakdown by her domineering mother, a rich widow.[34] Under the guidance of the benevolent Doctor Jacquith, she is cured to emerge as a poised and beautiful woman; following his advice, she decides to see life and takes a trip to South America. There, she has an affair with a charming married man; he is, however, unable to leave his family for her because of his daughter who is on the brink of madness, so Charlotte returns home alone. Soon afterward, she falls into depression and is hospitalized again; in the mental asylum, she encounters the daughter of her lover who immediately develops a traumatic dependence on her. Dr. Jacquith informs Charlotte that her lover's wife died recently, so that they are now free to marry; yet he is quick to add that this marriage would be an unbearable shock for the daughter—Charlotte is her only support, the only thing standing between her and the final slip into madness. Charlotte decides to sacrifice her love and to dedicate her life to mothering the unfortunate child; when, at the end of the film, her lover asks her for her hand, she promises him just deep friendship, refusing his offer with the phrase: "Why reach for the moon, when we can have the stars?"—one of the purest and therefore most efficient nonsenses in the history of cinema.

When her lover shows to Charlotte a picture of his family, her attention is drawn to a girl sitting aside and staring sadly into the camera; this figure arouses her immediate compassion and Charlotte wants to know all about her. Why? She identifies with her because she recognizes in her her own position, that of the neglected "ugly duckling." So when, at the film's end, Charlotte sacrifices her love life for the poor girl's rescue, she does not do it out of an abstract sense of duty: the point is rather that she conceives the girl's present situation, when her very survival depends on Charlotte, as *the exact repetition of her own situation* years ago when she was at her mother's mercy. Therein consists the structural homology between this film and "The Purloined Letter": in the course of the story, the same intersubjective network is repeated, with the subjects shifting to different positions—in both cases, an omnipotent mother holds in her hands the daughter's fate, with the one difference that in the first scene it was an evil mother driving the daughter to madness, while in the second scene a good mother is given a chance to redeem herself by pulling the daughter from the brink. The film displays poetic *finesse* by conferring a double role on Doctor Jacquith: the same person who, in the first scene, "sets free" Charlotte, i.e., opens up to her the perspective of an unchained sexual life, appears in the second scene as the bearer of prohibition who prevents her marriage by reminding her of her debt. Here, we have the "compulsion to repeat" at its purest: Charlotte cannot afford marriage since she must *honor her debt*. When, finally, she seems freed from the nightmare, "fate" (the big Other) confronts her with the price of this freedom by putting her into a situation where she herself can destroy the young girl's life. If Charlotte would not sacrifice herself, she would be persecuted by the "demons of the past": her happy marital life would be spoiled forever by the memory of the unfortunate child in the asylum paying the price, a reminder of how she betrayed *her own* past. In other words, Charlotte does not "sacrifice herself for the other's happiness": by sacrificing herself, she honors her debt to *herself*. So, when she finds herself face to face with a broken girl who can be saved only by means of her sacrifice, we could again say that "a letter arrives at its destination."[35]

Within this dimension of the outstanding debt, the role of the letter is assumed by an object that circulates among the subjects and, by its very circulation, makes out of them a closed intersubjective community. Such is the function of the Hitchcockian object: not the decried MacGuffin but the tiny "piece of the real" which keeps the story in motion by finding itself "out of place" (stolen, etc.): from the ring in *Shadow of a Doubt*, the cigarette lighter in *Strangers on a Train*, up to the child in *The Man Who Knew Too Much* who circulates between the two couples. The story ends the moment this object "arrives at its destination," i.e., returns to its rightful owner: the moment Guy gets back the lighter (the last shot of *Strangers on a Train* where the lighter falls out of dead Bruno's unclasped hand), the moment the abducted child returns to the American couple (in *The Man Who Knew Too Much*), etc. This object embodies, gives material existence to the lack in the Other, to the constitutive inconsistency of the symbolic order: Claude Lévi-Strauss pointed out how the very fact of exchange attests a certain structural flaw, an imbalance that pertains to the Symbolic, which is why the Lacanian mathem for this object is $S(\not{A})$, the signifier of the barred Other. The supreme exemplar of such an object is the ring from Richard Wagner's *Ring des Nibelungen*, this gigantic drama of the unbalanced symbolic exchange. The story opens with Alberich stealing the ring from the Rhine maidens, whereby it becomes the source of a curse for its possessors; it ends when the ring is thrown back into the Rhine to its rightful owners—the Gods, however, pay for this reestablishment of the balance with their twilight, since their very existence was founded upon an unsettled debt.

The imaginary and the symbolic dimension of "a letter always reaching its destination" are thus in their very opposition closely connected: the first is defined by the imaginary (mis)recognition (a letter arrives at its destination insofar as I recognize myself as its addressee, i.e., insofar as I find *myself* in it), whereas the second comprises the concealed truth that emerges in the "blind spots" and flaws of the imaginary circle. Let us just recall so-called "applied psychoanalysis," the standard "psychoanalytic interpretation" of works of art: this procedure always "finds itself," and the propositions on Oedipus complex, on sublimation, etc., are again and again confirmed since the search moves in an imaginary closed circle and finds only what it is already looking for—what, in a sense, it already has (the network of its theoretical preconceits). A letter traversing the symbolic circuit "arrives at its destination" when we experience the utmost futility of this procedure, its utmost failure to touch the inherent logic of its object. The way "a letter arrives at its destination" within the symbolic circuit therefore implies the structure of a slip, of "success through failure": it reaches us unbeknowst to us. In Agatha Christie's *Why Didn't They Ask Evans?*, the young hero and his girl friend find a mortally wounded man on the links who, seconds before his death, raises his head and says "Why didn't they ask Evans?" They set out to investigate the murder and, long afterward, when the dead man's mysterious phrase is completely forgotten, they concern themselves with the somewhat peculiar circumstances of the certification of a dying country gentleman's will: the relatives called as a witness a distant neighbor instead of using the servant Evans who was present in the house, so . . . "Why didn't they ask Evans?" Instantaneously, the hero and his girl friend realize that their question reproduces verbatim the phrase of the man who died on the links—therein consists the clue for his murder. What we have here is an exemplary case of how "a letter arrives at its destination": when, in a totally contingent way, it finds its proper place.

This reference to the letter and its itinerary enables us to distinguish between the two modalities of the crowd. When, apropos of his interpretation of the Freudian dream of Irma's injection, Lacan speaks of "l'immixion des sujets," "the inmixing of subjects," of the moment when the subjects lose their individuality by being reduced to little wheels in a nonsubjective machinery (in the dream itself, the moment of this reversal is the appearance of the three professors who exculpate Freud by enumerating mutually exclusive reasons for the failure of Irma's treatment), this machine is of course synonymous with the *symbolic order*. This mode of the crowd is exemplarily depicted in the paintings of Pieter Brueghel from the years 1559 and 1560 (*Dutch Proverbs, Fight between Carnival and Lent, Child Games*): the subject is here "beheaded," "lost in the crowd," yet the transsubjective mechanism which regulates the process (games, proverbs, carnivals) is clearly of a symbolic nature: it can be unearthed by means of the act of interpretation. In other words, it is the signifier which runs the show—through this very confusion and blind automatism, the letter nevertheless "arrives at its destination." How? Let us recall Eric Ambler's spy novel *Passage of Arms*, the story of a poor Chinese in Malaya in the early 1950s, after the breakdown of the Communist insurgency: upon discovering a forgotten hideout of Communist arms in the jungle, he plans to sell them in order to buy an old bus and thus become a small-scale capitalist. He thereby sets in motion an unforeseen chain of events which exceed by far his original intent: the rich Chinese who buys the arms resells them to an Indonesian pro-Communist guerilla, the transaction involves an "innocent" American tourist couple, the story moves from Malaya to Bangkok, then to Sumatra, yet all this improvisatory texture of accidental encounters brings us back to our starting point: at the end, the Chinese becomes the owner of an old, ramshackle bus, "the letter arrives at its destination," as if some hidden "cunning of Reason" regulated the chaotic flow of events. Something not dissimilar to this is at work in the quartets and quintets of Mozart's great operas; it suffices to mention the finale of *Le Nozze di Figaro*: the persons speak and sing over one another, there is an entire network of misapprehensions and false identifications, yet this chaos of comic encounters seems to be run by the hidden hand of a benevolent destiny which provides for the final reconciliation. An abyss separates this "immixture" from, say, the quintet in the third act of Wagner's *Meistersinger von Nürnberg* where all the voices efface their differences and yield to the same pacifying flow—not to mention the brutal irruption of the crowd that follows Hagen's "call to men (*Männerruf*)" in the second act of *Die Götterdämmerung*. The point here is the link between this crowd and the prelude to the opera with the sibyls no longer able to decipher the future course of events, since the cord of destiny is cut—the crowd enters the stage when history is no longer regulated by the texture of symbolic destiny, i.e., when the father's phallic authority is broken (one should remember that, the previous evening, Siegfried broke Wotan's spear). This crowd, the *modern* crowd, appeared for the first time in Edgar Allan Poe's "The Man of the Crowd": the anonymous observer watches through the windowpane of a cafe (this frame that introduces the distance between "inside" and "outside" is crucial here) the turmoil of the London evening crowd and decides to follow an old man; at dawn, after long hours of walking, it becomes clear that there is nothing to discover: "It will be in vain to follow; I shall learn no more of him, nor of his deeds." The old man is thus exposed as the "man of the crowd," the epitome of evil, precisely insofar as he embodies something that "doesn't allow itself to be read"—*es lässt sich nicht lesen*, as Poe himself puts it in German. This "resistance to being read" of the crowd designates of course the passage from the symbolic register to that of the Real.[36]

The real encounter

The motif of fate has brought us to the very brink of the third level, that of the Real; here, "a letter always arrives at its destination" equals what "meeting one's fate" means: "we will all die." A common pretheoretical sensitivity enables us to detect the ominous undertone that sticks to the proposition "a letter always arrives at its destination": the only letter that nobody can evade, that sooner or later reaches us, i.e., the letter which has each of us as its infallible addressee, is death. We can say that we live only in so far as a certain letter (the letter containing our death warrant) still wanders around, looking for us. Let us recall the ill-famed "poetic" statement of the Iranian president Ali Hamnei apropos of the sentence of death pronounced on Salman Rushdie: nothing can stop its execution, the bullet is already on its way, sooner or later, it will hit its mark—such is the fate of all and each of us, the bullet with our name on it is already shot. Derrida himself emphasizes the lethal dimension of writing: every trace is condemned to its ultimate effacement. Note the fundamental ambiguity of the very word "end": "aim" and "annihilation"—the closing of the letter's circuit equals its consumption. The crucial point here is that the imaginary, the symbolic, and the real dimension of "a letter always arrives at its destination" are not external to each other: at the end of the imaginary as well as the symbolic itinerary, we encounter the Real. As was demonstrated by Lacan apropos of Freud's dream of Irma's injection, the dual mirror relationship culminates in the horrifying confrontation with the abyss of the Real, exemplified by the flesh of Irma's throat:

> the flesh one never sees, the foundation of things, the other side of the head, of the face, the secretory glands *par excellence*, the flesh from which everything exudes, at the very heart of the mystery, the flesh in as much as it is suffering, is formless, in as much as its form in itself is something which provokes anxiety.[37]

The fascinating image of a double is therefore ultimately nothing but a mask of horror, its delusive front: when we encounter ourselves, we encounter death. The same horror emerges with the fulfillment of symbolic "destiny," as is attested by Oedipus: when, at Colonnus, he closed the circuit and paid all his debts, he found himself reduced to a kind of soap bubble burst asunder—a scrap of the real, the leftover of a formless slime without any support in the symbolic order. Oedipus realized his destiny

> to that final point which is nothing more than something strictly identical to a striking down, a tearing apart, a laceration of himself—he is no longer, no longer anything, at all. And it is at that moment that he says the phrase I evoked last time—*Am I made man in the hour when I cease to be?*[38]

The unpaid symbolic debt is therefore in a way constitutive of our existence: our very symbolic existence is a "compromise formation," the delaying of an encounter. In Max Ophuls's melodrama *Letter from an Unknown Woman*, this link connecting the symbolic circuit with the encounter of the Real is perfectly exemplified. At the very beginning of the film "a letter arrives at its destination," confronting the hero with the disavowed truth: what was for him a series of unconnected, ephemeral love affairs that he only vaguely remembered destroyed a woman's life. He assumes responsibility for this by means of a suicidal gesture: by deciding not to escape and to attend the duel he is certain to lose.

However, as is indicated in Lacan's above-quoted reading of the dream of Irma's injection, the Real is not only death but also life: not only the pale, frozen, lifeless immobility but also 'the flesh from which everything exudes," the life substance in its mucous palpitation. In other words, the Freudian duality of life and death drives is *not* a symbolic opposition but a tension, and antagonism, inherent to the presymbolic Real. As Lacan points out again and again, the very notion of life is alien to the symbolic order. And the name of this life substance that proves a traumatic shock for the symbolic universe is of course *enjoyment*. The ultimate variation on the theme of a letter that always arrives at its destination reads therefore: "you can never get rid of the stain of enjoyment"—the very gesture of renouncing enjoyment produces inevitably a surplus enjoyment that Lacan writes down as the "object small a." Examples offer themselves in abundance, from the ascetic who can never be sure he does not repudiate all worldly goods because of the ostentatious and vain satisfaction procured by this very act of sacrifice, to the "sense of fulfillment" that overwhelms us when we submit to the totalitarian appeal: "Enough of decadent enjoyment! It's time for sacrifice and renunciation!" This dialectic of enjoyment and surplus enjoyment—i.e., the fact that there is no "substantial" enjoyment preceding the excess of surplus enjoyment, that enjoyment itself is a kind of surplus produced by renunciation—is perhaps what gives a clue to so-called "primal masochism."[39]

Such a reading, however, leads beyond Lacan's "Seminar on 'The Purloined Letter,' " which stays within the confines of the "structuralist" problematic of a senseless, "mechanical" symbolic order regulating the subject's innermost self-experience. From the perspective of the last years of Lacan's teaching, the letter which circulates among the subjects in Poe's story, determining their position in the intersubjective network, is no longer the materialized agency of the *signifier* but rather an *object* in the strict sense of materialized enjoyment—the stain, the uncanny excess that the subjects snatch away from each other, forgetful of how its very possession will mark them with a passive, "feminine" stance that bears witness to the confrontation with the object-cause of desire. What ultimately interrupts the continuous flow of words, what hinders the smooth running of the symbolic circuit, is the traumatic presence of the Real: when the words suddenly stay out, we have to look not for imaginary resistances but for the object that came too close.

NOTES

1 Pascal Bonitzer, *Le Champ aveugle*, (Paris: Cahiers du Cinéma/Gallimard, 1982), pp. 49–50.

2 Ibid., p. 49.

3 Gilles Deleuze, *L'Image-mouvement* (Paris: Editions de Minuit, 1983), pp. 234, 236.

4 Cf. Jacques Lacan, "Seminar on 'The Purloined Letter,' " in John P. Muller and William J. Richardson, eds., *The Purloined Poe* (Baltimore and London: Johns Hopkins University Press, 1988), p. 53.

5 Among the more recent films which are centered on the efficacy of the final scene, mention should be made of Peter Weir's *Dead Poet's Society*: is the whole story not a kind of buildup to the final pathetic crescendo when the pupils defy the school authorities and express their solidarity with the fired teacher by standing on their benches?

6 The fact that this final dialogue takes place in complete silence—we read the words in interposed titles as in silent movies—confers on it an additional intensity: it is as if silence itself has begun to speak. An intrusion of the voice at

this point would ruin the whole effect, more precisely: it would ruin its sublime dimension. This scene alone more than justifies Chaplin's "eccentric" decision to produce a silent movie in the era of sound, because the whole efficacy of the sequence is due to the fact that we—the spectators—know that movies already talk and thus experience this silence as the absence of the voice.

7 Jacques Lacan, *The Four Fundamental Concepts of Psycho-Analysis* (London: Tavistock Publications, 1977), chapters 17 and 20.

8 Michel Chion, *Les Lumières de la ville* (Paris: Nathan, 1989).

9 It should be noted that *City Lights* itself germinated from a similar idea. It was originally to be the story of a father who lost his sight in an accident; to avoid the psychic traumatism that knowledge of his blindness would cause his small daughter, he pretends that the clumsy acts which result from his blindness (his overturning a chair, his numerous false steps, etc.) are comical imitations of a clown, meant to amuse her; unsuspecting of the true state, the girl accepts this explanation and laughs heartily at her father's misadventures.

10 This split between the ideal figure of the rich man and the tramp as the ideal figure's objective support enables us also to locate the paradox of self-destructive female curiosity, at work from Richard Wagner to contemporary mass culture. That is to say, the plot of Wagner's *Lohengrin* turns on Elsa's curiosity: a nameless hero saves her and marries her, but enjoins her not to ask him who he is or what is his name (the famous air "Nie solst du mich befragen" from act 1)—as soon as she does so, he will be obliged to leave her . . . Elsa cannot stand it and asks him the fateful question; so, in an even more famous air ("In fernem Land," act 3), Lohengrin tells her that he is a knight of the Grail, the son of Parsifal from the castle of Montsalvat, and then departs on a swan, while the unfortunate Elsa collapses dead. How not to recall here Superman or Batman where we find the same logic? In both of these cases, the main female character has a presentiment that her partner (the confused journalist in *Superman*, the eccentric millionaire in *Batman*) is really the mysterious public hero, but the partner puts off as long as possible the moment of revelation. What we have here is a kind of forced choice attesting to the dimension of castration: man is split, divided into the weak everyday fellow with whom sexual relation is possible and the bearer of the symbolic mandate, the public hero (knight of the Grail, Superman, Batman); we are thus obliged to choose: as soon as we force the sexual partner to reveal his symbolic identity, we are bound to lose him.

So when Lacan says that the "secret of psychoanalysis" consists in the fact that "there is no sexual act, whereas there is sexuality," the act is to be conceived precisely as the performative assumption, by the subject, of his symbolic mandate, as in the passage in *Hamlet*, where the moment when, finally—too late—Hamlet is able to act is signaled by his expression "I, Hamlet the Dane": this is what is not possible in the order of sexuality, i.e., as soon as the man proclaims his mandate, saying "I . . . Lohengrin, Batman, Superman," he excludes himself from the domain of sexuality.

11 William Rothman, "The ending of 'City Lights,' " in *The "I" of the Camera* (Cambridge: Cambridge University Press, 1988), p. 59.

12 Cf. Jacques Lacan, *Le Séminaire, livre VII: L'Ethique de la psychanalyse* (Paris: Editions du Seuil, 1986).

13 Or, to mention an example from western movies: it is easy to love Indians portrayed as helpless, brutalized victims, as in *The Broken Arrow* or *Soldier Blue*, but the situation is far more ambiguous in John Ford's *Fort Apache* where they are portrayed as victorious, militarily superior, overrunning the US cavalry like a blast of wind.

14 Jacques Lacan, *Le Séminaire, livre VII, p. 133.*

15 It would be interesting to read *Limelight* as a film which is complementary to *City Lights*: at the end of *City Lights*, the tramp "begins to live" (is recognized in his true being), whereas at the end of *Limelight*, he dies; the first film begins with his uncovering (the Mayor unveils the monument), the second ends with the veiling of his body; in the first film, he becomes at the end the full object of another's gaze (and is thereby recognized as a subject), whereas in the second film he himself turns into a pure gaze; in the first film, the mutilation of the girl, his love, refers to her eyes (blindness), in the second to her feet (paralysis: the original title of the film was *Foot-lights*); etc. The two films have thus to be approached in a Lévi-Straussian manner, as two versions of the same myth.

16 Cf. Jacques Derrida, "The Purveyor of Truth," in *The Post Card: From Socrates to Freud and Beyond* (Chicago: University of Chicago Press, 1987).

17 Cf. Jacques Lacan, "Seminar on 'The Purloined Letter,' " p. 53.

18 Since this recourse to common sense takes place more often than one might suspect, *systematically* even, within the "deconstruction," one is tempted to put forward the thesis that the very fundamental gesture of "deconstruction" is in a radical sense *commonsensical*. There is namely an unmistakable ring of common sense in the "deconstructionist" insistence upon the impossibility of establishing a clear cut difference between empirical and transcendental, outside and inside, representation and presence, writing and voice; in its compulsive demonstration of how the outside always already smears over the inside, of how writing is constitutive of voice, etc. etc.—as if "deconstructionism" is ultimately wrapping up commonsensical insights into an intricate jargon. Therein consists perhaps one of the hitherto over-looked reasons for its unforeseen success in the USA, the land of common sense *par excellence*.

19 What is crucial here is the difference between the letter's symbolic circuit and its itinerary in what we call "reality": a letter always arrives at its destination on the symbolic level, whereas in reality, it can of course fail to reach it. This difference is strictly homologous to that established by Lacan apropos of the two possible readings of the phrase "You are the one that will follow me" (Jacques Lacan, *Le Séminaire, livre III: Les Psychoses* (Paris: Editions du Seuil, 1981), pp. 315–19):

1) read as a statement ascertaining a positive state of things, it can of course be falsified if it proves inaccurate, i.e., if you do *not* follow me;

2) read as a bestowal of a symbolic mandate, or designation, i.e., as the establishment of a pact giving birth to a new intersubjective relation, it cannot simply be falsified by your factual behavior: you *remain* "the one that will follow me" even if, in reality, you do *not* do it—in this case, you simply do not live up to your symbolic title which nevertheless determines your place in the symbolic network. In other words, read in this second sense, the determination "the one that will follow me" functions as a "rigid designator" in the Kripkeian sense: it remains true "in all possible worlds," irrespective of your factual behavior.

20 As to these readings, cf. Barbara Johnson's "The Frame of Reference: Poe, Lacan, Derrida," in *The Purloined Poe.*

21 Cf. Michel Pêcheux, *Language, Semantics and Ideology* (London: Macmillan, 1982).

22 Cf. Barbara Johnson, op. cit., p. 248.

23 Michel Pêcheux, op. cit., p. 107.

24 An exemplary case of such a (mis)recognition is found in Joseph Mankiewicz's *Letter to Three Wives* where each of the three wives on a Sunday trip recognizes herself as addressee of the letter sent to them by the local *femme fatale* announcing that she has run away with one of their husbands: the letter stirs up the trauma of each of them, each of them becomes aware of the failure of her marriage.

25 Cf. Jacques Lacan, "Intervention on Transference," in Charles Bernheimer and Claire Cahane, eds., *In Dora's Case* (London: Virago Press, 1985).

26 As for the paradoxes of the "Beautiful Soul," cf. Slavoj Žižek, *The Sublime Object of Ideology* (London: Verso Books, 1989), pp. 215–17.

27 G. W. F. Hegel, *Philosophy of Right* (Oxford: Clarendon Press, 1942), p. 8.

28 Therein consists the elementary Hegelian procedure; Hegel demonstrates the "nontruth" of some proposition not by comparing it with the thing as it is "in itself" and thus ascertaining the proposition's inaccuracy, but by comparing the proposition *with itself*, i.e., with its own process of enunciation: by comparing the intended meaning of the proposition with what the subject effectively said. This discord is the very impetus of the dialectical process, as is attested at the very beginning of the *Phenomenology of Spirit* where "sense certainty" is refuted by means of a reference to the universal dimension contained in its own act of enunciation.

29 Cf. Jacques Derrida, "Freud and the Scene of Writing," in *Writing and Difference* (Chicago: University of Chicago Press, 1978), where it is demonstrated by rigorous analysis how it is not possible to differentiate in a clear-cut way between "primary" and "secondary" processes: the "primary" process (subjected to the logic of the unconscious: condensations, displacements, etc.) is always already (re)marked by the "secondary" process that characterizes the system of consciousness/preconscious.

30 *Stricto sensu*, there *is* a subjective position within which a letter does *not* arrive at its destination, within which the repressed does *not* return in the shape of symptoms, within which the subject does *not* receive from the Other his own

message in its true form: that of a *psychotic*. "A letter arrives at its destination" only with the subject entering the circuit of communication, i.e., capable of assuming the dialectical relationship toward the Other *qua* locus of truth. However, according to Lacan's famous formula of the psychotic forclusion ("what was foreclosed from the Symbolic returns in the Real"), even in psychosis the letter *does* ultimately reach the subject, namely in the form of psychotic "answers of the Real" (hallucinations, etc.).

31 Elaborated in Jacques Derrida, *La Vérité en peinture* (Paris: Flammarion, 1978).

32 As for this topology, cf. Jacques-Alain Miller, "Théorie de la langue," *Ornicar?* 1 (1975).

33 Karl Marx, *Grundrisse* (Harmondsworth: Penguin Books, 1972), p. 107.

34 We rely here on the perspicacious analysis by Elizabeth Cowie, "Fantasia," *m/f* 9 (1984).

35 There is, however, another side to this story: Charlotte's act of renunciation can also be read as an attempt to elude the inherent impossibility of the sexual relationship by positing an external hindrance to it, thus preserving the illusion that without this hindrance, she would be able to enjoy it fully. In short, the trick is here the same as that of "courtly love": "A very refined manner to supplant the absence of the sexual relationship by feigning that it is us who put the obstacle in its way" (Jacques Lacan, *Le Séminaire, livre XX: Encore* (Paris: Editions du Seuil, 1975) p. 65).

36 When, with the advent of capitalism, the symbolically structured "community" was replaced by the "crowd," community became in a radical sense *imagined*: our "sense of belonging" does not refer anymore to a community we experience as "actual," but becomes a performative effect brought about by the "abstract" media (press, radio, etc.) (cf. Benedict Anderson, *Imagined Communities* London and New York: Verso Books, 1983). Every community, from the most "primitive" tribes onward, was of course always already "staged" by symbolic rituals; yet it was only with capitalism that the community became "imagined" in the precise sense of being dialectically opposed to the atomized, "actual" economic life. What we have in mind here is not only the fact that, in contrast to the precapitalist ethnic communities, the concept Nation is a product of the expansion of the media (the role of the press in eighteenth and ninteenth centuries, Hitler and radio, Moral Majority's TV evangelism, etc.), but that a more refined logic is at work from political identification up to TV quiz shows and sexuality. Let us recall Stuart Hall's analysis of Thatcherism's political appeal (cf. his *Hard Road to Renewal* (London and New York: Verso Books, 1988)): the Thatcherite interpellation succeeded insofar as the individual recognized himself/herself not as a member of some actual community but as a member of the imagined community of those who may be "lucky in the next round" by way of their individual entrepreneurship. The hope of success, the recognition of oneself as the one who *may* succeed, overshadows the actual success and already functions as a success, the same as in a TV quiz show where, in a sense, "taking part in it" already is to win: what really matters is not

the actual gains but being identified as part of the community of those who *may* win. Today, such a logic has penetrated even the most intimate domain of sexuality, as attested by the success of "minitel" (the network of personal computers connected by phone) in France: upon entering the circuit of minitel communication, I choose a pseudonym for myself and then exchange the most obscene sexual fantasies with others whom I also know only by their pseudonyms . . . The point of it, of course, is that, within this imagined community of anonymous participants, everybody knows that these fantasies will never be "realized": gratification is procured by the flow of signifiers itself—it is as if "minitel" were made to exemplify Lacan's thesis according to which enjoyment is primarily enjoyment in the signifier. It seems therefore that today's predominant economy of enjoyment repeats the paradox of quantum physics where possibility (the possible trajectories of a particle) as such possesses a kind of actuality: to imagine a possible gratification of desire equals its actual gratification.

37 *The Seminar of Jacques Lacan, Book II: The Ego in Freud's Theory and in the Technique of Psychoanalysis* (Cambridge: Cambridge University Press, 1988), pp. 154–55.

38 Ibid., p. 226.

39 In other words, if we subtract from enjoyment its surplus, we are left with nothing at all; the closest scientific analogy to it is perhaps the notion of *photon* in physics. When physicists refer to the mass of a particle, they usually refer to its mass when it is at rest. Any mass other than a rest mass is called relativistic mass; since the mass of a particle increases with velocity, a particle can have any number of relativistic masses—the size of its relativistic mass depends upon its velocity. The total mass is thus composed of the rest mass plus the surplus added by the velocity of its movement. The paradox of photons is, however, that *they don't have any rest mass*: their rest mass equals zero. The photon is thus an object which exists only as a surplus, as the acceleration due to its velocity; in a way, it is "without substance"—if we subtract the relativistic mass that depends upon its velocity, i.e., if we "quiet it down" and attempt to seize it in its state of rest, "as it really is," it dissolves. And it is the same with the "object small a" *qua* surplus enjoyment: it exists only in its distorted state (visually, for example, only insofar as it is viewed from aside, anamorphotically extended or contracted)—if we view it "straight," "as it really is," there is nothing to see.

2

WHY IS *WOMAN* A SYMPTOM OF MAN?

2.1 WHY IS SUICIDE THE ONLY SUCCESSFUL ACT?

The act as an answer of the real

The miracle of Roberto Rossellini's encounter with Ingrid Bergman, this true act of grace that stirred his creativity and caused it to take another direction, exemplifies in an almost uncanny way how "a letter always arrives at its destination." The background of the story is well known: in 1947, at the height of her fame as the leading Hollywood star, Ingrid Bergman saw Rossellini's *Open City* and *Paisan*, his two neorealist masterpieces, in a small New York theater. Deeply affected, she wrote a letter to Rossellini which attests to her transferential relationship with him even before the two of them met personally—a case of love *before* first sight. She was obsessed by the idea of helping Rossellini gain well-deserved international fame by putting her stardom at his disposal; so she offered herself for any role, if he had any use for a Swedish actress who spoke fluent English, some German and only two words of Italian: "Ti amo!" (I love you!) However, a series of accidents almost prevented her letter from reaching him:

> An Italian she met in America told her she could reach Rossellini by writing to Minerva Studios. Then, the studio headquarters burnt down just after her letter arrived; sifting through the ashes, they found the letter, but when the studio tried to contact Rossellini, he kept hanging up, since he was in a dispute with them at the time. When the letter finally managed to get to him, he had to have his secretary translate it from English—and then asked her who Ingrid Bergman was. Once apprised of her international fame, he quickly responded with an urgent telegram on May 8, his birthday, that it was "absolutely true that I dreamed to make a film with you." . . .[1]

A lie pure and simple, opportunistic flattery, or was it? What to think then of the fact that in Rossellini's most famous film, *Open City* from 1945, the two central negative characters, the lesbian Nazi and the Gestapo torturer, are named *Ingrid* and *Bergmann*? In a way, Rossellini effectively *had* already had dreams on the "Ingrid Bergman" theme . . . What were his thoughts upon receiving a letter signed by a person whose name condensed two utter impersonations of evil from his film?[2] Wasn't this a kind of "answer of the Real" to his reckless playing with film illusion, an experience close to that of Casanova when, as if in response to his magic prattle, nature reacted with a violent thunderstorm? Ingrid Bergman thus entered Rossellini's life with the traumatic impact of an *act*: although her letter appeared as a shock, the place for her within Rossellini's symbolic space had already been carved out far in advance.

How should we conceive the notion of act at work here, i.e., the act in its suicidal dimension?[3] Today, it is already part of received wisdom, a sign of good manners so to speak, to reject with derision the supposedly "naive," "commonsensical" opposition of words and acts or things, an opposition upon which phrases of the type "you only talk instead of acting!" "not only in words, but also in deeds," and so forth are based. Everybody now knows that "we can do things with words": more than forty years have passed since J. L. Austin wrote his standard manual on this theme. And indeed, is not the very kernel of psychoanalysis embedded in the dimension of language as speech *act*? Is it not confined to this dimension by the very fact that it is a *talking cure*, an attempt to reach and transform the real of the symptom solely by means of words, i.e., without having recourse to an immediate operation on the body (via electrotherapy, pharmacotherapy, etc.)? (We can thus determine with precision the moment when Wilhelm Reich ceased to be a psychoanalyst: when he abandoned the medium of the word and started to rely on bodily massage to release neurotic tensions.) And, closer to our domain, does not Lacan, at the very moment when he elaborated his notion of the autonomous symbolic order, formulate a kind of theory of the speech act (performative) *avant la lettre*? Is not the fundamental proposition of his first *Seminars* that intersubjective reality is composed of utterances which, by means of their very act of enunciation, *make* the subject what it asserts to be—utterances of the type "you are my wife, my teacher," and so forth, in other words: interpellations, utterances whereby the subject, by recognizing itself in their call, becomes what they purport it to be? And is not herein also the accent of Lacan's conception of the functional role of remembering past traumas? The point is not to arrive at the factual truth of some long-forgotten event—what is effectively at stake here is, quite literally, the *recollection* of the past, i.e., the way this remembrance of the past bears on the subject's *present* position of enunciation, how it transforms the very place from which the subject speaks (is spoken). Herein lies the "effect of truth" intended by the psychoanalytic cure: when I draw a childhood trauma out of the shadowy world of "repression" and integrate it with my knowledge, this radically transforms the symbolic horizon that determines my present "self-understanding"—after accomplishing it, I am not the same subject as before.

However, it is obvious that Lacan's thesis on suicide as the only successful act doesn't enter this frame: the matrix of the act enabling us to grasp suicide as the act par excellence is definitely *not* that of a speech act, of a performative. Which is then this matrix? Instead of risking an immediate answer, let us return to Rossellini, since his central obsession was precisely that of a suicidal, "impossible" act of freedom beyond the scope of a performative.

Germany, Year Zero: The word no longer obliges

Rossellini was perfectly aware of the crucial role of the performative dimension in structuring intersubjective space: an entire series of his films is centered on the dialectic of "playing a role," of assuming performatively a symbolic mandate. This dialectic was taken to its extreme in *General della Rovere*, a tragicomic story about Bertone, a petty thief and swindler (played by Vittorio de Sica). The story takes place during the German occupation of Italy; Bertone is arrested by the Gestapo and forced to collaborate. Because of his ressemblance to General della Rovere, the legendary partisan leader, he is obliged to pass himself off as della Rovere in a prison full of members of the resistance (unbeknownst to the partisans, the real della Rovere had already been caught and shot by the Germans). The idea of the Germans is that Bertone, posing as della Rovere, should make inquiries among the prisoners about the organization of the resistance and its other leaders. However, events take an unforeseen turn when Bertone becomes more and more accustomed to his role and ends by insisting on it even at the price of his life: rather than give the Germans the names they seek, he lets them shoot him as "General della Rovere" . . . As Leo Braudy succinctly put it, "the importance of the film lies in its acceptance of artifice—role-playing, the assumption of disguise—as a way toward moral truth . . . [This film] introduces the idea that role-playing and disguise can lead to a liberation and realization of the self."[4] The dialectic at work here is that of symbolic identification, of assuming a symbolic mandate: insisting on a false mask brings us nearer to a true, authentic subjective position than throwing off the mask and displaying our "true face." As long as poor Bertone, under the pressure of circumstances, just pretends to be della Rovere, we have the comic situation of a common little man occupying by chance the hero's place; as soon as he is prepared to forfeit his very life for this "role," the situation acquires tragic dimensions, his very insistence on the mask becomes an authentic ethical deed. Such a dialectic—developed by Rossellini even more pointedly in his *Rise to Power of Louis XIV*—implies that there is more truth in a mask than in what is hidden beneath it: a mask is never simply "just a mask" since it determines the actual place we occupy in the intersubjective symbolic network; what is effectively false and null is our "inner distance" from the mask we wear (the "social role" we play), our "true self" hidden beneath it. The path to an authentic subjective position runs therefore "from the outside inward": first, we pretend to be something, we just act as if we are that, till, step by step, we actually become it—it is not difficult to recognize in this paradox the Pascalian logic of "custom" ("act as if you believe and belief will come by itself"). The performative dimension at work here consists of the symbolic efficiency of the "mask": wearing a mask actually *makes us* what we feign to be. In other words, the conclusion to be drawn from this dialectic is the exact opposite of the common wisdom by which every human act (achievement, deed) is ultimately just an act (posture, pretense): the only authenticity at our disposal is that of impersonation, of "taking our act (posture) seriously."[5]

This logic of act *qua* identification with a mask, *qua* assuming a symbolic mandate is, however, overshadowed in Rossellini's films by another, radically heterogeneous logic that comes forth in the moments of *epiphany*; as a rule, these epiphanies are read in a Christian perspective, as moments of grace that agitate and illuminate the hero—but is this really the right way to approach them? Let us take a closer look at this question by focusing upon three films, all of which are structured as a preparation or a reaction to the traumatic moment of epiphany: *Germany, Year Zero*; *Stromboli*; *Europa '51*. Each of these films is characterized by a certain structure of *lure*: it sets a trap to be avoided, i.e., if we perceive it in a "spontaneous" way, we are inevitably led astray.

Germany, Year Zero is a story about Edmund, a boy of ten living with his elder sister and sickly father in the ruins of occupied Berlin in the summer of 1945. He is left to the street and keeps his family by way of petty street crimes and black-market peddling. He falls more and more under the influence of his homosexual Nazi teacher, Henning, who fills him with lessons on how life is a cruel struggle for survival where one must deal mercilessly with the weaklings who are just a burden to us. Edmund decides to apply this lesson to his father who constantly moans and groans that he will never recover his health and that he wants to die, since he is only a burden to his family: granting his request, he mixes a fatal dose of medicine into the father's glass of milk. After the father's death, he wanders around aimlessly among the ruins of the Berlin streets; a group of children refuse to let him join their game, as if they have somehow guessed his horrible deed, so he awkwardly plays hopscotch alone for a few moments, but he is unable to let himself go in the game—childhood is lost for him, he is already cut off from human community. His sister calls him, but he can no longer accept her solace, so he hides from her in an abandoned, half-ruined apartment house, walks to the second floor, closes his eyes and jumps. The last shot of the film shows his tiny body lying amidst the concrete ruins. The scene for which the entire film was shot is of course the final wandering of Edmund in the ruins of Berlin and his suicide. Wherein lies the meaning of this act? The reading which offers itself immediately is quite obvious: the film is a story of how the morally corrupted Nazi ideology can spoil even a child's innocence and induce him to accomplish parricide. Once he becomes aware of the true dimension of his deed, he kills himself under the pressure of unbearable guilt.

Is this reading the only one possible? A closer examination quickly reveals a series of uneasy details that disturb this image. True, Edmund acts, he passes over to the act, while the teacher just chatters pathetically about the right of the strong, so that when Edmund tells him about his parricide, the teacher shrinks back in horror. Are we, however, for all that, justified in asserting that Edmund simply took the lesson of his teacher literally and consequently acted upon it? Was his act really *caused* by the teacher's word, so that we are concerned with a causal chain linking words and deeds? The least we can add is that, by means of his act, Edmund not only complies with the teacher's lesson, "applying" it to his own family, but at the same time meets his father's explicit will to die. His act is therefore somehow indeterminable, it cannot be properly located, being at the same time an act of supreme cruelty and cold distance *and* an act of boundless love and tenderness, attesting that he is prepared to go to extremes to comply with his father's wishes. This coincidence of opposites (cold, methodical cruelty and boundless love) is *a point at which every "foundation" of acts in "words," in ideology, fails*: this "foundation" simply falls short of the abyss announced in it. Edmund's act, far from "taking literally" and realizing the most corrupted and cruel ideology, implies a certain surplus which eludes the domain of ideology as such—it is an act of "absolute freedom" which momentarily suspends the field of ideological meaning, i.e., which interrupts the link between "words" and "deeds." Precisely by being emptied of every "positive" (ideological, psychological) content, Edmund's act is an act of freedom as defined by F. W. J. Schelling:

an act founded only in itself, not in any kind of ideological "sufficient grounds."[6] It is for this reason that in Edmund's parricide, pure evil coincides with the most perfect childish innocence: in the very act of murdering his father, Edmund becomes a saint. The use of the term "saint" is here not careless: a couple of years after *Germany, Year Zero*, Rossellini shot *Francesco, giullare di Dio*, a film on Saint Francis, in which he put the break of Saint Francis with all worldly institutional ties, his return to the state of blessed innocence where we "have all" precisely insofar as we have "lost all," in line with Edmund's voidance of and isolation from ordinary human community.[7] Edmund's radical "emptying" is displayed by his very reticent way of acting, especially in the scene in which he provides his father with the glass of poisoned milk. Edmund watches his father with an inexpressive, tired, pale gaze, with no trace of fear, compassion, regret, or any other sentiment. Any kind of "identification" with Edmund is thereby thwarted—we, the viewers, cannot shiver with Edmund, feel his tension, regret, or horror at his act: "Edmund, who in a more conventional film would be the focus of audience identification, here seems rather a kind of null set, an empty integer, a focal point of effects."[8] The null set, the empty integer, these are Lacanian names for the subject of the signifier, i.e., for the subject, insofar as it is reduced to an empty place without support in imaginary or symbolic identification.[9] Edmund is in fact pure, "demonic" evil, but what we must bear in mind is that precisely for this reason, he embodies the pure spirituality of a will delivered from every "pathological" motivation.

Edmund is excluded from community, "symbolically dead": not only does he find himself excluded from concrete human community, what is at stake here is a far more radical experience of exclusion from—of asserting a distance with respect to—the big Other itself, the symbolic order. What propels him into act is an awareness of the ultimate insufficiency and nullity of every ideological foundation: he succeeds in occupying that impossible/real empty place where *words no longer oblige*, where their performative power is suspended. *This* is "Germany, Year Zero": Germany in the year of absolute freedom when the intersubjective bond, the engagement of the Word is broken. True, we can call this—the distance taken from the Other—also "psychosis," but what is "psychosis" here if not another name for freedom?[10]

So when, after the parricide, Edmund tells his teacher: "You just talked about it, I did it!" this utterance in no way suggests a shift of responsibility to the teacher, i.e., an argument in the manner of "Don't blame me, it was you who told me to proceed this way!" but quite to the contrary, a cold, impassionate ascertaining of the above-mentioned absolute *gap* that separates words and deeds. And, following the immanent logic of the film, the acceptance of this gap is the very opposite of evil embodied in a corrupting, all-pervading voice, most forcefully in the famous scene of Edmund trying to sell the record of one of Hitler's speeches to two British soldiers: he puts the record on a portable phonograph and, all of a sudden, Hitler's voice resounds through the debris-filled hallways; the accidental passersby grow stiff, marveling at the sudden reappearance of this uncannily familiar voice . . . It is such a disembodied voice that materializes the invisible pervasiveness of the corrupt Nazi ideology, while the entire accent of the scene is precisely on the fact that Edmund is *not* enchanted by this or by any of the other ideological voices which bombard him from all sides: not only the teacher's voice, but also his sister's voice offering him the haven of family just before his suicide. What propels him to act is no voice, no superego imperative, but precisely the accepted distance from all voices.[11]

In this sense, *Germany, Year Zero* is the exact opposite of Hitchcock's *Rope* (shot only a year later). The fundamental problem of both films is the same: that of the relationship of words and deeds, as exemplified by the realization of a dreadful ideology; both films occur as a reaction to the traumatic experience of Nazism: the realization of such a monstrous ideology, how was it possible? At least in *Rope*, Hitchcock shrinks from the abyss Rossellini was able to confront (which is why *Rope* is to be counted among Hitchcock's failures): what is wrongly attributed to *Germany, Year Zero* is effectively the thesis of *Rope*. When the homosexual couple strangles their best friend, they do it to win recognition from professor Caddell, their teacher who preaches the right of Supermen to dispose of the useless and weak (the same as Henning in *Germany*); when Caddell is confronted with the literal realization of his doctrine—when, following the Lacanian definition of communication, he gets back from the other his own message in its inverted, true form—he is shaken and shrinks back from the consequence of his words, i.e., he is not prepared to recognize in them his own truth (again, the same as Henning in *Germany*). Hitchcock, however, remains at this insight: the "rope" from the film's title is the rope linking words and deeds, and the film turns out to be an admonition against "playing with words"—never play with dangerous ideas since you can never be sure that there won't be a psychotic taking them "literally"; nobody in the film, neither the professor nor the murderous couple, is capable of breaking this bond and attaining the point of freedom.[12]

Europa '51: Escape into guilt

Edmund's suicide has therefore nothing whatsoever to do with remorse: he just lets himself be drawn into the vertiginous abyss he discovered in committing the parricide. And it is the same abyss that swallows the child in *Europa '51*, a film which is in many aspects complementary to *Germany*: in *Germany*, the moment of epiphany arrives at the end, it functions as the dénouement, whereas the entire story of *Europa* consists of the display of consequences for its characters of a traumatic "encounter with the Real" which takes place at the very beginning.

Europa '51 is the story of Irene, the wife in a rich Roman family, whose young son desperately seeks contact with her, while she is more interested in receptions and social life. Her son suddenly attempts suicide (by throwing himself into the void in the middle of a spiral staircase) and soon afterward dies from a blood clot. His death brings about in Irene an all-pervasive feeling of guilt, as if it had been her insipid life and neglect of her son which drove him to death; she breaks completely with her former way of life and sets out to search for new meaning in sacrifice and helping people: following the advice of her cousin, a Communist, she gets a low-paid job in a factory; she seeks an answer in the Church and tries helping the poor and working among them, but nothing can satisfy or appease her. When she tries to persuade a small robber from the neighborhood to surrender to the police instead of reporting him herself, she finally transgresses the law; the court of law finds her irresponsible due to the shock caused by the death of her child and sends her to a psychiatric ward for observation. After a series of tests, a cold and distanced psychiatrist proclaims her insane; the family leaves her and, at the end of the film, we see her alone in a sterile cell, while in front of the hospital, the poor whom she tried to help gather and hail her as a new saint . . .[13]

The trap laid by the film is the very "obvious" reading according to which Irene breaks down because of the unbearable pressure of guilt that weighs upon her as soon as she becomes aware that she was deaf to her son's desperate appeal. Read this way, the film is reduced to the usual criticism of the so-called "alienation of contemporary society" where the noise of bustling social life renders us deaf to the desperate cry of our neighbor. If, however, the end of the film, when Irene breaks off all worldly family ties and assumes a "saintly" attitude of abandonment, is to have any sense, then we must question the authenticity of the very guilt which emerges apropos of the son's suicide: this guilt, far from being authentic, functions already as an escape, i.e., it conceals a far more radical traumatism. In psychoanalytic theory, one talks a lot about the transference or the "projection" of guilt, i.e., about the way the subject gets rid of his responsibility via a paranoiac "projection" of guilt onto the Other (the Jew, for example); perhaps, we should rather reverse the relationship and conceive the very act of assuming guilt as an escape from the real traumatism—we don't only escape *from* guilt but also escape *into* guilt, take refuge in it. To grasp this paradox, we must relate the subjective experience of guilt to the inconsistency of the big Other (the symbolic order), i.e., to the fact that the big Other is "always already dead." It is in this sense that we should interpret the famous Freudian dream about the father who doesn't know he is dead: his figure persists, retains its consistency, till he is told the truth. Therefrom the typical obsessional compulsion: I must prevent at any price the Other from learning (that it is dead, impotent)—better for me to die than for the Other to get to know the horrible truth . . . In short, the subject takes the guilt upon himself: insofar as he sacrifies himself by assuming the guilt, the Other is saved from the devastating knowledge of its inconsistency, impotence, inexistence. Who among us has not had this experience apropos of a person toward whom we are in a relationship of transference: better for me to assume guilt quickly than for the other's (father's, the loved woman's) stupidity, impotence, etc., to come into public view—love is easily recognizable precisely by way of this readiness to assume the role of the scapegoat.[14]

The proper way to determine more closely this logic of guilt in its relation to the big Other's inconsistency is via the contradictory nature of the very notion of big Other. That is to say, in ideological discourse, the agency of the big Other is present in two mutually exclusive modes.

First of all, the "big Other" appears as a hidden agency "pulling the strings," running the show behind the scenes: divine Providence in Christian ideology, the Hegelian "cunning of Reason" (or, rather, the popular version of it), the "invisible hand of the market" in the commodity economy, the "objective logic of History" in Marxism-Leninism, the "Jewish conspiracy" in Nazism, etc. In short, the distance between what we wanted to achieve and the effective result of our activity, the surplus of the result over the subject's intention, is again embodied in another agent, in a kind of meta subject (God, Reason, History, Jew). This reference to the big Other is of course in itself radically ambivalent. It can function as a quieting and strengthening reassurance (religious confidence in God's will; the Stalinist's conviction that he is an instrument of historical necessity) or as a terrifying paranoiac agency (as in the case of the Nazi ideology recognizing behind economic crisis, national humiliation, moral degeneration, etc., the same hidden hand of the Jew). These two contradictory aspects are united in the figure of the psychoanalyst *qua* "subject supposed to know" (Lacan): in the psychoanalytic cure, his very presence functions as a kind of pawn, it guarantees that the inconsistent string of "free associations" will retroactively receive meaning. At the same time, however, the presence of the analyst materializes a menace to the analysand's enjoyment, it threatens to rob him of his enjoyment through the dissolution of his symptoms—when the analytic cure approaches its final stage, it usually provokes in the analysand a paranoiac fear that the analyst is after his innermost treasure, his kernel of secret enjoyment . . . As can immediately be perceived, the reassuring and the threatening aspects are not symmetrically disposed: the supposed subject *assures* the analysand of the meaning and *menaces* his enjoyment. Both aspects are actually already present in the anti-Semitic figure of the Jew who *simultaneously* guarantees meaning—if we accept the premise of the Jewish conspiracy, things suddenly "become clear," we are able to recognize a unique pattern behind the apparent economic and moral chaos—and deprives us of our rightful enjoyment.

The crucial point not to be overlooked is, however, that the ideological "big Other" functions at the same time as the precise opposite of the hidden agent pulling the strings: the agency of pure semblance, of an appearance which is nevertheless *essential*, i.e., which should be preserved at any price. This logic of the essential appearance was carried to the extreme in "real socialism," in which the whole system aimed at maintaining the appearance of the people united in their support of the Party and in the enthusiastic construction of Socialism—ritualized spectacles followed one after another in which nobody "really believed" and everybody knew that nobody believed, but the Party bureaucrats were nonetheless uncommonly frightened by the possibility that the appearance of belief would disintegrate. They perceived this disintegration as a total catastrophe, as the dissolution of the entire social order. The question to be asked here is simply: if nobody "really believed," and if everybody knew that nobody believed, *what* was then the agency, the gaze for whom the spectacle of belief was staged? It is here that we encounter the function of the "big Other" at its purest. In everyday reality, life may be dreadful and dull, but all is well as long as all this remains hidden from the gaze of the "big Other." It is for *his* gaze that the spectacle of the happy and enthusiastic people must be staged again and again. If the "big Other" in the first meaning of the term functions as a "subject supposed to know," here it functions on the contrary as the "subject supposed *not* to know," as the agency from which vulgar everyday reality must be hidden.[15] In short, to recall again the Freudian dream of the father who does not know that he is dead, what must be kept from the big Other (incarnated in the gaze of the leader) is the simple fact that he is dead.

The last terrifying and spectacular example of this compulsive logic of the pure appearance is the fall of Ceaucescu. His crucial mistake, probably the immediate cause of his downfall, was his decision, after the slaughter in Timisoara, to organize a gigantic old-style rally of support in Bucharest to prove to the "big Other" that the appearance was still maintained. The crowd, however, was no longer prepared to play the game and the spell was broken . . . The usual explanation, according to which Ceaucescu was a megalomaniac who lost contact with reality, was sincerely convinced about popular support for his regime and *therefore* organized the rally obviously falls short. As if the ramified network of the Securitate is not evidence enough that, for years, he was systematically preparing to crush popular revolt against his rule! Ceaucescu definitely did not believe in the support of the people. What he did believe in was the big Other.[16] Moments like the mass rally in Bucharest when "the spell was broken," i.e., when the "big Other" disintegrated, exemplify perfectly how we can *lose something we never possessed*. Was not the crucial turning point in the decomposition of Eastern European "really existing socialism" the sudden awareness of the subjects that, in spite of the tremendous force of the apparatuses of repression, the Communist party is actually *powerless*, that it is only as strong as they, the subjects, make it, that its strength is their belief in it? And is this turning point not best rendered by the paradox that the Party thus lost what it never had? The paradox to be explained is namely the following: the subjects, of course, never really believed in the Party, in communism, etc., Party rule was from the very beginning experienced as an imposed dictature—if, however, the Party *never possessed legitimacy* in the eyes of the people, how to account for the fact that the above-described moment when "the spell was broken" was, for all that, experienced as a *loss of legitimacy*? The key lies in the status of the "big Other" *qua* the order of "essential appearance": although the subjects "never really believed in it," they nevertheless *acted as if* they believed, *as if* the Party ruled with full legitimacy, they followed the "external" ritual, made the proper acclamations when it was necessary, etc. In other words, what is lost in a loss of what we never possessed is the "essential appearance" which ruled our lives.

It is therefore here, in the relationship to the Communist leader, that we encounter the link connecting the guilt with the Other's inconsistency at its purest: if something goes wrong, we can attest our devotion to the cause by readily assuming responsibility for the failure and so saving the purity of the revolutionary project itself. Perhaps therein consisted also the logic of the Stalinist purges, i.e., the mystery of the dedicated Communists who unhesitatingly confessed to the most horrid counterrevolutionary crimes: their maneuver was to keep intact the communist idea, to prevent the Other from learning the truth and disintegrating. According to Lacan, the same mechanism is at work in the experience of "original sin": God did not only die, He was always already dead, He only did not always know about it, and the sense of man's "original sin" is precisely to spare Him the experience of his "inexistence" (inconsistency, impotence) by assuming guilt. The logic of "original sin" is therefore again: better for me to be throughout guilty than for Him to learn about His death.[17]

This "inexistence of the Other" that we conceal by all too willingly assuming guilt is thus what is at stake in *Europa '51*: at the end of the film, Irene doesn't simply get rid of her guilt, rather, she experiences her guilt itself as a kind of delusive maneuver destined to conceal the ontological void that swallowed her son. Her attempt to take refuge in communism and Christianity, the two main ideologies of "Europe '51," is thus nothing but a desperate attempt to recover the traumatic encounter of the Real (her son's suicidal act) by means of integrating it into a symbolic universe of guilt, locating it within an ideological field, and thus conferring meaning upon it: "Irene is therefore attracted by ideological constellations which fascinate her as, for the moment, at least, they enable her to integrate the scandal of her son's death into a transcendent logic."[18] And what takes place toward the end of the film when Irene assumes the subjective position of the saint, i.e., of an objectival remainder-excrement, is precisely *separation* in the strict Lacanian meaning of the term: separation of *a* (object) from I (symbolic identity), a falling out of the object from the symbolic network, the assumption of a distance from the symbolic universe.

Stromboli: The act of freedom

Separation is also enacted toward the end of *Stromboli*, the first of Rossellini's Bergman movies. *Stromboli* is a story about Karin, an Estonian émigrée who, at the end of the Second World War, finds herself in a refugee camp in Italy. After repeated failures to obtain an Argentinian visa, she marries a poor Italian fisherman from the volcanic island of Stromboli as a last desperate attempt to escape the camp. Life on the island goes on within the confines of a closed community where a primitive patriarchal atmosphere reigns: there is "authentic" contact with nature, but also customary beating of women . . . Karin is soon stifled by her new life and resolves to run away: she takes a long walk across the mountain with the crater to the island's other shore, where a boat leaves for the mainland. As Karin ascends the volcano, however, smoke and fumes from the crater surround and choke her and she fades away. After this terrifying "encounter with the Real," the American and Italian versions of the film distinctly divide. In the American version (put together by RKO against Rossellini's will), Karin later wakes up to a bright morning and descends back toward the village, while an obtrusive voiceover tells us exactly what to think: "Out of her terror and her suffering, Karin had found a great need for God. And she knew now that only in her return to the village could she hope for peace." The Italian version, however, where the last word was Rossellini's, leaves the dilemma open: the film ends with Karin repeating offscreen "My God! Oh merciful God!" and with a shot of the billowing smoke of the volcano. Asked if she is leaving or returning to the village at the end, Rossellini replied.

> I don't know. That would be the beginning of another film. . . . There is a turning point in every human experience in life—which isn't the end of the experience or of the man, but a turning point. My finales are turning points. Then it begins again—but as for what it is that begins, I don't know.[19]

By this very irresolution of its ending, *Stromboli* marks the proper dimension of the act: it ends at the precise point at which the *act* is already accomplished, although no *action* is yet performed. The act done (or, more appropriately: endured) by Karin is that of *symbolic suicide*: an act of "losing all," of withdrawing from symbolic reality, that enables us to begin anew from the "zero point," from that point of absolute freedom called by Hegel "abstract negativity." The moment of this symbolic suicide can be located in a precise way: it takes place between the two mentions of God. Karin reaches her lowest point of despair and dejection when, on running from the village (the social link), she finds herself surrounded by the volcano's smoke and fumes. In the face of the primordial power of the volcano, all social ties pale into insignificance, she is reduced to her bare "being there": running away from the oppressive social *reality*, she encounters something incomparably more horrifying, the *Real*. Sobbing wildly, she cries out: "I'll finish it, but I haven't the courage; I'm afraid." Then she cries out the name of God twice, but as an expression of extreme frustration and exhaustion, and breaks down. Fade in to a shot of a quiet, sunny morning; Karin, who fell asleep on the crater's brink, awakens and again says "Oh God!" twice, but the same words are now "transformed into an act of homage to the magnificent stillness all around her."[20] To use Hegelian terms: the previous experience of a loss is converted into the *loss of a loss itself*—now, she is aware that what, a moment ago, she was so afraid to lose, is totally null, i.e., is already in itself a kind of a loss. We could also say that Karin experiences the meaning of God's tautology: her entire experience could be written down as "God is . . . God," denoting the ultimate coincidence of God *qua* all-destructive fury and God *qua* blissful serenity. After we pass through the "zero point" of the symbolic suicide, what a moment ago appeared as the whirlpool of rage sweeping away all determinate existence changes miraculously into supreme bliss—*as soon as we renounce all symbolic ties*. And the *act* in the Lacanian sense is nothing but this withdrawal by means of which we *renounce renunciation itself*, becoming aware of the fact that we have nothing to lose in a loss.[21] What Karin didn't have the courage to finish the previous night is precisely this act of symbolic suicide, this withdrawal *from* symbolic reality which is to be opposed strictly to the suicide "*in* reality." The latter remains caught in the network of symbolic communication: by killing himself, the subject attempts to send a message to the Other, i.e., it is an act that functions as an acknowledgment of guilt, a sobering warning, a pathetic appeal (like the recent Lithuanian political self-incinerations), whereas the symbolic suicide aims to exclude the subject from the very intersubjective circuit.

The trap laid by *Stromboli* consists therefore in the reading of its end that offers itself as "obvious": through the experience of epiphany, Karin becomes aware of the frivolity and pointlessness of her aversion to the damp life in the village; reborn, she calmly accepts her destiny . . . However, as we have seen, the whole point of Rossellini's ending is that it stops short of this conclusion. What lies ahead of Karin is undoubtedly what, in a vulgarly pathetic way, we call "a new life": sooner or later, she will return to the village, make peace with her husband or return to the mainland and assume new symbolic mandates, a new place in the community, in one way or another, she will begin again to be active—but the film ends *before* Karin finds her place in a new symbolic identity (or reassumes the old one), *before* the new performative, the new "founding word."[22] There is of course something exceptional, excessive even, in such an encounter with the Real, with the abyss of the "abstract freedom": it takes place only in the utmost intimacy of what some call the "mystic experience." The emphasis of Lacan is, however, that such a passage through the "zero point" of symbolic suicide is at work in *every* act worthy of this name. What is namely an act?[23] Why is suicide the act *par excellence?* The act differs from an active intervention (action) in that it radically transforms its bearer (agent): the act is not simply something I "accomplish"—after an act, I'm literally "not the same as before." In this sense, we could say that the subject "undergoes" the act ("passes through" it) rather than "accomplishes" it: in it, the subject is annihilated and subsequently reborn (or not), i.e., the act involves a kind of temporary eclipse, *aphanisis*, of the subject. Which is why every act worthy of this name is "mad" in the sense of radical *unaccountability*: by means of it, I put at stake everything, including myself, my symbolic identity; the act is therefore always a "crime," a "transgression," namely of the limit of the symbolic community to which I belong. The act is defined by this irreducible *risk*: in its most fundamental dimension, it is always *negative*, i.e., an act of annihilation, of wiping out—we not only don't know what will come out of it, its final outcome is ultimately even insignificant, strictly secondary in relation to the NO! of the pure act.[24]

Today, as communism falls apart everywhere, it is worth recalling the *act* which started it all, an act contemporary to *Germany, Year Zero* and *Stromboli*: Tito's "No!" to Stalin in 1948, i.e., the split of Yugoslav Communists with the Moscow-dominated international communist movement. The negative dimension was here far more decisive than its positive outcome or motivation: what really counted was simply the fact that a Communist party which held power said "No!" to Stalin's hegemony. The positive reasons in the name of which this break was accomplished were probably not clear to its bearers themselves; we could even risk a cynical hypothesis that all later inventions because of which Yugoslavia is today in such a mess (worker's self-management) sprang from the desperate attempts of the Party ideologues to "rationalize" the "No!" of the pure act, to found it upon some positive ideological project. What we must bear in mind here is this hiatus: the break with Stalin was not a break in the name of worker's self-management (as was claimed by later apologists), it was an act of pure risk, of refusal, of "persisting on one's own," and it was only later that this refusal assumed positive, determinate existence in the ideological project of self-management. With their "No!" to Stalin, Tito and his companions crossed their Rubicon without being sure of what awaited them on the other bank, of what would become of them. It should also be clear, now, why an act, although it belongs to the Real, is possible only against the background of the symbolic order: the greatness of an act depends strictly on the place *from which* it was accomplished. In other words, as it has already been pointed out by numerous political historians, Tito's "No!" had such a subversive impact only because it was pronounced *by a Communist*, only because he resisted Stalin *as a Communist*. (For this reason, there was no great pressure on Yugoslavia to become part of Western political or military alliances.) If Tito had "changed sides," passed over to the West and "restored capitalism," nothing really subversive would have happened: we would simply have had a case of communist defeat in the Cold War, the West would have appropriated a part of Stalin's empire; it was precisely by his insistence that he was acting *as a Communist* that Tito made a breach into the communist monolith.[25] One of the usual Habermasian reproaches to the Lacanian ethic concerns its alleged incompatibility with the spirit of *polis*, of community: is not, in the eyes of Lacan, the ultimate ethical achievement the suicidal ecstasy, the full acceptance of our "being toward death" which evidently suspends the social dimension? Is not every public deed as such a kind of betrayal of the subject's "authentic" desire, i.e., the death drive? We can see, now, where this reproach runs short: the "authentic" suicidal gesture and the public deed are not to be opposed in an external way, since a "suicidal" gesture, an *act*, is at the very foundation of a new social link.

With an act, *stricto sensu*, we can therefore never fully foresee its consequences, i.e., the way it will transform the existing symbolic space: the act is a rupture after which "nothing remains the same." Which is why, although History can always be explained, accounted for, afterward, we can never, as its agents, caught in its flow, foresee its course in advance: we cannot do it insofar as it is not an "objective process" but a process continuously interrupted by the scansion of acts. The new (the symbolic reality that emerges as the aftermath of an act) is always a "state that is essentially a by-product,"[26] never the result of advance planning. There are numerous examples of such acts: From de Gaulle's "No!" to Pétain and to French capitulation in 1940, Lacan's dissolution of the *Ecole freudienne de Paris* in 1979, up to the mythical case of the act of transgression, Caesar's crossing of the Rubicon—all of them gestures of a masculine leader. However, we shouldn't forget that the paradigmatic case of such an act is *feminine*: Antigone's "No!" to Creon, to state power; her act is literally suicidal, she excludes herself from the community, whereby she offers nothing new, no positive program—she just insists on her unconditional demand. Perhaps we should then risk the hypothesis that, according to its inherent logic, the act as real is "feminine," in contrast to the "masculine" performative, i.e., the great founding gesture of a new order; in the case of Lacan, his dissolution of the *Ecole freudienne* would be "feminine," and he would pass over to the "masculine" side only by his gesture of founding the new *Ecole de la Cause*. The line should be drawn from Antigone to Simone Weil, the Catholic mystic and French resistance fighter who ended her life in London by means of suicidal starvation and served Rossellini as the model for Irene in *Europa '51*. In this perspective, the difference masculine/feminine no longer coincides with that of active/passive, spiritual/sensual, culture/nature, etc. The very masculine *activity* is already an escape from the abysmal dimension of the feminine *act*. The "break with nature" is on the side of woman, and man's compulsive activity is ultimately nothing but a desperate attempt to repair the traumatic incision of this rupture.

2.2 THE "NIGHT OF THE WORLD"

Psychoanalysis and German idealism

By identifying the act as a suspension of constituted reality, as the subject's withdrawal from it, we attain the level at which it becomes possible to elaborate the link that connects the psychoanalytic theory of drives and the philosophy of German idealism (Fichte, Schelling,

Hegel), the latter's notion of reality as something constituted, "posited" by the subject.

The dimension of psychoanalytic theory lost with the ascent of positivist *ego psychology* is the former's opposition to the common-sensical (and at the same time scientific) approach which accepts so-called "external reality" as such, as something *given* in advance, and reduces the problem of the "psychical apparatus" to the question of how (if at all) this apparatus succeeds in accommodating itself to reality, in connecting, "coupling" with it. In this perspective, the definition of "normalcy" is a psychical apparatus open to reality, whereas the psyche is "pathogenic" if, instead of establishing proper contact with reality, it builds its own "disjointed" universe. It was of course the classical Marxist criticism of "conformist" psychoanalysis which opposed itself to such a notion of reality: the "reality" to which conformist psychoanalysis refers as a norm of psychic "sanity" is not neutral reality as such, but the historically specified form of *social* reality. By offering as its ideal the subject "adjusted to reality," conformist psychoanalysis makes itself subservient to existing social reality, to its relations of domination, categorizing critical distance from it as "pathological."

The scope of this criticism is, however, limited by the fact that it still retains the notion of accordance of psychic apparatus with reality, although only as a "regulative idea" to be realized in the nonalienated society to come. A step further (or a step backward into a nonhistorical absolutization of the split, if we look at it with the eyes of the above-mentioned Marxist criticism) was already accomplished by Freud himself, whose theoretical starting point was an original, irreducible, so to speak constitutive *discord* between the logic of the psychic apparatus and the demands of reality: it is because of this discord that "discontent in civilization" is something that defines the *condition humaine* as such. "By its own nature," the psychic apparatus is not adjusted to reality: it runs following the "pleasure principle," which cares nothing for the limitations imposed by reality; thereupon, the conditions of self-preservation enforce upon the psychic apparatus a renunciation of the absolute predominance of the "pleasure principle," its transformation into the "reality principle." The point not to be missed here is that the reign of the "reality principle" is not something that the psychic apparatus could arrive at following the immanent, spontaneous path of "maturation," but something imposed, extorted by means of a series of traumatic cuts ("complexes," integrations of losses): our most "natural" openness to reality implies that the prohibitions which exert pressure upon the inherent logic of the psychic apparatus have successfully broken it down and become our "second nature."

However, even such a notion of the irreducible discord between the psychic apparatus "spontaneously" striving for the reign of a pure "pleasure principle" and the demands of reality still accepts "reality" as something simply given in advance, as a positive entity independent of the psychic apparatus, which, *from without*, exerts its pressure and disturbs the balanced functioning of the psyche. True, we are thus far from any kind of preestablished harmony between the psychic apparatus and reality: the focal object of psychoanalytic theory is the traumatic process by means of which the psychic apparatus is forced out of the closed circuit of the "pleasure principle" and into connecting with reality; yet "reality" is still simply here, given in advance as that to which the psyche must adjust itself. By introducing the dimension of "beyond the pleasure principle," the late Freud accomplishes here two further steps which—insofar as we think out all their consequences, as was done by Lacan—change completely the picture presented above. The hypothesis of a "death drive" concerns directly this point: its implication is that the foreign body, the intruder which disturbs the harmonious circuit of the psychic apparatus run by the "pleasure principle," is not something external to it but strictly *inherent* to it: there is something in the very immanent functioning of the psyche, notwithstanding the pressure of "external reality," which resists full satisfaction. In other words, even if the psychic apparatus is entirely left to itself, it will not attain the balance for which the "pleasure principle" strives, but will continue to circulate around a traumatic intruder in its interior—the limit upon which the "pleasure principle" stumbles is internal to it.[27] The Lacanian mathem for this foreign body, for this "internal limit," is of course *object petit a: objet a* is the reef, the obstacle which interrupts the closed circuit of the "pleasure principle" and derails its balanced movement—or, to refer to Lacan's elementary scheme:

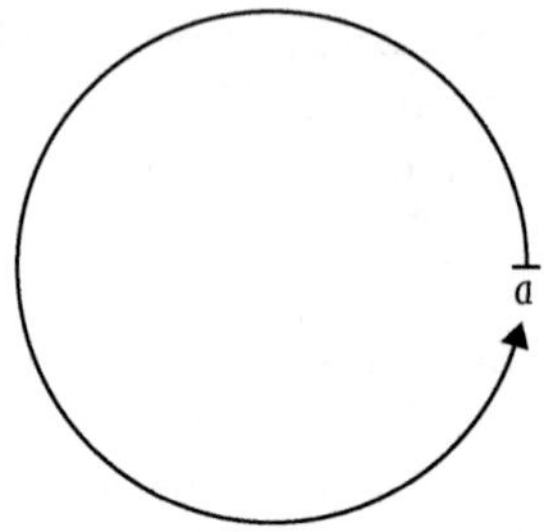

And the final step to be taken is to grasp this inherent impediment in its *positive* dimension: true, the *objet a* prevents the circle of pleasure from closing, it introduces an irreducible displeasure, but the psychic apparatus finds a sort of perverse pleasure *in this displeasure itself*, in the neverending, repeated circulation around the unattainable, always missed object. The Lacanian name for this "pleasure in pain" is of course enjoyment (*jouissance*), and the circular movement which finds satisfaction in failing again and again to attain the object, the movement whose true aim coincides therefore with its very path toward the goal, is the Freudian *drive*. The space of the drive is such a paradoxical, curved space: the *object a* is not a positive entity existing in space, it is ultimately nothing but a certain *curvature of the space itself* which causes us to make a bend precisely when we want to get directly at the object. It is for this reason that Lacan was so fascinated by the paradoxes of courtly love: the lady is such a paradoxical object which curves the space of desire, i.e., which offers us as the way to attain it only endless detours and ordeals—more precisely, the lady is in herself nothing at all, a pure semblance which just materializes the curvature of the space of desire.[28] The resemblance of the depicted Lacanian scheme to a cross section of an eye is by no means accidental: *object a* effectively functions as a rift in the closed circle of the psychic apparatus governed by the "pleasure principle," a rift which "derails" it and forces it to "cast a look on the world," to take into account reality. This is how we should conceive Lacan's thesis that *object a* serves as a support to reality: access to what we call "reality" is open to the subject *via* the rift in the closed circuit of the "pleasure principle," *via* the embarrassing intruder in its midst. The place of "reality" within the psychic economy is that of an "excess," of a surplus which disturbs and blocks from within the autarky of the self-contained balance of the psychic apparatus—"reality" as the external necessity which forces the psychic apparatus to renounce the exclusive rule of the "pleasure principle" is correlative to this inner stumbling block.[29]

How should we then conceive the relationship between *object a*, this strange body in the very heart of the psychic apparatus, and so-called "external reality"? The crucial point not to be missed is that *objet a* functions as the inherent, internal "excess" which impedes *from within* the "smooth running" of the psychic apparatus, as its immanent antagonism, whereas reality always, by definition, appears as an *external* limit; the Lacanian name for such an internal self-impediment is, of course, the *Real*. The radical conclusion to be drawn from it is that—contrary to the commonsensical external opposition of "pleasure principle" and "reality principle" (upheld also by the early Freud)—"reality" is not something given in advance but something the ontological status of which is in a way secondary, in other words: something *constituted* in the precise meaning this term acquired in German idealism. What we call "(external) reality" *constitutes* itself by means of a primordial act of "rejection": the subject "rejects," "externalizes" its immanent self-impediment, the vicious circle of the drive antagonism, into the "external" opposition between the demand of its drives and those of the opposed reality. It is here that, within psychoanalysis, the achievement of German idealism "returns" what was "repressed" in post-Hegelian thought: the process of constitution *qua* the subject's *prehistory*, i.e., what must have gone on *before* the subject could establish a relationship with "external reality"—the process which, with Fichte, acquires the form of the I's absolute act of positing (of itself as) the object, and which, with Schelling, appears as the antagonism of God's prehistory, resolved when God speaks out his Word.

The fiction of reality

Psychoanalysis thus conceives "reality" as something constituted, "posited" by the subject, in the precise meaning this term acquired in German idealism. The "year zero" from the title of the Rossellini's film is that "dark passage" through the zero point, that "eclipse of (constituted) reality," that withdrawal of the subject into itself, that "night of the world," the experience of the pure self *qua* "abstract negativity," about which Hegel speaks in a manuscript for the *Realphilosophie* of 1805–1806:

> The human being is this night, this empty nothing, that contains everything in its simplicity—an unending wealth of many presentations, images, of which none happens to occur to him—or which are not present. This night, the inner of nature, that exists here—pure self—in phantasmagorical presentations, is night all around it, here shoots a bloody head—there another white shape, suddenly here before it, and just so disappears. One catches sight of this night when one looks human beings in the eye—into a night that becomes awful . . .[30]

And the symbolic order, the universe of the Word, emerges only against the background of the experience of this abyss, as is demonstrated by Hegel in the same manuscripts, when he points out that this inwardness of the pure self "must enter also into existence, object becoming, opposite this innerness to be external; return to being. This is language as name-giving power . . . Through the name the object as individual being is born out of the I."[31]

The first association that comes to mind apropos of these fragments is of course the traditional "deconstructionist" reproach to Hegel: true, Hegel acknowledges this radical withdrawal of the subject into itself, this "night of the world," but only as a passing moment which is quickly sublated (*aufgehoben*) in a new spiritual reality of names—negativity is thus again reduced to a vanishing point within the self-mediation of the Spirit . . . However, such a reading, in spite of its convincing, even self-evident character—in a series of his statements, Hegel seems to purport it in an unequivocal way—falls short of the crucial accent of Hegel: the experience of "abstract negativity," the "psychotic" withdrawal of the subject into self (the "night of the world"), is not a passing moment, sublated in the final result of the dialectical movement, the positive articulation of concrete content—the point is rather that this very concrete articulation of the positive spiritual content is nothing but *a form in which the radical negativity (the "night of the world") assumes determinate being*. In the famous paragraph 32 of the

Preface to the *Phenomenology of Spirit*, Hegel says precisely this when he praises the power of Understanding;

> the most astonishing and mightiest of powers, or rather the absolute power. The circle that remains self-enclosed and, like substance, holds its moments together, is an immediate relationship, one therefore which has nothing astonishing about it. But that an accident as such, detached from what circumscribes it, what is bound and is actual only in its context with others, should attain an existence of its own and a separate freedom—this is the tremendous power of the negative; it is the energy of thought, of the pure "I." Death, if that is what we want to call this non-actuality, is of all things the most dreadful, and to hold fast what is dead requires the greatest strength . . . [The life of Spirit] is this power, not as something positive, which closes its eyes to the negative, as when we say of something that it is nothing or is false, and then, having done with it, turn away and pass on to something else; on the contrary, Spirit is this power only by looking the negative in the face, and tarrying with it. This tarrying with the negative is the magical power that converts it into being.[32]

We already know how the negative is converted into being: through language as name-giving power, i.e., through the emergence of the symbolic order. Hegel's statements on how understanding breaks up the living organic whole and confers autonomous existence on what is effective only as a moment of concrete totality are to be read against the background of the fundamental Lacanian notion of the signifier *qua* the power which mortifies/disembodies the life substance, "dissects" the body and subordinates it to the constraint of the signifying network. Word is murder of a thing, not only in the elementary sense of implying its absence—by naming a thing, we treat it as absent, as dead, although it is still present—but above all in the sense of its radical *dissection*: the word "quarters" the thing, it tears it out of the embedment in its concrete context, it treats its component parts as entities with an autonomous existence: we speak about color, form, shape, etc., as if they possessed self-sufficient being. The power of understanding consists in this capacity to reduce the organic whole of experience to an appendix to the "dead" symbolic classification. In our everyday attitude, we are "spontaneous Bergsonians": we bemoan the fate of immediate life experience, we point out how the fullness of life flow escapes forever the network of language categories, we laugh at those who become so entangled in the fictitious world of symbols that they lose the taste of effective life. Hegel is, on the contrary, full of wonder for this mortifying faculty of understanding before which the living substance is utterly helpless, for this tremendous power that tears apart what "naturally" belongs together and is thus able to subordinate the very reality of the life process to symbolic "fictions"; for him, this inversion where fiction subjugates reality rather proves *the inherent ontological nullity of what we call "reality."* For what is the "life of Spirit" if not a life process governed by (what appears to our everyday view as) fictitious nonentities? Let us just take the case of the ethical-political arrangement of a given community: its symbolic identity is bestowed upon it by a series of legal, religious, and other values which regulate its life; these values are literally "fictions," they exist nowhere, they possess no substantial ontological consistency, they are present only in the form of symbolic rituals which enact them. The entire legal order, for example, is founded upon fictions concerning "moral," physically nonexistent persons which appear as entities with their own will, and rights, entities which declare wars, and make treaties, etc. ("our state concluded peace with its neighbor," "the company bought raw materials," "the Fatherland is humiliated" . . .). The point here is not the cynical insipidity that "these are all just fictions" but the fact that because of these "fictions" thousands die in wars, lose their jobs . . . In other words, although such a "fiction" effectively exists only in its real effects (the state is actual only in the real activity of its citizens, the Fatherland only in the patriotic feeling and acting of those who recognize themselves in its call), we cannot *reduce* it to these effects and purport that, for example, "the Fatherland is *nothing but* the sum of these actual individual deeds"—on the contrary, these very deeds assume their ontological consistency only by way of reference to the symbolic fiction "Fatherland." The Fatherland as the cause for which we fight "is nowhere in reality," but in spite of this, we cannot explain the very "material" reality of fights and sufferings without reference to it. To resort to the traditional philosophical terms, Lacans avoids here the idealist as well as the nominalist trap: the "big Other" (the symbolic order) of course possesses no substantial actuality, it doesn't exist as a Platonic world apart, yet neither can it be reduced to a nominalistically conceived "abbreviation" for the multitude of individual, really existing entities. Precisely insofar as it is a "dead scheme," we must presuppose it as an ideal point of reference which, in spite of its inexistence, is "valid," i.e., dominates and regulates our actual lives. In a somewhat poetic manner we could say that man is the animal whose life is governed by symbolic fictions. *This is the way "tarrying with the negative" takes place, this is the way negativity as such acquires positive, determinate being: when the very actual life of a community is structured by reference to symbolic fictions.* In our everyday lives, we accept this as something so self-evident that we don't even notice the oddness of what is going on—to become fully aware of it, a philosophical experience of "wondering" is necessary.

One of the lessons of Lacanian psychoanalysis—and at the same time the point at which Lacan rejoins Hegel—is the radical discontinuity between the organic immediacy of "life" and the symbolic universe: the "symbolization of reality" implies the passage through the zero point of the "night of the world." What we forget, when we pursue our daily life, is that our human universe is nothing but an embodiment of the radically inhuman "abstract negativity," of the abyss we experience when we face the "night of the world." And what is the *act* if not the moment when the subject who is its bearer *suspends* the network of symbolic fictions which serve as a support to his daily life and confronts again the radical negativity upon which they are founded?[33]

In other words, Hegelian "absolute negativity" *coincides thoroughly* with the abyss which separates the Kantian subject's phenomenal experience from the thing in itself. Hegel's aim is not to prove that we can attain the thing in itself, that we can overcome the barrier which to Kant appeared untraversable; what he accomplishes is just a kind of shift of perspective by means of which this abyss is no longer conceived as a barrier limiting our powers, separating us from the thing itself, but as the very power of separation, of introducing a radical split into the thing itself. Another way to approach the same problem is *via* the relationship language/reality. For traditional philosophy, their disjunction goes unsaid: to speak about a thing is not the same as to do it. One of the main endeavors of contemporary philosophy is to undermine the self-evident character of this disjunction by way of showing how speech is in itself a species of activity, even a privileged one. The principal thesis of philosophical hermeneutics, for example, is that the "reality" which we encounter within our practical, active relationship to the objects around us is always already disclosed through the symbolic medium: reality "is" only as interpreted by language, language is its ultimate ontological horizon. The late-Wittgensteinian approach, on the other hand, conceives language directly as a form of activity, as "expressive behavior" embedded in a specific life form—we "do things with words"; etc. It is the merit of these orientations to invalidate the commonsense attitude best rendered by phrases like "empty words are not enough, we must set to work, do it instead of just talking about it"; against such platitudes, one is tempted to propose the opposite motto "enough of empty acts, it is time we pass from acts to words!" That is to say, every activity is situated in some horizon of meaning which alone renders it possible, so that by "pronouncing the right word" which introduces a break in this symbolic background, one cannot continue to act in the same way as before.

Yet what all these orientations have in common is that they perceive the abyss which separates "things" from "words" as a *problem*, as something one has to overcome—Hegel, on the contrary, perceives it as the Spirit's supreme accomplishment, he sees in it the Spirit's "infinite" power to disengage itself from the immediacy of what is simply given, to break up its organic unity. For him, the true theoretical problem is not how to leap over the abyss which separates acts from words, but how to conceive this abyss itself: the absolute act, the act stronger than all interventions in reality, is the act by means of which we disjoin the "great chain of being" and acquire distance from it. The only way to "overcome" the abyss that separates acts from words is to thematize the *act* which opens up this abyss, i.e., to render visible the radical *violence*, the breach in the Real, which forms the hidden reverse of the calm contemplative distance from reality. *This* act is overlooked by the traditional contemplative attitude as well as by post-Hegelian attempts to overcome this distance by conceiving speech as a modality of acting. Or, to put it in Kierkegaardian terms: we effectively "overcome" the abyss that separates words from acts only by way of experiencing the word in its violent and contingent "becoming," before it acquires the features of *logos*, the universe of symbolic necessity.[34]

What we call "culture" is therefore, in its very ontological status, *the reign of the dead over life,* i.e., the form in which the "death drive" assumes positive existence. Herein lies also the fundamental "Hegelian" lesson of Rossellini's films: the act *qua* real, transgression of a symbolic limit, does not enable us to (re)establish a kind of immediate contact with the presymbolic life substance, it throws us, on the contrary, back into that abyss of the Real out of which our symbolic reality emerged. Now we can further specify the lure of Rossellini's Bergman films: they always contain some picture of "authentic," substantial life, and it seems as if the heroine's salvation depends on her ability to immerge into this substantial "authenticity": Karin in *Stromboli* must accept life in the closed island community; Irene in *Europa '51* should find herself in the naive but authentic faith of the poor who at the end proclaim her a saint; the English couple in *Voyage to Italy* overcome the restraint of their relationship through contact with the spontaneous life feeling of the Italian crowd . . . The strategy of these films is precisely to denounce this lure as such, to present it in its falseness: Karin in *Stromboli* is "reborn" by experiencing a horror before which the misery of the island community pales—the life of the fishermen is thus exposed in all its nullity; at the end of *Europa '51*, Irene definitely renounces religious ideology—her beatification by the poor outcasts is just a cruel irony, proof of a missed encounter between her and them; what the English couple cruising Italy come across behind the vivacious Italian crowd is the inert presence of ancient statues and ruins. In all three cases, we have therefore a movement *from reality to the Real,* to what, in reality itself, is "more than reality": the volcano is what is "on the island more than island itself," its excess of the Real, just as sainthood is what is "in religious ideology more than ideology," the nonideological kernel in its heart, and, finally, the same as the old ruins which are what is "in Italy more than Italy," a mute witness to some past, long-lost enjoyment.[35] In all three cases, the heroine is able to perceive this fissure of the "substance" insofar as she occupies the position of a *stranger,* i.e., insofar as her gaze is *external*: those who find themselves *within* the substance are necessarily blinded. The mechanism that renders them blind is that of the *sacrifice*: the elementary function of the sacrifice is *to heal the fissure of the Other.* What holds together a "substantial" ("primordial") community is its rite of sacrifice, and the position of a "stranger" is defined precisely by his refusal to partake in this rite.

The fascination of the sacrifice

In the last pages of his *Four Fundamental Concepts of Psycho-Analysis*, Lacan directly opposes psychoanalytic experience to the fascination of the sacrifice: the heroism demanded by psychoanalysis is not the heroic gesture of assuming upon oneself the sacrifice, of accepting the role of sacrificial victim but, on the contrary, the heroism of *resisting the temptation of the sacrifice*, of confronting what the fascinating image of the sacrifice *conceals*. Lacan himself draws our attention to the political dimension of the sacrificial logic, pointing out how the drama of Nazism reenacts:

> the most monstrous and supposedly superseded forms of the holocaust. . . . [T]he offering to obscure gods of an object of sacrifice is something to which few subjects can resist succumbing, as if under some monstrous spell. . . . But for whoever is capable of turning a courageous gaze towards this phenomenon—and, once again, there are certainly few who do not succumb to the fascination of the sacrifice in itself—the sacrifice signifies that, in the object of our desires, we try to find evidence for the presence of the desire of this Other that I call here *the dark God*.[36]

What is then concealed by the fascinating spectacle of the sacrifice? Lacan relates the sacrifice to the *desire of the Other*, to the enigmatic *Che vuoi?* What does the Other want of me? In its most fundamental dimension, sacrifice is a "gift of reconciliation" to the Other, destined to appease its desire. Sacrifice conceals the abyss of the Other's desire, more precisely: it conceals the Other's lack, inconsistency, "inexistence," that transpires in this desire. *Sacrifice is a guarantee that "the Other exists"*: that there is an Other who can be appeased by means of the sacrifice. The trick of the sacrifice consists therefore in what the speech-act theorists would call its "pragmatic presupposition": *by the very act of sacrifice, we (presup) pose the existence of its addressee* that guarantees the consistency and meaningfulness of our experience—so, even if the act fails in its proclaimed goal, this very failure can be read from within the logic of sacrifice as *our* failure to appease the Other. Insofar as this abyss of the Other's desire emerged in all its violence with the Jewish religion—i.e., insofar as the fundamental position of the Jewish believer is that of a perplexed *Che vuoi?*—What does He want of me?—it was unavoidable for it to break with the logic of sacrifice: sacrifice would mean that we betrayed the abyss of *Che vuoi?* and translated God's desire into a demand that can be appeased by means of a sacrifice. And—at this point, we can follow René Girard[37]—it was precisely for this reason that we encounter in the Jewish religion the first appearance of a subject who *resists* assuming the role of a scapegoat/victim: Job. Job's refusal to play his part in the sacrificial rite is the exact reverse of his perplexion in front of his calamities: instead of identifying heroically with his evil fate, he continues to raise the question of the meaning of it all, of what God wants of him with it. We witness here what is perhaps the greatest ethical revolution in the history of mankind: the moment when the subject refuses the allotted role of the victim, the moment when the social perspective of sacrificing the scape-goat is confronted with the perspective of the victim itself; what is here so subversive and pathbreaking, what confers upon the story of Job its dramatic tension and at the same time its truth, is the very *confrontation* of the two perspectives. That is to say, if we were to dispose only of the point of view of the community demanding sacrifice, we would remain within the "totalitarian" universe; if, on the other hand, we were to be limited to the victim's voice, we would have a subjective point of view with nothing attesting to its truth. The effect of truth proceeds solely from the confrontation of the two perspectives: first, the sacrificial discourse places the subject in the position of a sacred victim, depicting him as an untouchable, horrendous entity, in short: as an *object* in the psychoanalytical sense, with all the transferential energy invested in it; then, we are all of a sudden transposed into his own perspective, brought face to face with the uncanny scene in which it is not simply a subject but the thing itself which starts to talk.

Today, in our universe of mass culture, the figure which comes closest to this role of a scapegoat embodying sacred violence is the "serial killer," the madman who, with no "rational ground," compulsively repeats murderous acts.[38] It is for this reason that Fred Walton's *When a Stranger Calls*, perhaps the best variation on a theme of anonymous phone menaces, is of special interest. The first part of the film is narrated from the point of view of a young girl baby-sitting in a suburban family mansion: the children are asleep on the first floor, while she watches television in the sitting room. After the first threatening calls repeating the demand "Did you check the children?" she alerts the police who advise her to lock all the doors firmly, not to allow anybody to enter the house and to try to engage the molester in long conversation enabling the police to trace the call. Soon afterward, the police locate their source: another telephone within the same house . . . The molester was there all the time and has already killed the children. The killer appears thus as an unfathomable object with whom no identification is possible, a pure Real provoking unspeakable terror. At this point in the story, however, the film takes an unexpected turn: we are suddenly transposed into the perspective of the killer himself, witnessing the miserable everyday existence of this lonely and desperate individual—he sleeps in an asylum, wanders around decrepit cafes, and attempts in vain to establish contact with his neighbors; so that when the detective hired by the murdered children's father prepares to stab him, our sympathies are wholly on the poor killer's side.

Again, there is nothing subversive about the two points of view in themselves: if the story were narrated from the sole perspective of the young baby-sitter, we would have the standard case of a victim threatened by a phantom-like, bodyless and, for that reason, all the more horrifying menace; if we were limited to the murderer's self-experience, we would have the standard rendition of the murderer's pathological universe. The entire subversive effect hangs upon the rupture, the passage from one perspective to the other, the change which confers upon the hitherto impossible/unattainable object a body, which gives the untouchable thing a voice and makes it speak—in short, which *subjectivizes* it.[39]

Girard, however, falls short of his own conception when he reduces Job to a kind of forerunner, announcer, of Christ, the true paradigm of a victim who speaks out and subjectivizes himself: Christ's gesture, as a gesture of love, *conceals* the anxiety-provoking abyss of the Other's inconsistency, thereby performing the turn from the religion of anxiety (Judaism) into that of love (Christianity). That is to say, in what consists the lure of love? When in love, I love somebody because of the *objet a* in him/her, because of what is "in him more than himself"—in short, the object of love cannot give me what I demand of him since he doesn't possess it, since it is an excess in its very heart. What defines love is this basic discord or gap (elaborated by Lacan apropos of the relationship of Alcibiades to Socrates in Plato's *Symposion*):[40] the lover [*erastes*] seeks in the beloved [*eromenos*] what he lacks, but, as Lacan puts it, "what the one lacks is not what is hidden within the other"—the only thing left to the beloved is thus to proceed to a kind of exchange of places, to change from the object into the subject of love, in short: to *return love*. Therein consists, according to Lacan, love's most sublime moment: in this inversion when the beloved object endeavors to deliver himself from the impasse of his position, from the impossibility of complying with the lover's demand, by assuming himself the position of the lover, by reaching his hand back to the lover and thus answering the lover's lack/desire with his own lack. Love is based upon the illusion that this encounter of the two lacks can succeed and beget a "new harmony." Therein consists also the supreme sublimity of Christ's gesture: what is this gesture if not a *sign of God's love for man?* In reply to the believer's love for Him, in reply to the hands that the believer stretches toward Him, God himself changes into a lover and reaches back toward man—concealing thereby the abyss of the Otherness that no sacrifice could appease, i.e., with which no relationship of exchange is possible.[41]

Considering that the voice to which psychoanalysis opens the space to articulate itself by lending an ear to it is precisely that of the victim *qua* object of fascination (female hysteric), one can only wonder at the fact that even some Lacanians reduce psychoanalysis to a kind of heroic assumption of a necessary, constitutive sacrifice—those for whom psychoanalysis ends when the analysand is able to accept a fundamental renunciation as a condition of access to desire ("symbolic castration"). Lacan is as far as possible from such an ethic of heroic sacrifice: the lack to be assumed by the subject is not its own but that of the Other, which is something incomparably more unbearable. The Other itself doesn't possess what the subject lacks, and no sacrifice can compensate for this lack of the Other. Now, we can also see how alien is to Lacan any glorification of the "big Other" as the structural order that "pulls the strings" and regulates the subject's self-experience, i.e., the standard "structuralist" thesis that the subject, in his imaginary self-experience, misrecognizes the signifying mechanism that effectively "runs the show": the supreme illusion consists precisely in this reliance on the consistency of the "big Other." The "big Other doesn't exist," as Lacan puts it: it is just a subject's presupposition—the (presup)position of an immaterial, ideal order, i.e., of Another Place that guarantees the ultimate meaning and consistency of the subject's experience.[42]

Herein consists the crucial difference between the Lacanian big Other and the Althusserian big Other materialized in Ideological State Apparatuses: the way Althusser almost compulsively again and again reminds us of the *materiality* of ideology, of its material existence in ideological institutions and rituals, is deeply symptomatic and functions as a kind of theoretical denial. It testifies to the fact that Althusser misrecognizes the specific agency of the "ideal," "immaterial" big Other in the shape of the symbolic order guaranteeing meaning to the historical contingency. This "big Other" is retroactively posited, i.e., presupposed, by the subject in the very act by means of which he is caught in the cobweb of an ideology. The subject, for example, *(presup)-poses* the big Other in the guise of Historical Reason or divine Providence in the very moment and gesture of conceiving himself as its executor, as its unconscious tool. This act of (presup)position which makes the big Other exist is perhaps the elementary gesture of ideology, and it is precisely at this place that we should locate the above-mentioned difference between suicide *qua* "demonstrative" act and suicide *qua* suspension of the symbolic order: the "demonstrative" suicide still addresses the big Other, whereas the "symbolic" suicide cancels the very presupposition of the "big Other"—in a way, it is the negative, the reversal, the "undoing" of the founding ideological gesture of (presup)posing the Other. In this precise sense, i.e., insofar as Rossellini's films endeavor to enact this suspension, they are unideological, they enable us to break out of the ideological closure.

This "withdrawal" of the subject from the Other is what Lacan calls "subjective destitution": not an act of sacrifice (which always implies the Other as its addressee) but an act of abandonment which sacrifices the very sacrifice. The freedom thus attained is a point at which we find ourselves not only without the other *qua* our neighbor, but without support in the Other itself[43]—as such, it is unbearably suffocating, the very opposite of relief, of "liberation." That is to say, "liberation" always implies a reference to the Other *qua* Master: ultimately, nothing liberates as well as a good Master, since "liberation" consists precisely in our shifting the burden onto the Other/Master. So-called "free associations" in a psychoanalytic cure are the supreme proof of it: by means of them, the analysand liberates himself from the pressures and constraints of censorship, he can prattle freely—but only because he can rely on the analyst, the "subject supposed to know," the "master of signification" (as Lacan put it in the 1950s) whose very presence guarantees him that retroactively, at the end, his prattle will obtain meaning and consistency. The freedom attained by the act is the very opposite of this freedom: by undergoing it, all the burden falls back upon the subject since he renounces any support in the Other.

In conclusion, we can now also define the trap laid by Rossellini's films on the level of their form. It is already a commonplace of cinema theorists to oppose Rossellini to "manipulators" who create meaning by artificial interventions in the cinematic material (e.g., montage): in contrast to such a procedure, Rossellini is supposed to let the unorganized material itself speak, i.e., to renounce the position of the artist *qua* Master who pulls the strings and to limit his role to that of a collector/observer of cinematic material, keeping his mind open for the contingency of the Real. In Rossellini's films, meaning does not result from the author's conscious manipulation, it emerges from the material itself by means of miraculous, unpredictable acts of grace (André Bazin[44] attempted thus to detect the roots of Rossellini's Christianity in the very formal qualities of his films). But if this were the case, Rossellini would proceed somewhat in the manner of the analysand in free associations: stringing contingent fragments of the Real and relying on the presence of the big Other (God) to produce meaning, i.e., still implying the Other *qua* guarantee of meaning. What Rossellini effectively does is, rather, the exact opposite: all the time, we can sense in his films a tremendous effort of "manipulation," of bringing under control the excess of the Real, and the features that are usually taken as proofs of his "modernism" (e.g., "empty time" which subverts the linear narration) are precisely monuments of his *failure* to attain his goal; Rossellini's greatness lies in the fact that he intentionally included in his films traces of their own failure—what is "modern" about them is that the tension between "manipulation" and material is acknowledged as part of the artistic endeavor itself.

Every one of his films is an ultimately failed attempt to come to terms with the Real of some traumatic encounter. What are *Open City*, *Paisan*, and *Germany, Year Zero* if not three attempts to come to terms with the trauma of fascism? What are *Stromboli*, *Europa '51*, and *Voyage to Italy* if not attempts to integrate, to master the traumatic encounter with Ingrid Bergman, her *act* of saying "No!" to Hollywood and joining Rossellini at the height of her stardom, this tremendous decision, an effective "act of madness" that nothing in Rossellini's own life, full of opportunistic maneuvering, can match.[45] True, all his films in which she stars display frenetic activity to balance the dignity of her act, to recompense for it—but *the act was hers*.

NOTES

1 Peter Brunette, *Roberto Rossellini* (Oxford: Oxford University Press, 1987), p. 375.

2 And, on the other hand, what were *her* thoughts upon seeing this strange "Ingrid Bergmann" in *Roma*? This is indubitably the reason why she responded so enthusiastically to this film: beyond the fascination with the film as such, she was interpellated as pure Evil embodied in the Ingrid/Bergmann couple.

3 Should one point out how Bergman's choice of Rossellini attests to the "suicidal" determination to obliterate her symbolic status in Hollywood and to (re)create herself *ex nihilo*?

4 Quoted in Brunette, op. cit., p. 387.

5 The very term "act" is extremely interesting from the Lacanian perspective: the multiplicity of its meanings condenses the whole Imaginary-Real-Symbolic triad—*Imaginary*: fake, show, performance; *Real*: doing, exertion, stroke; *Symbolic*: edict, decree, ordinance, enactment. In German, where one of the meanings of "Akt" is also "the painting of a nude human body," we can even imagine an entire scenario: first, we are seduced by the image of a naked woman; then, we "accomplish the (sexual) act"; finally, we inscribe our conquest in the list, i.e., in an act (the stage which was crucial for don Giovanni).

6 Cf. F. W. J. Schelling, *Über das Wesen der menschlichen Freiheit* (Frankfurt: Suhrkamp Verlag, 1978).

7 The homology between the subjective position of the psychoanalyst and that of the saint runs like a thread through the last years of Lacan's teaching: in both cases, we assume the position of an object-excrement, of a remainder which embodies the inconsistency of the symbolic order, i.e., of an element which cannot be integrated into the machinery of social *usefulness*, of a point of pure expenditure. True, we often encounter with Lacan also statements which point in the opposite direction, like those which put psychoanalytic associations in the same series as concentration camps—but is the opposition here really insurmountable? Is it not rather that the moment "saints" endeavor to "socialize," to "go

marchin'in" and organize themselves as a social order, we get *monasteries*: a totally regulated world which can serve as a model for concentration camps, with the exception that, instead of torturing their victims, monks torture *themselves*, assuming the heavy burden of abstinence? Were not the Jesuit missions in seventeenth-century Paraguay ("reducciones" (reductions), as they were called at that time) concentration camps of a sort with their most thorough regulation of one's entire life, including its most intimate details (Hegel ironically recalls that Jesuits even rang a bell at midnight to remind their Indian subjects of their marital duties)?

8 Brunette, op. cit., p. 84.

9 The problem of how Rossellini can render the most intimate moment, absolute abandonment, of the act of freedom is therefore a pseudoproblem: he can render it precisely insofar as it is a totally "empty" act, an act that "hides nothing," not an act of indescribable fullness. In other words, we cannot identify with Edmund not because of the unattainable depth of his "inner struggle" but because there is simply *nothing to identify with*.

10 This freedom is of course not to be conceived in the common sense of "unprincipled behavior," as when we "ignore our engagements": it is precisely such "unprincipled deceivers" who remain thoroughly attached to the power of the word—by the very act of deception, they count on the trustworthiness of the word and thus stay within its field. Their position is simply split, inconsistent, in contrast to Edmund where we find no trace of a split, i.e., where cold firmness immediately coincides with childish innocence.

11 Cf. Jacques Rancière, "La Chute des corps," in *Roberto Rossellini* (Paris: Cahiers du Cinéma, 1989).

12 According to Lesley Brill (cf. his *The Hitchcock Romance* (Princeton: Princeton University Press, 1988)), Hitchcock's *oeuvre* divides into two series, "romances" and "ironic" films, precisely with reference to the relationship between words and deeds. In "romances," the movement has a direction "from outside inward," which is why they are dominated by the performative force of the word. The couple, linked by an external contingency, first pretends to be in love, whereupon, step by step, the external link grows into authentic love; these films therefore end with a successful communication, with an establishment of an authentic intersubjective link. Their opposite is "ironic" films culminating in *Psycho*: here, a mask remains just a mask, the word fails in its performative enforcement, so that instead of communication, we get a psychotic dissolution of the social link.

13 It is this new community of believers emerging as a by-product of Irene's act that enables us to locate properly Rossellini's seemingly unintelligible, even cynical comment on Edmund's suicide in *Germany* as "a true light of hope": ". . . from there is born a new way of living and of seeing, the accent of hope and faith in the future and in men" (Quoted from Brunette, op. cit., p. 86). Rossellini is quite aware of the illusory character of this new community of hope and faith; what he is really interested in is the suicidal act of radical

withdrawal upon which it is only possible to found a new community—the experience of total abandonment, the passage through the "point zero" which is forgotten once we find ourselves *within* the new community.

14 Here, we should supplement the standard psychoanalytic interpretation of the son's sentiment of guilt toward his father according to which the repressed parricidal desire returns in the inversed form of guilt: one of the most traumatic experiences for the son is the moment when he is forced to acknowledge the fact that father is "dead" (an impotent impostor whose mask of authority conceals utter helplessness); by assuming guilt, the son endeavors to keep immaculate the image of father *qua* representative of the Law. In other words, the very parricidal desire is already a lure destined to obscure the father's impotence.

15 One of the shapes assumed by the "subject supposed not to know" in ideology is also the myth of the "noble savage" living in a world not yet spoiled by our corrupt civilization. The enlightened Westerners follow here a typical obsessional economy: the "noble savage" should be kept in ignorance at any price whatsoever, we should prevent him the access to our degenerated knowledge which would undermine his blissful way of life. The ambiguity of this guardianship was already noted by Aldous Huxley in his *Jesting Pilate*, where he remarked how Englishmen are full of admiration for the wisdom of Indians who preserve their old traditions and resist the pressure of our way of life, they are prepared to acknowledge their unfathomable spiritual depth, inaccessible to us, vulgar materialists and utilitarians; what, however, causes an almost unbearable disquiet and resistance is *an Indian who masters our own knowledge and technology better than us* . . . In short, one is always ready to acknowledge to the Indian his "radical alterity"—what triggers real panic is his excessive *resemblance*, is the point at which he becomes "more like ourselves than we."

16 How, then, should we combine these two aspects of the ideological big Other? The solution is simpler than it may seem. The appearance which must be maintained at whatever cost by means of the totalitarian spectacle is precisely the appearance that the Party is an instrument of historical necessity, fulfilling a noble mission, the appearance that the decisions of the Party are authorized by the big Other of the meaning of History. In other words, *the appearance to be maintained at any cost is none other than that there is meaning hidden behind the appearance*, behind the apparent historical contingency—the appearance of the "big Other" in the first sense of the term. It is for that reason that the ideology of "real socialism" incessantly accentuated the deep *love* of the people for the Party and their leader: "love" is to be conceived here in a strict psychoanalytical sense, as a relation of transference to the "subject supposed to know."

17 The ethical imperative upon which this attitude is founded is of course that of "saving the other's face": to do everything, better to die than allow the other to lose face. Therein consists the most elementary dimension of what we call "tact" or "consideration": how to disagree with the other, how to *refuse his demand*, without making him lose face. Contrary to the first impression, the

"face" referred to here is not imaginary, it concerns the level of symbolic identity: it defines the place to which the subject is assigned within the intersubjective symbolic network; the dizziness that seizes us when we "lose face" in public manifests our loss of support in the "big Other." (Which is why we encounter the clearest version of the ethics of "saving the other's face" in Japan, i.e., in a society with the most rigidly defined structure of symbolic mandates.)

18 Alain Bergala, "Celle par qui le scandale arrive," in *Cahiers du Cinéma* 356 (February 1984), p. 11.

19 Quoted in Brunette, op. cit., p. 126.

20 Ibid., p. 124.

21 Is not the same conversion at work in Freud's famous dream of Irma's injection? The dual, imaginary dialogue with Irma, dominated by Freud's narcissistic interests, culminates in a look into her open mouth; suddenly, this horror (where the throat's opening clearly corresponds to the crater in *Stromboli*) changes miraculously into a sort of ataraxia, the subject floats freely in symbolic bliss—as soon as the dreamer (Freud) renounces his narcissistic perspective.

22 Already apropos of Edmund's suicide in *Germany, Year Zero*, Rossellini speaks about a "kind of abandonment to rest that has to come before any new action" (Brunette, op. cit., p. 86): this is the act in the Lacanian sense of the term—the withdrawal that, so to speak, clears the space for a new action.

23 Cf. Jacques-Alain Miller, "Jacques Lacan: Bemerkungen über sein Konzept des *passage à l'acte*," *Wo es war* 7–8 (Wien: Hora Verlag, 1990).

24 Here, we could also establish a link with the notion of act as recently elaborated by Ernesto Laclau: the act located at the point of undecidability of a symbolic structure (cf. his introduction to *New Reflections on the Revolution of Our Time* (London: Verso, 1990)). The irreducible "unaccountability" of an act attests to the fact that what defines an act is a temporality irreducible to space: the act introduces a cut separating "afterward" from "before," a discontinuity which cannot be accounted for within a spatial disposition of elements. In this sense, act runs counter to the tendency to reduce time to space, i.e., temporal succession to spatial, synchronous coexistence, at work in art as well as in the scientific practice of our century. What is cubism in painting, for example, where the object is depicted simultaneously from different points of view, if not an attempt to translate the temporal succession of the gaze circulating around the object into spatial coexistence of different perspectives within the synchronous unity of a picture? And it is probably more than a coincidence that, at the same time, the theory of relativity paved the way for a notion of the universe as a time-space continuum, i.e., for a "static" picture of the universe where time is conceived as the fourth dimension of space which can be traversed in both directions, the same as with its first three dimensions. On that account, the universe no longer "develops in time": it is always already given *in toto*. In contrast to this conception, the irreducible temporality of act presupposes the paradoxical ontology of a space where there is always, constitutively, something

"amiss," "out of joint," "not at its own place." The famous line from *Hamlet* that the time is "out of joint" should be "reflected into itself," as Hegel would say: from the experience of a certain period of time as "out of joint," corrupted, abnormal, pathological, we should pass to a "derailment," imbalance, that pertains to the very *form* of time: time as such implies spatial imbalance, a universe where the thing is always "wanting (at) its own place." It is against this background that we should conceive "being thrown into the world" (*Geworfenheit*) as the fundamental determination of "being there" (*Dasein*) with Heidegger: time is the irreducible horizon of our understanding of being precisely because "being there" ("man") is in an ontologically constitutive way "out of its place," i.e., finds itself thrown into a place which is not "its own."

25 Which is why today's disintegration of communism, in spite of the tremendous consequences of what is going on, produces no *acts*.

26 Cf. Jon Elster, *Sour Grapes* (Cambridge: Cambridge University Press, 1983).

27 The best indicator of this inherent impasse of the "pleasure principle" is the actual state of the popular ideology in the USA, so-called "nonism," i.e., NON-ideology: the attitude of radical renunciation (of pollution, of fat and cholesterol in food, of stressful situations . . .). In short, the final price for a pleasure-oriented life is that the subject is bombarded from all sides by superego prohibitions: don't eat fat and beef, avoid food with pesticides, don't smoke, don't pollute—a new empirical confirmation of Lacan's paradoxical inversion of the famous Dostoyevski's proposition from the *Brothers Karamazov*: "If God doesn't exist, then everything is permitted": nothing at all is permitted—not even the most innocent pleasures of eating, drinking, and smoking.

More precisely, we can get anything, but in an aseptic, substanceless form—anything, including the most cruel fantasies, like that of "Ratman," Freud's famous analysand (of being tortured by a rat who penetrates the anus). A recent hushed-up scandal with a movie star revealed that the staging of this fantasy is currently fashionable in Hollywood: a veterinarian cuts off the teeth and claws of a mouse; the mouse is then put in a bag and his tail tied to a string; when the bag is deep in the anus, the excitement is provided by the animal's desperate motion till it suffocates; then it is pulled out by the tail . . . (The problem of the Hollywood star was that he pulled the string too hard, so that the dead mouse stayed within and the star had to seek medical help). Here we have the paradox of consumption "nonism": you can get everything, but in a form robbed of substance—cake without sugar and fat, beer without alcohol, coffee without caffeine, mouse without teeth and claws . . .

28 We all know the crucial step accomplished by the theory of relativity, the step from the thesis that matter "curves," "bends," space to the thesis that what we call "matter" is *nothing but* the curvature of space—perhaps, this homology enables us to grasp the Lacanian proposition on the purely formal status of *objet a*: far from being the positive, material *cause* of the curvature, of derailing the path of desire, *object a*—insofar as it is perceived as a positive entity (the lady in courtly love, for example)—is nothing but a chimerical materialization

of the curved structure of the space of desire itself. And since the only "substance" ("matter") acknowledged by psychoanalysis is enjoyment, we can also say that enjoyment is ultimately nothing but a certain purely formal curvature of the space of pleasure/displeasure, a curvature which makes us experience pleasure in displeasure itself.

29 As for the paradoxes of "beyond the pleasure principle," cf. the incisive developments of Joan Copjec in "The Sartorial Superego," *October* 50 (Cambridge, MA: MIT Press, 1989).

30 Quoted from Donald Phillip Verene, *Hegel's Recollection* (Albany: SUNY Press, 1985), pp. 7–8.

31 Ibid., p. 8.

32 G. W. F. Hegel, *Phenomenology of Spirit* (Oxford: Oxford University Press, 1977), pp. 18–19.

33 Herein consists ultimately Hegel's theory of the necessity of war: wars are necessary so that individuals are not drowned in the closed circuit of their everyday lives, i.e., to remind them of the abyss of negativity upon which their life is founded—a clear proof of how, within the movement of the dialectical process, negativity is not simply "sublated" in its positive result.

34 On another level, it is the same with psychoanalysis. That is to say, one knows the trite reproach according to which psychoanalysis is only capable of decomposing the personality structure and cannot offer a positive alternative to the pathological structure it demolished. Idiotic as this reproach may sound, there is a kind of logic in it—why, indeed, is "psychoanalysis" not followed by "psychosynthesis"? The answer, of course, is that a successful psychoanalysis as such already *is* the required "synthesis," insofar as it explains the genesis of the split, i.e., conceives it "in its becoming." Therein consists also the relevance of Lacan's theory of the "mirror stage" to the field of philosophy; as Lacan points out, the paranoiac feelings of persecution that characterize the mirror stage are constituted by a stagnation similar to "the faces of actors when a film is suddenly stopped in midaction": "Now, this formal stagnation is akin to the most general structure of human knowledge: that which constitutes the ego and its objects with attributes of permanence, identity, and substantiality, in short, with entities or 'things' that are very different from the *Gestalten* that experience enables us to isolate in the shifting field, stretched in accordance with the lines of animal desire" (Jacques Lacan, "Aggressivity in Psychoanalysis," in *Ecrits: A Selection* (New York: Norton, 1977), p. 17.)

What Lacan renders visible here is "Platonism in its becoming": he does not refute Platonism by directly denouncing the illusory nature of *eidos* but by exposing the genesis of the subject's fixation on the immobile *eidos*.

35 According to Alain Bergala, the fundamental feature of Rossellini's Bergman films consists in the fact that the third element disturbing the harmonious relationship of the couple is not the usual third member of a love triangle but some radically heterogeneous element of a wholly nonpsychological nature: the volcano in *Stromboli*, ideologies (communism and Catholicism) in *Europa '51*,

the statues and ruins of Naples in *Voyage to Italy* (cf. Bergala, op. cit., p. 10). What we should add to this is that in each of the three cases, this disturbing element is of a different nature: the volcano in *Stromboli* is *real* (Bergala himself identifies it as a "Thing in itself" upon which every experience of meaning breaks down), in *Europa '51* we have *symbolic* ideologies, whereas the ruins from *Voyage* clearly function as *sinthome*, signifying fragments, fragments of a culture, which are at the same time the congealment of a lost enjoyment.

36 Jacques Lacan, *The Four Fundamental Concepts of Psycho-Analysis* (London: The Hogarth Press, 1977), p. 275.

37 Cf. René Girard, *Job: The Victim of His People* (London: Athlone Press, 1987).

38 Which is why Hannibal Lecter, the sadist/mastermind psychiatrist from Thomas Harris's serial-killer novels (*The Red Dragon, Silence of the Lambs*), is the closest mass culture can get to the figure of the Lacanian analyst.

39 We encounter a homologous inversion in the foremost hard-boiled novels and films: the moment when the *femme fatale* subjectivizes herself. She is first rendered from the perspective of her (masculine) social environment and appears as a fatal object of fascination which brings perdition and leaves behind ruined lives, "empty shells"; when we are finally transposed into her point of view, it becomes manifest that she herself cannot dominate the effects of "what is in her more than herself," of the *object* in herself, upon her environment—no more than men around her, she is a helpless victim of fate.

40 Cf. Jacques Lacan, *Le Séminaire, livre VIII: Le Transfert* (Paris: Editions du Seuil, 1991), chapters 2 to 11.

41 Which is why, in the psychoanalytic process, the analyst should *not* reach his hand back to the analysand, i.e., answer the transferential love by his own love: only by means of this refusal of the analysand's demand of love, only by persisting in the mute position of death, can he induce the analysand to assume the truth of his desire beyond transference.

42 Another reason for the psychoanalyst to remain silent: by demanding nothing from the analysand, his silence suspends the illusion of interpellation and thus forces the analysand to confront his own act of positing the Other.

43 The "psychotic" dimension of this withdrawal from the Other is best manifested by the psychotic's fundamental attitude of *Un-Glauben*, dis-belief in the symbolic order that guarantees the reality's consistency: this dis-belief engenders the typical psychotic idea that the "world" is just my hallucination induced by some Evil Manipulator.

44 Cf. his articles on Rossellini in Vol. IV of *Qu'est-ce que le cinéma?* (Paris: Les Editions du Cerf, 1962).

45 In other words, his films with Bergman are *allegorical*: their diegetic content (their "enunciated") is an allegory of the intersubjective conditions of their process of production. (As to this notion of allegory, see Fredric Jameson, "Allegorizing Hitchcock," in *Signatures of the Visible* (New York and London: Routledge, 1990).)

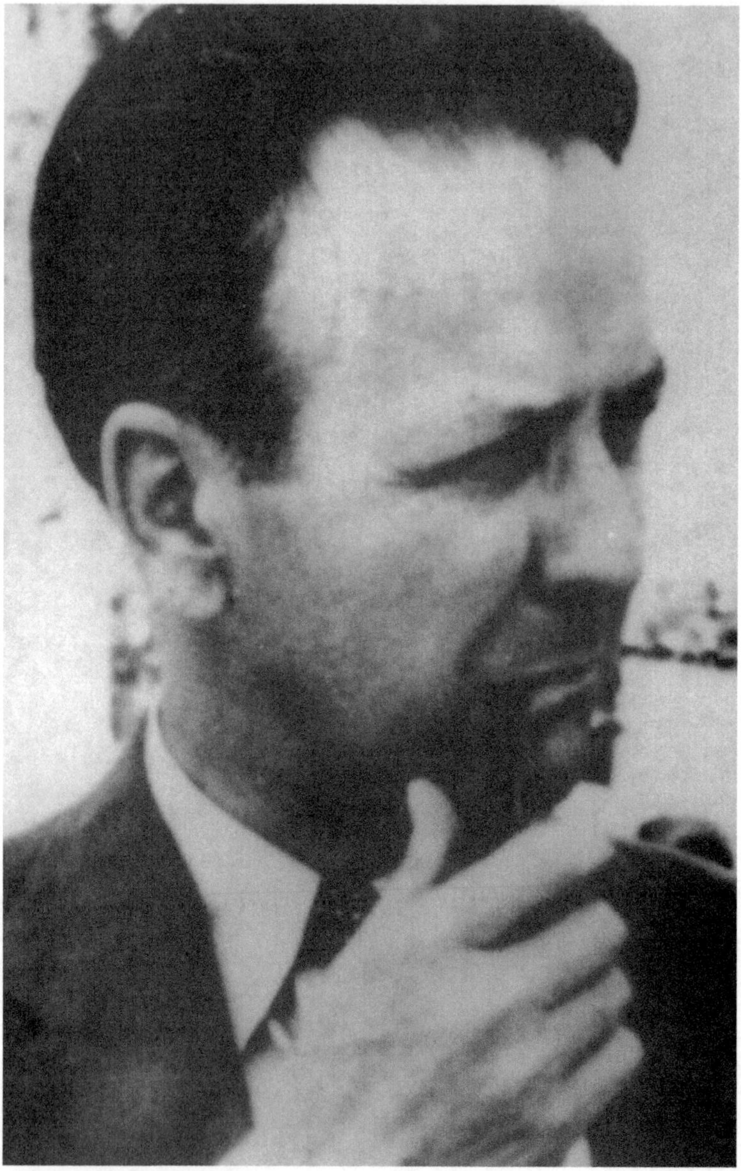

3

WHY IS EVERY ACT A *REPETITION*?

3.1 BEYOND "DISTRIBUTIVE JUSTICE"

Why was Chandler's *Playback* a failure?

The obvious failure of Raymond Chandler's last novel, *Playback* (1958), is usually explained by the decline of his creative impetus which is then tracked down to his alcoholism, born of despair after his wife's death; yet the function of this escape into psychology is, as always, to allow us to elude the inherent logic of the failure. In order to detect it, one has to bear in mind that *Playback* grew out of a screenplay written in 1947–1948 which, due to a series of unfortunate circumstances, was never shot; here is Chandler's initial treatment for the screenplay:

> The crucial week in the life of a girl who decides to spend it in a tower suite in a hotel, under an assumed name, her identity thoroughly concealed with great care, to accept what comes, and at the end of the week to jump to her death.
>
> During this week the frustrations and tragedies of her life are repeated in capsule form, so that it almost appears that she brought

> her destiny with her, and that wherever she went the same sort of thing would happen to her.[1]

What we have here is the skeleton of an entire ethical narrative: at the beginning, there is a *forced choice* which marks the subject's existence with *guilt* (the traumatic death of the girl's husband in *Playback*); this traumatic situation is then *repeated*, "replayed," opening up to the subject the possibility to "redeem" himself/herself by means of a suicidal *act*. The crucial change brought about by novelization was of course the introduction of the first-person narrative: the story is now told as it is seen through the eyes of Philip Marlowe and thus changed into a "normal" hard-boiled detective novel. Therein consists the ultimate reason of its failure: it endeavors to incorporate into the hard-boiled universe a subjective position (an ethical attitude) which is formally excluded from it, i.e., the presence of which renders visible the falsity of the very perspective from which the story is being told. To put it briefly, the subjective position of Marlowe—a cynical romantic sticking to his values against the wicked world whose corruption is embodied in the *femme fatale*—is founded upon the misrecognition of the ethical attitude embodied in the girl's suicidal act. Which is why the interest of *Playback* (the novel) consists in its very failure: as the confrontation of two incompatible logics (incompatible since one of them implies the "repression" of the other), it reveals the inherent limitation of the hard-boiled universe.

We encounter the same ethical narrative of the act *qua* suicidal repetition of a forced choice in William Styron's *Sophie's Choice*. The traumatic original situation takes place in a German concentration camp where a Nazi officer confronts Sophie with an impossible choice: she has to choose one of her two children to survive, while the other will be sent to a gas chamber; if she refuses to make the choice, both of them will die. Driven into a corner, Sophie chooses the younger son, thus contracting a burden of guilt which drives her into madness. At the end of the novel, she exculpates herself by means of a suicidal gesture: torn between her two loves, a psychotic failed artist to whom she is indebted for saving her life after her arrival in America, and a young beginning writer, she chooses the first and together they commit suicide.[2] Although "Sophie's choice" functions today as a true *casum* evoked in numerous ethical treatises, one should note how, as a rule, attention is focused on the original situation of forced choice and on its disturbing ethical implications (How should one perform in such a situation? Is not the proper attitude to refuse the choice as such, whatever the costs?), whereas the problem of *repetition*, i.e., of the suicidal act by means of which the subject can later exculpate himself, is singularily absent from the debate.

"Distributive justice" and its exception

This uneasiness betrays the fact that "Sophie's choice" subverts far more than the hard-boiled universe: it saps the very foundations of the notion of justice which regulates our everyday commerce, namely the notion of "distributive justice." Let us just recall its most elaborate articulation, John Rawls's *Theory of Justice*,[3] an attempt to give liberal ethics a radical antiutilitarian, Kantian twist. In a thoroughly Kantian fashion, Rawls "evacuates" the ethical domain, i.e., empties it of all "pathological" (contingent, empirical) objects. That is to say, Rawls's crucial thesis is his affirmation of the primacy of Justice over the good: justice has to be defined prior to and independently of what we take for good, it cannot be deduced from the notion of good. In contemporary secular societies in which a multitude of world views coexist, every particular, determinate notion of the supreme good is experienced as an ultimately "contingent" entity; consequently, no unity—the ideological "cement" holding them together—can be defined in the terms of some common good. What is thereby refuted is also every form of utilitarianism which renders Justice dependent on the "calculus of pleasures," on the maximizing of the Good for the greatest possible number of people—to refer to psychoanalytical terminology, Rawls takes up a position "beyond the pleasure principle," as well as beyond its inherent prolongation, the reality principle. This is what is at stake in the distinction he elaborates between the rational and the reasonable: the Rational consists of the "calculus of pleasures," of the economy of expenses and gains at the level of the reality principle, it is the agency which tells us when it is profitable to renounce the present pleasure for the sake of the long-term gain, i.e., to obey a social norm although this obedience is detrimental to our short-term interests;

whereas Justice concerns ethical principles which are to be followed irrespective of the "rational" consideration of our "pathological," contingent interests. Rawls's central notion of the "veil of ignorance" aims precisely at this erasure of the subject's "pathological" considerations: the ethical subject acts *as if he does not know where (which position within society) he speaks from*, he is constituted by means of this abstraction from his position of enunciation.

The paradox of the subject of Justice is thus that the total transparency of his object entails the total impenetrability of the place from which he speaks: on the one hand, he is supposed to be totally informed about the society on which he is called to pass a judgment, about the position of all its subjects, about their interests and their views; on the other hand, the reverse of this supposition of total knowledge is a radical ignorance of the way the subject himself is "embedded" in the social universe—a "reasonable" judgment must express a standpoint which the subject would agree with even if his position on the social scale were the lowest.[4] This erasure of the "pathological" content of the subject's position of enunciation can be written in Lacanian mathems as S → $, i.e., the passage from the "pathological" subject full of particular interests to the emptied, "barred," subject of Justice; in other words, the subject is irreducibly *split* into the "pathological" subject made of "flesh and blood" and the ethical subject, a kind of symbolic fiction, an abstract participant of the "original situation" in which the social contract was made. The status of this social contract—the symbolic pact *qua* original social fact prior to any utilitarian "calculus of interests"—is also that of a symbolic fiction: the only way to pass a coherent ethical judgment on the present state of actual society is to proceed from the fiction of the "original situation" in which the subjects concluded the social contract, covering with the "veil of ignorance" the "pathological" determination of themselves *qua* beings of flesh and blood. The Lacanian notion of the Ego-Ideal (as opposed to the ideal ego) is to be located precisely at this fictitious place of the "original situation," the place from which the subject looks at himself so that he is able to pass ethical judgment—that is to say, judgment on the distribution of goods, since, according to Rawls, Justice ultimately concerns the distribution of goods, i.e., is distributive justice.

However, as was demonstrated by Jean-Pierre Dupuy,[5] "Sophie's choice" presents a limit case which, like the apocryphal grain of sand, disturbs the logical mechanism of distributive justice. The crucial point is that "Sophie's choice" is *not* just another case of the standard sacrificial situation in which we sacrifice the rights of the individual for the larger benefit of the community (as in a situation of extreme interethnic tensions where the utilitarian logic tells us that it is "rational" to put to death some innocent individuals since we know that this sacrifice will calm passions and thus spare a far greater number of lives). It is easy to defend the antiutilitarian liberal standpoint against such a logic of the scapegoat into which the collective guilt is projected: one has simply to affirm the right of the individual not to be wronged for the sake of the allegedly higher interests of the community. Yet, in "Sophie's choice," nobody is less harmed if she refuses the choice: in this case, both of the children die. In other words, this situation *does* stand Rawls's test of the "veil of ignorance": even if one occupies the position of the sacrificed child, the "reasonable" thing to do is to accept the sacrifice since the victim does not lose anything by it, only others gain. As pointed out by Dupuy, what we encounter here is not just the limit of utilitarianism but the limit of reason as such: "Sophie's choice" is not only "rational" but also "reasonable" in Rawls's sense, yet our ethical intuition tells us unmistakably that there is something wrong with it . . . Consequently, the paradox "Sophie's choice" presents for Rawls's theory is the following: the fundamental attitude of this theory is "antisacrificial," i.e., its ultimate aim is to undermine the traditional ethics of the individual's sacrifice for the benefit of the community and to replace it with the ethics of tolerance, of individual rights, etc.; yet its own axioms, when applied to "Sophie's choice," legitimate the sacrificial choice. In this sense, we can say that this version of the sacrificial situation presents a "blind spot" of Rawls's theory: a strange body which is ultimately incompatible with it, yet which, at the same time, cannot be inherently refuted and therefore has to be excluded (sacrificed?) in advance if the theory is to maintain its consistency. In a somewhat naive formulation, we could say that Rawls' ethics is "not made for sacrificial situations": Rawls does not offer a better answer of how to act in a sacrificial situation, what he offers are rather principles which, if followed, prevent the very rise of sacrificial situations.[6]

Sacrifice, traditional and utilitarian

It may seem that we have condensed in the figure of "sacrificial logic" two incompatible ethical attitudes, the traditional communitarian one and the utilitarian one; however, it can be shown that we are dealing here with a split inherent to sacrificial logic which concerns a shift in the status of knowledge. The traditional sacrificial logic was described in a paradigmatic way by René Girard:[7] guilt is projected onto the scapegoat whose sacrifice allows us to establish social peace by localizing violence; as if in recognition of this beneficial role he plays, the victim thus gains the aura of sanctity. The crucial component of this "generative scapegoating" is of course that society "really believes" in the scapegoat's guilt: the "social function" of the scapegoating lies in its by-product, in the way it guarantees the social pact, yet it can perform this function only insofar as it is not directly posited as its aim. The utilitarian sacrifice implies on the contrary a cynical-manipulative attitude: the organizer of the scape-goating in no way believes in the victim's guilt, his point is simply that one has to give preference to the interests of the community over the rights of the individual—the individual's sacrifice is acceptable insofar as it prevents the disintegration of the social fabric. The problem with this cynical-"enlightened" logic of the sacrifice is that it presupposes and needs the "other" ("ordinary people") in the role of the simpleton who "really believes" in the scapegoat's guilt—otherwise, there is no point in the sacrifice. To render visible the dubious nature of this presupposition, we have only to think of the Stalinist monster trials as the most explicit form of cynical-utilitarian sacrificial logic (apart from fascist anti-Semitism): the answer to the question "Did the prosecutors really believe in their victim's guilt?" is far more difficult and ambiguous than it may seem. A "true" Stalinist would probably say: even if, on the level of immediate facts, the accused are innocent, they are all the more guilty on a deeper level of historical responsibility—by the very insistence on their abstract-legal innocence, they have given preference to their individuality over the larger historical interests of the working class expressed in the will of the Party . . . This argument clearly resumes the paradox of the sacred space at work in traditional sacrificial logic: as soon as a man finds himself occupying the place of the sacred victim, his very being is stigmatized and the more he proclaims his innocence, the more he is guilty—since his guilt resides in his very resistance to the assumption of "guilt," i.e., the symbolic mandate of the victim conferred on him by the community. What the victim has to do in order to be "equal to his task" is therefore to assume the burden of guilt in full consciousness of his innocence: the more he is innocent, the greater is the weight of his sacrifice.

In other words, the reference to the simpletons who are supposed to "really believe" in the victim's guilt and for the sake of whom the entire spectacle of scapegoating is staged, is deeply ambiguous: by means of it, the utilitarian manipulator *transposes onto the other his own (unconscious) belief*, like the parents who "of course do not believe in Santa Claus, we just pretend to believe in order not to disappoint our children . . ." The break separating the manipulating utilitarian who justifies scapegoating by its social benefits from traditional sacrificial logic is therefore far less clear-cut than it may seem, it is rather a case of continuous gradation: manipulation itself must be supported by the presupposition of a naive believer, and traditional sacrifice itself is never "pure" but contains always an element of "manipulation." To put it succinctly, the split is inherent to both versions of the sacrifice, both resort to the fetishistic logic of "I know very well (that the victim is innocent), but nevertheless . . ." This continuous passage is rendered possible by their common feature: the assumption that "sacrifice pays," which results from the foundation of ethics in the common Good. On the other hand, the Kantian revolution, by repudiating this foundation of ethics in the common Good (and its corollary, the ethical valuation of an act by its actual consequences),[8] breaks without reserve with the sacrificial logic in its traditional as well as its utilitarian versions—from what quarter then do the paradoxes arise with which Rawls becomes entangled in his endeavor to elaborate the contours of an antisacrificial ethics?

Le père . . .

At this precise point, a reference to psychoanalytic theory comes to our assistance: the fundamental insight behind the notions of the Oedipus complex, incest prohibition, symbolic castration, the advent of the

Name of the Father, etc., is that a certain "sacrificial situation" defines the very status of man *qua* "parlêtre," "being of language." That is to say, what is the entire psychoanalytic theory of "socialization," of the emergence of the subject from the encounter of a presymbolic life substance of "enjoyment" and the symbolic order, if not the description of a sacrificial situation which, far from being exceptional, is the story of everyone and as such *constitutive?* This constitutive character means that the "social contract," the inclusion of the subject in the symbolic community, has the structure of a *forced choice*: the subject supposed to choose freely his community (since only a free choice is morally binding) does not exist prior to this choice, he is constituted by means of it. The choice of community, the "social contract," is a paradoxical choice where I maintain the freedom of choice only if I "make the right choice": if I choose the "other" of the community, I stand to lose the very freedom, the very possibility of choice (in clinical terms: I choose psychosis). What is sacrificed in the act of choice is of course the Thing, the incestuous Object that embodies impossible enjoyment—the paradox consisting in the fact that the incestuous Object *comes to be through being lost*, i.e., that it is not given prior to its loss. For *that* reason, the choice is forced: its terms are incomparable, what I cede in order to gain inclusion in the community of symbolic exchange and distribution of goods is in one sense "all" (the Object of desire) and in another sense "nothing at all" (since it is in itself impossible, i.e., since, in the case of its choice, I lose all). This is the point which clearly marks the specificity of psychoanalysis: all other theories conceive the incest prohibition as a term in an act of exchange which ultimately "pays," whereby the subject gets something in return (cultural progress, other women, and so forth), whereas psychoanalysis insists that the subject gets nothing in exchange (and also gives nothing).[9] In short, this renunciation is "pure," a pure negative gesture of withdrawal which constitutes the space of possible gains and losses, i.e., of the distribution of goods: women become an object of exchange and distribution only after the "mother thing" is posited as prohibited. Therein consists the psychoanalytic reading of Kant: the primacy of Justice over the Good implies that the supreme Good (the Thing in itself *qua* incestuous Object) is posited as impossible/unattainable.

In the last years of his teaching, Lacan formulated this choice as the alternative of *"le père ou pire,"* "the Father or worse"—the choice is not between good and bad but between bad and worse. The forced choice of community, i.e., the subordination to the authority of the Name of the Father, is "bad" since, by means of it, the subject "gives way as to his desire," and thus contracts an indelible guilt (as Lacan says, the only thing that the subject can be guilty of in psychoanalysis is to give way as to his desire).[10] This guilt constitutive of the subject, which is at the root of what Freud calls the "discontent" that pertains to culture, can help us to explain why the Lacanian mathem for the subject is $, that is to say: the subject crossed off, evacuated, reduced to the empty gesture of a forced choice. Which is why the time for the subject is never

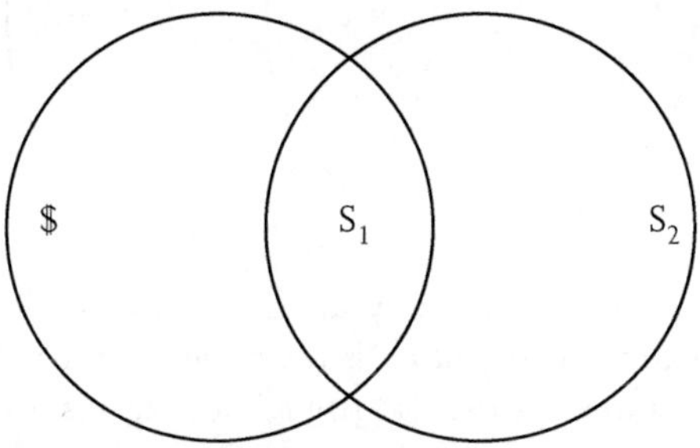

present: the subject constitutes himself when, all of a sudden, the presubjective X is posited as the one who *has already chosen*; social reality is "subjectivized" when, all of a sudden, it is imputed to the subject as something that he has freely chosen.[11] Consequently, the scheme of alienation that Lacan proposes in his *Four Fundamental Concepts of Psycho-Analysis* has to be taken quite literally, as a choice between the two signifiers: the subject cannot "have it all" and choose himself as nonbarred, all he can choose is a partial mark, one of the two signifiers, the symbolic mandate that will represent him, designate his place in the intersubjective network, function as his stand-in in the Other—in other words, in which he will be *alienated*. In the case of "Sophie's choice," the dyad S_1–S_2 can be read as the two children out of which she is forced to choose one; in *Romeo and Juliet*, S_1–S_2 is the couple of two Names of the Father, Montague and Capulet: if Romeo and Juliet would prefer to remain members of a community, one of them would have to renounce his/her Name and adjoin the other's. Yet the two of them did not "give way as to their desire": by means of their suicidal gesture, they *repeated* the fundamental choice into which they were born by disowning their respective Names, *separating* themselves from the totality of S_1–S_2 and thereby choosing themselves as "worse"; the same as with Sophie who, in her repeated choice, chooses herself as "worse," as nonsymbolizable *object*. The Lacanian mathem for this "worse"

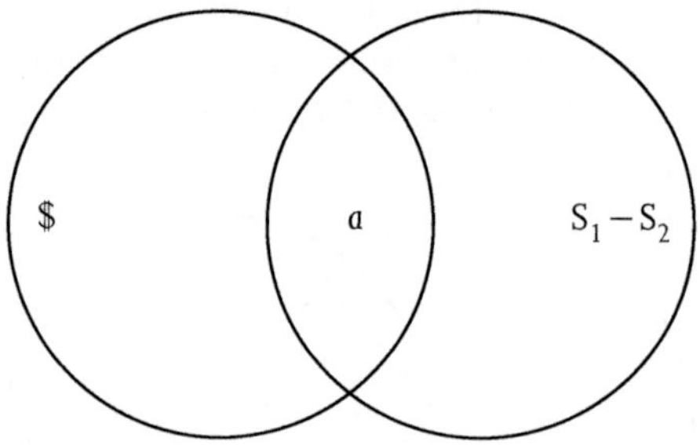

element which presents the only alternative to the "bad" choice of the Father is namely *objet petit a*: *"le père ou pire"* ultimately amounts to the alternative "Father or the *objet petit a*." It is against this background that one has to grasp Lacan's thesis that "a madman is the only free man": the "madman" (the psychotic) is the subject who has refused to walk into the trap of the forced choice and to accept that he has "always already chosen"; he took the choice "seriously" and chose the impossible opposite of the Name of the Father, i.e., of the symbolic identification which confers us a place in the intersubjective space. Which is why Lacan insists that psychosis is to be "located within the register of ethics": psychosis is a mode "not to give way as to our desire," it signals our refusal to exchange enjoyment for the Name of the Father.[12]

. . . ou pire

Thereby, we have already indicated that Lacan's last word is not the forced choice. The original position of man *qua* being of language is decidedly that of *alienation* in the signifier (in the symbolic order): the first choice is necessarily that of the Father, which marks the subject with the indelible guilt pertaining to his very (symbolic) existence. This alienation is best exemplified by the Kantian moral subject: the split subject subordinated to the moral imperative, caught in the vicious circle of the superego where he is all the more guilty the more he obeys its command. Yet Lacan's wager is that it is possible for the subject to get rid of the superego pressure by *repeating* the choice and thus exculpating himself of his constitutive guilt. The price of it is exorbitant: if the first choice is "bad," its repetition is in its very formal structure "worse" since it is an act of *separation* from the symbolic community: Lacan's supreme example is here of course Antigone's suicidal "No!" to Creon.

Therein consists the Lacanian definition of the authentic ethical act: an act which reaches the utter limit of the primordial forced choice and repeats it in the reverse sense. Such an act presents the only moment when we are effectively "free": Antigone is "free" after she has been excommunicated from the community. In our time, such acts seem almost unthinkable: their pendants are usually disqualified as "terrorism," like the gesture of Gudrun Ensslin, leader of the "Red Army Faction," a Maoist "terrorist" organization, who killed herself in the maximum-security prison in 1978. Her story was told in Margaretha von Trotta's film *The Times of Plumb* (the parallel between her destiny and that of Antigone has already been drawn in Volker Schloendorf's episode in the omnibus *Germany in Autumn*). Today, when Antigone is as a rule "domesticated," made into a pathetic guardian of the community against tyrannical state power, it is all the more necessary to insist on the scandalous character of her "No!" to Creon: those who do not want to talk about the "terrorist" Gudrun, should also keep quiet about Antigone. Was not Antigone's gesture repeated by RAF sympathizers who took part in Gudrun's funeral—masked, since they knew they were being filmed by the police? What was really disturbing about the RAF "terrorism" was not the bombs but the refusal of the forced choice, of the fundamental social pact, implied in their attitude. How, then, should one answer the reproach that RAF members "went too far" when, in the name of their "mad" choice, they suspended the most elementary ethics? One should assume it fully—on condition that "suspension of the ethical" is grasped here in its precise Kierkegaardian sense (the obvious "Kierkegaardian" overtone of the terms we used to determine the act—"repetition," "choice of freedom," "guilt"—should suffice to legitimize this turn). The fundamental ethical gesture is the subject's alienation in the universality of the symbolic pact, whereas the religious marks the suspension of the ethical, i.e., the moment of the "mad" decision when, instead of the I, the symbolic identity, the universal law, we choose *a*, the exception, the particular object that sticks out from the symbolic order. In short, the leap into the religious *repeats* the ethical forced choice and thereby exculpates us of the guilt implied in it.

Repetition: imaginary, symbolic, real

Repetition as act is to be distinguished from its other modalities; that is to say, the status of the repetition with Kierkegaard is triple, according to his triad of the *esthetical*, *ethical*, and *religious* stages (or, to name their Lacanian equivalents, Imaginary, Symbolic, and Real).[13]

In the *esthetical* stage, the impossibility of repetition is experienced under the guise of the imaginary deadlocks that the subject encounters when he endeavors to resuscitate the fullness of past pleasures. In his *Repetition*, Kierkegaard exemplifies this deadlock by means of the failure of his (i.e., the narrator's) return to Berlin: every attempt to restore some past intense experience is doomed to result in an anticlimax—even if, on the level of "reality," the thing is exactly the same (Kierkegaard goes to the same restaurants and theaters, visits the same friends), it now leaves him cold and indifferent . . .

In the *ethical* stage, repetition assumes the form of the universal norms of conduct: instead of chasing the elusive moments of esthetical pleasure, we rely upon the certitude of repetition. Repetition is a sign of maturity when the subject has learned to avoid the twin traps of impatient hope in the New and of nostalgic memory of the Old: we find satisfaction in the return of the Same, like the happy marital couple who has overcome the yearning for exotic adventures, yet is still able to avoid melancholic remembrance of past passions. The deadlock which pushes Kierkegaard toward the next (religious) stage is of course the experience of how, at this stage too, repetition is impossible: the ideal point at which we overcome the futile yearning for the New without falling into a nostalgic backward-directed attitude, is never present as such. The structure of subjective time is such that, from hopeful expectations, from "too early," we are thrown all of a sudden into melancholic remembrance, into "too late." In other words, the self-referential paradox consists in the fact that the ideal point between hope and memory *is present precisely and only in the mode of hope or memory*: in youthful zeal we hope to find peace in a beloved spouse one never gets tired of; in old age we remember the happy time fulfilled with the reliable rhythm of repetition . . .

The most succinct determination of the status of repetition in the *religious* stage is of course its *reflection into itself*: insofar as repetition is not possible, it is possible to repeat this very experience of impossibility, i.e., the failure to attend the Object. This is how Lacan conceives the difference between repetition of a signifier and repetition *qua* traumatic encounter with the Real: the repetition of a signifier repeats the symbolic *trait unaire*, the mark to which the object is reduced, and thus constitutes the ideal order of the Law, whereas "traumatism" designates precisely the reemergent failure to integrate some "impossible" kernel of the Real. What Kierkegaard has in mind here is, ultimately, the well-known opposition of two attitudes to history: when we are thrown into historical "becoming," caught in its flow, we experience the abyss of history's "openness," we are forced to choose; afterward, when we cast a retrospective gaze on it, its course loses the character of "becoming" and appears as the manifestation of some "eternal" necessity. It is therefore in the name of this abyss of free decision that Kierkegaard turns against the retrospective "comprehension of history" which endeavors to account for the necessity of what took place: those who "comprehend history" are nothing but "backward-turned prophets," they are no better than those who pass forward prophecies—both are forgetful of the free decision involved in the act of becoming: if we observe the past as necessary, we forget that it is something that came into existence.[14] By means of the repetition of the past, we undermine this image of history *qua* the linear process of the unfolding of an underlying necessity and unearth its process of becoming: to "repeat" the October Revolution, for example, means not to look at it as a link in the chain of historical necessity but to render visible the existential deadlock of its participants, the weight of decisions they were forced to assume within that unique constellation.

Kierkegaard's crucial point is that what we have here is precisely repetition, *not* remembrance: we do not "transpose ourselves into the spirit of the past" from a standpoint of an external, neutral gaze; the past appears in its "openness," in its possibility, only to those whose present situation is threatened by the same abyss, who are caught in the same deadlock. In this sense Kierkegaard conceives the Christian attitude as the experience of our "simultaneousness with the humiliated Christ of the Gospel": in the act of repetition by means of which we became Christians we do not identify with Christ *qua* Master but with a humiliated originator of a scandalous act. The same "simultaneousness" with the past of catastrophic failures and humiliations is referred to in Walter Benjamin's *Theses on the Philosophy of History* where he determines revolution as repetition which suspends linear historical progress: when a revolution conceives itself as repetition of past failed revolutionary attempts, these attempts are rendered visible in their very "openness," as desperate acts to break the "great chain of (historical) being." Revolution "delivers" the past failed attempts by *repeating them in their "possibility,"* it retroactively realizes their potentials which were crushed in the victorious course of "official" history.[15] The specific dimension of this repetition, in which, to the gaze of those stimatized by the utmost actual threat, the past appears in its "possibility," is that of theology—it is perhaps somewhat easier to understand thus why the concept of repetition was eminently theological for Kierkegaard.

Repetition and postmodernity

Now we can approach from a new perspective also the ill-famed problem of the postmodern loss of proper historical sense, i.e., its lack of appreciation of the common tradition which unites us with our past. The experience of how we are "embedded" in a historical continuum is allegedly superseded by the logic of *nostalgia*, by the fascination with an etheric image of the past wrested from its historical context. Benjamin's concept of repetition *qua* stasis, suspension of the historical continuum, forms an appropriate antidote to this reproach, since, in it the two terms exchange their respective "value": for Benjamin, "truth" lies on the side of the anhistorical stasis, whereas History is always "false," a narrative of the victor who legitimizes his victory by presenting the previous development as the linear continuum leading to his own final triumph. How, then, should we deal with this antagonism of the two perspectives on history, of the partisans of historicity who deplore the loss of historical sensitivity in the postmodern nostalgia and of the Benjaminian reliance upon the delivering power of the "anhistorical" repetition which interrupts the historical continuum? The first step is of course to grasp this antagonism as inherent to each of the two terms, historicity and anhistorical repetition. The "historical sense" is inherently torn between awareness of the way the very place from which we speak is determined by a "decentered" historical tradition, and between "historicism," i.e., the Master's gaze which, viewing history from a safe metalanguage distance, constructs the linear narrative of "historical evolution." The postmodern anhistorical stasis, on the other hand, is torn between repetition *qua* suspension of movement by means of which we "synchronize" our menaced position with that of our predecessors, and between repetition *qua* aced position with that of our predecessors, and between repetition *qua* nostalgia, the proper object of which is not the image of the past but rather the very gaze enraptured by this image—nostalgia always relies on such a reflexive turn, what really fascinates us in it is the gaze still able to immerse itself "naively" in the etheric image of the lost past. In both cases, the logic of the "fall" (from historical awareness into historicism; from repetition *qua* stasis into nostalgia) is the same, it implies our exclusion from the process, our acquiring an external distance; yet the crucial thing is that in the double form in which this antagonism is experienced, the terms are linked diagonally (historicity proper is opposed to nostalgia and historicism to repetition), so that we obtain a kind of Greimasian semiotic square.

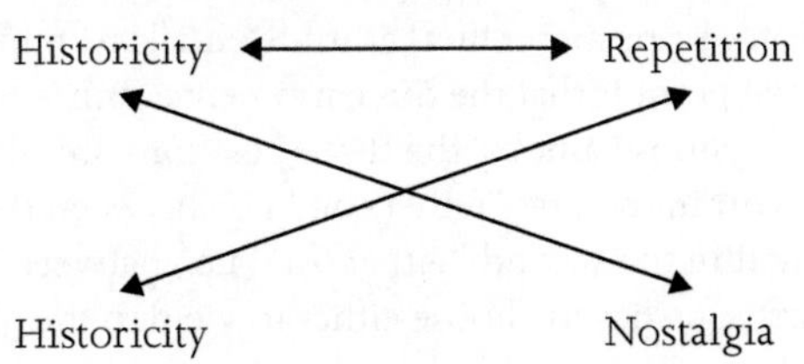

The key to this enigma consists in the basic paradox of historicity as opposed to historicism: what distinguishes it is precisely the presence of an *unhistorical kernel*. That is to say, the only way to save historicity from the fall into historicism, into the notion of the linear succession of "historical epochs," is to conceive these epochs as a series of ultimately failed attempts to deal with the same "unhistorical" traumatic kernel (in Marxism, this kernel is of course the class struggle, class antagonism)—in short, to conceive the founding gesture of each new epoch as *repetition* in the precise Kierkegaardian-Benjaminian sense. The most succinct definition of historicism is therefore: historicity *minus* the unhistorical kernel of the Real—and the function of the nostalgic image is precisely to fill out the empty place of this exclusion, i.e., the blind spot of historicism. In other words, what the nostalgic image conceals is not the historical mediation but on the contrary the unhistorical traumatic kernel which returns as the Same through all historical epochs (in Marxist terms, the nostalgic image of idyllic precapitalist society as opposed to capitalist antagonism ultimately conceals the class struggle which is what *remains the same* in the passage from feudalism to capitalism).

"Either/or" redoubled

The double opposition (historicity vs. nostalgia, historicism vs. repetition) can be arranged into a narrative succession: in a first moment, we refuse nostalgic stasis in the name of historical sense; in a second moment, we become aware of how this historical sense itself turns into its opposite, into historicism, if we do not take into account the unhistorical kernel in its midst—the affirmation of historical sense proper implies its punctual suspension. This narrative succession offers us also the matrix of Kierkegaard's triad *esthetical, ethical, religious*, where the middle term (*ethical*) undergoes the same split, which is why the very affirmation of a proper ethical attitude entails its punctual suspension. The crucial point is that the three moments cannot be "synchronized": we never choose among the three positions simultaneously, we choose either within the first "either/or," i.e., between the *esthetical* and the *ethical*, or within the second "either/or," i.e., between the *ethical* and the *religious*. First, one has to choose either to yield to the pleasure of the moment or to opt for the universality of moral law; then, one has to choose either to accept the universality of moral law as the ultimate horizon or to be prepared to suspend it for the sake of the religious demand. That is to say, the problem of the *religious* suspension of the *ethical* emerges only *after we have already chosen the ethical.*[16]

The shift of perspective at work here can be exemplified by means of the dialectic of law and violence: first, law appears as opposed to particular acts of violence that subvert it, the subject is torn between "pathological" impulses to transgress law and between the ethical injunction to obey it; then, the ground is suddenly swept from under his feet when he experiences how the reign of law itself is founded upon violence, i.e., how the imposition of the reign of law consists in the universalization of a violence which thereby becomes "legal." This violent reverse of the law is—to put it in Kierkegaard's terms—"the law in becoming." The experience of this reversal can be rendered palpable apropos of today's spontaneous ideological perception of the threats to the existing world order: now, with the disintegration of "really existing socialism," the neutral, universal medium, the presupposed measure of the "normal" state of things, is organized around the notion of capitalist democracy (the market, pluralism, etc.), whereas those who oppose it are more and more reduced to "irrational," marginal positions ("terrorists," "fundamentalist fanatics"). As soon as some political force threatens too much the circulation of capital—even if it is, for example, a benign ecological protest against woodcutting—it is instantly labeled "terrorist," "irrational," etc. Perhaps, our very survival depends on our capacity to perform the above-described reversal and to locate the true source of madness in the allegedly neutral measure of "normalcy" which enables us to perceive all opposition to it as "irrational." Today when the media bombard us with shocking revelations about different versions of "madness" that threaten the "normal" circuit of our everyday lives, from serial killers to religious fundamentalists, from Saddam Hussein to narco-cartels, one has to rely more than ever on Hegel's dictum that the true source of evil is the very neutral gaze which perceives Evil all around.

In a first approach, all this has nothing to do with Kierkegaard's notion of the *religious*; yet things become clearer as soon as we consider that Kierkegaard's aim was to reaffirm the Christian attitude in its "scandalous" reverse, before it settled down into a force of law and order, i.e., to reaffirm it as an *act*, as was the very appearance of Christ in the eyes of the keepers of the old law, before Christ was "christianized," made part of the new law of Christian tradition. This scandalous "suspension of the Ethical" (of the old Jewish law) inherent to the Christian attitude is what Kierkegaard wants to resuscitate in his furious polemics against institutionalized Christianity ("Christendom") that occupied the last years of his life. One is here tempted to reread Kierkegaard's insistence that every believer must "repeat" Christ's scandal—i.e., Christianity in its "becoming," before it turned into an established necessity—through the perspective of G. K. Chesterton's perspicacious remark about how the detective story "keeps in some sense before the mind the fact that civilization itself is the most sensational of departures and the most romantic of rebellions . . . It is based on the fact that morality is the most dark and daring of conspiracies."[17] This is what is ultimately at stake in the *second* "either/or": the experience of how the *ethical* attitude is the only true subversion. To paraphrase Chesterton, when the true Christian believer stands alone, fearless amid the knives and fists of the servants of established necessity, it does certainly serve to remind us that it is the agent of belief who is the original and subversive figure, while the esthetic footpads yielding to pleasures are merely placid old cosmic conservatives, happy in the immemorial respectability of apes and wolves. Or, to paraphrase Brecht from his *Three-Penny Opera*: we enter the religious when we say to ourselves "What is a transgression of the law against the transgression that pertains to the law itself? What are the petty human crimes against the voice of God ordering Abraham the senseless sacrifice of his son? Which human crime can approach the cruelty of God's trifling with human destiny?"[18]

3.2 IDENTITY AND AUTHORITY

The "exception reconciled in the universal"

What one should not miss here is the inherent link between this suspension of the Ethical and Kierkegaard's notion of authority: by means of his readiness to sacrifice his beloved son, Abraham attests his unconditional submission to God's authority; if he would judge God's demand as to its content ("How can He demand of me something so atrocious?"), God's authority would be submitted to his judgment and thereby devalorized. In other words, God's proper authority is experienced only in the religious suspension of the Ethical: if God would only be a power which confers supplementary authority on ethical commands, he would lose his proper authority and function as an *esthetical supplement to the ethics*, i.e., a kind of imaginary creature procuring ordinary people, enslaved to imagination, to obey the abstract ethical imperatives. As we have already pointed out, this religious suspension of the Ethical is not its simple external abolition but its inherent condition of possibility, i.e., precisely that which confers on the Ethical its *identity*. The same point can be rendered also in terms of the universal and its constitutive exception: the religious "suspension of the Ethical" refers to an exception which does not relate to the universal as its external transgression but, precisely *qua* exception, founds it:

> The rigorous and determinate exception who although he is in conflict with the universal still is an offshoot of it, sustains himself . . . The exception who thinks the universal in that he thinks himself through; he explains the universal in that he explains himself. Consequently, the exception explains the universal and himself, and if one really wants to study the universal, one only needs to look around for a legitimate exception. The legitimate exception is reconciled in the universal.[19]

At the very point at which Kierkegaard opposes himself most violently to the alleged Hegelian "tyranny of the Universal," he is of course at his closest to Hegel: what is the Hegelian "concrete Universal" if not the "exception reconciled in the Universal," i.e., the unity of the abstract Universal with its constitutive exception? The most ill-famed Hegelian example here is of course that of the state *qua* a rational totality of individuals who "made" themselves by means of their labor: the State achieves its actuality in the person of the monarch who is immediately, i.e., in his very nature, what he is in his symbolic determination (one becomes King by birth, not by one's merits). The King's exception is therefore an exception "reconciled in the Universal" since it founds it; the abstract, prereligious ethical republicanism *à la*

Fichte would of course protest against this royal exception, condemning it as an unbearable affront to republican principles, it would call upon us to treat the King the same way we treat other citizens, whereas the Hegelian speculation demonstrates how the very ethical universality, in order to sustain itself, requires an exception, a point at which it is suspended.[20] Yet to avoid repeating over again such commonplaces, let us refer to an entirely different domain, to a certain peculiarity of Theodor W. Adorno's style. As was pointed out by Fredric Jameson, the rhythm of his essays always contains a sudden halt, the refined dialectical analysis is abruptly cut off with a proposition which clearly recalls the good old Marxist invectives ("ideology of late capitalism," "expression of the class position of big capital," etc.). Where does the necessity of these repeated lapses into "vulgar sociologism" come from? Far from attesting to Adorno's theoretical weakness, they present the way thought's constitutive limit is inscribed within the thought itself; that is to say, such a "vulgar-sociological" reference

> gestures towards an outside of thinking—whether system itself in the form of rationalization, or totality as a socioeconomic mechanism of domination and exploitation—which escapes representation by the individual thinker or the individual thought. The function of the impure, extrinsic reference is less to interpret, then, than to rebuke interpretation as such and to include within the thought the reminder that it is itself inevitably the result of a system that escapes it and which it perpetuates.[21]

The crucial point here is that these "vulgar-sociological" references concern the level of *content*, they point toward the "social content" of the interpreted phenomena—thereby, we finally reached the paradox we were aiming at all the time. Dialectical analysis is ultimately analysis of form, it endeavors to dissolve the positivity of its object in the totality of its formal mediations. Within the standard "poststructuralist" perspective, it would therefore seem that such "vulgar" references denote the moment of "closure," the moment when the given field is "sutured" and blinds itself to its constitutive outside. Jameson's point is on the contrary that it is *precisely such "vulgar-sociological" references which keep the field of the analysis of form open, i.e., which prevent the thought from falling into the trap of identity and mistaking its limited form of reflection for the unattainable form of thought as such*. In other words, the function of the "vulgar-sociological" reference is to represent within the notional *content* what eludes notion as such, namely the totality of its own *form*: in it, that which escapes reflection, the form of its own totality, acquires positive existence under the guise of its opposite. Is it necessary to point out how it is precisely here, where Adorno purports to break the closed circle of the Hegelian self-transparency of the notion, that he remains thoroughly Hegelian? More precisely: it is only here that he attains the proper level of the Hegelian speculative identity: what Hegel calls "speculative identity" is precisely the identity of the form, of the totality of dialectical mediation which eludes the thought's grasp, with some unmediated bit of content referred to in the "vulgar-sociological" gesture (or, in the case of the state, the identity of the state *qua* rational totality with the "irrational," biological positivity of the King's body). The proper dialectical approach therefore includes *its own suspension*, a point of exception which is constitutive of the dialectical analysis.

That is the ill-famed dialectical "coincidence of the opposites": the pure form of dialectical mediation maintains its distance from the positive content it mediates only by means of its coincidence with the most inert, "nonmediated," remainder of this content; and the Lacanian "Real" ultimately denotes such a nonmediated leftover which serves as a support of the symbolic structure in its formal pureness.[22] Yet the paradox of identity resides in the fact that it is precisely through this remainder of the Real—through this supplementary remark which maintains its nonidentity and openness—that the system (Hegelian state, Adorno's theoretical edifice) *achieves its identity with itself*: as Hegel puts it, a state without the monarch at its head is not actually a state, and the same goes for Adorno's theory which, devoid of the "vulgar-sociological" sallies, would remain a maze of disconnected associations.

The vicious circle of dialectics and its remainder

By means of taking into account this paradox of the Hegelian notion of identity, one can prove false the extremely influential critique of the logic of self-reflection proposed in the 1960s by Dieter Henrich; its basic argument is that the self-reflective model of self-consciousness necessarily implicates us in a vicious circle.[23] According to Henrich, the self-reflective model of self-consciousness conceives the relationship of consciousness to itself as that of mirroring self-objectivization: the consciousness makes itself its own object; this capacity to make oneself one's own object by way of reflection distinguishes man from animal. In self-consciousness, the I splits into the I-subject and the I-object which are at the same time identical (self-consciousness consists in their coincidence). Problems arise as soon as we consider the fact that self-consciousness does not exist prior to self-reflection—the "object" comprehended by consciousness in the act of self-consciousness is the very consciousness conscious of itself. This way, one necessarily gets entangled in an impasse: if what the I comprehends, makes its object in the act of self-reflection is already in itself self-consciousness, then self-reflection does not explain self-consciousness, does not render its inherent structure, since it presupposes it as something already there; if, on the contrary, the I-object is not in itself self-consciousness, then the I-subject and the I-object are not identical and we do not have to do with self-consciousness . . . Self-reflection is thus either superfluous (it presupposes as already there what it purports to explain, i.e., self-consciousness) or it destroys the phenomenon to be explained (insofar as it implies the nonidentity of the I-subject and the I-object).

Against the background of this critique, Henrich redefines the standard textbook image of the relationship between Fichte's and Hegel's philosophy: the fundamental insight of Fichte's thought, its permanent living source, is an awareness of this impasse of self-reflection, and his entire philosophical development bears witness to the effort to find a way out of it. The successive stages of Fichte's philosophy, the new and newer drafts of the "doctrine of science (*Wissenschaftslehre*)," are so many attempts to tackle an insistent traumatic kernel which "returns as the same." Fichte first endeavors to extricate himself from it by means of the notion of the pure self-positing of the I: he conceives the identity of the I with itself (I = I) as the absolute starting point of philosophy. The "I" is an activity which coincides absolutely with its own self-positing, it "is" only insofar as it posits itself by means of its consciousness of itself; as such, it is the original unity of subject and object, of being and doing. In more contemporary terms, one could say that what Fichte aims at here is the notion of a pure performative: I = I designates the absolute coincidence of the enunciated (the propositional content) with its process of enunciation, i.e., a content which consists of nothing but the act of its own positing. Here, however, one encounters the first difficulty: the absolute identity of the I with itself *qua* self-positing, this point of pure self-transparency, is something that forever eludes the empirical I, since the latter is forever entangled in a network of relations to the "non-I," to the objects around it—in Hegelese, *the self-positing I remains forever a presupposition*: something that is never "posited as such," present in the transparency of an actual I. What right do we have then to attribute to this pure performative self-positing the character of an "I," if, precisely, it never possesses its fundamental characteristic, the transparent self-presence? In his late philosophy, Fichte draws the appropriate conclusion from the fact that the point which is forever inaccessible to the actual subject is the very point of his absolute self-identity, and conceives the absolute as transsubjective, as a foundation out of which the I emerges . . . It is not difficult to see how this failed encounter (I = I is first presupposed, then dethroned and conceived as a moment of some trans-subjective absolute) repeats the fundamental deadlock of self-reflection.[24]

The gist of Henrich's critique of Hegel is that this insight into the constitutive impasse of self-reflection gets lost with Hegel: Hegel reaffirms self-reflection as "absolute," as a circular movement capable of positing its own presuppositions, of "sublating" them without rest.[25] The price Hegel has to pay for this is numerous nonthematized equivocations, hidden shifts of meaning, which blur the vicious circle of the movement of reflection: according to Henrich, the only way out of this vicious circle is to presuppose a kind of "self-acquaintance (Selbstvertrautheit)" of the I which precedes self-reflection, i.e., to avoid reducing self-consciousness to self-reflection. However, the notion of dialectical identity whose contours we already designated enables us to point out exactly where this criticism misfires: the vicious circle of reflection cannot be an argument *against* Hegel, since Hegel—like Henrich—is not ignorant of the necessity to presuppose some surplus which eludes dialectical mediation. Their crucial difference lies elsewhere, it concerns the fact that *Hegel locates this surplus on the opposite end from*

Henrich: not in an inner "self-acquaintance," prior to reflective, self-objectivizing distance of the subject from itself, but in a radically contingent externality of some material, inert, nonrational remainder. This object is the correlate of the subject: it confers on the subject the minimum of consistency and thereby prevents the subject from collapsing into the vicious circle's abyss. Let us recall again the above-mentioned examples: Adorno's dialectical edifice would crumble into its vicious circle without the support in the "dogmatic," "vulgar-sociological" propositions; the state *qua* a rational totality would disintegrate without the body of the monarch *qua* an idiotic remainder of nonmediated nature . . . All these (and numerous other) examples follow the same fundamental logic whose most concise expression is the Hegelian paradox of phrenology "the Spirit is a Bone":[26] the true speculative identity is not a sublation of all particular moments in a spiritual totality, but the identity of this very totality of rational mediation with an inert, immediate, nonrational "piece of the real"—what Lacan would call the collapse of the big Other (the rational symbolic order) into *petit a*, the inert leftover.

In other words, *rational totality clings to an inert "piece of the real" precisely insofar as it is caught in a vicious circle*. For that reason, Hegel converts the Fichtean I = I into the absolute contradiction Spirit = Bone, i.e., into the *point of absolute nonmirroring*, the identity of the subject *qua* void with the element in which he cannot recognize his mirror image, with the inert leftover, the bone, the rock, the hindrance which prevents the absolute self-transparency of the pure performative: the subject is posited as correlative to an object which precisely cannot be conceived as the subject's objectivization. And what Henrich calls "prereflective self-acquaintance" designates simply the gesture of "subjectivization" by means of which the subject "forgets" how his existence clings on an external piece of contingent reality and thereby establishes himself as self-present inwardness. The step accomplished by Hegel is then to conceive the Fichtean deadlock as its own solution: it is not difficult to notice how the paradoxical logic of this inert surplus feature repeats the deadlock of reflection: this feature is *stricto sensu* superfluous (added to the reflective totality of self-mediation), yet simultaneously a foreign body which undermines its consistency.

Identity and fantasy

Thereby we reach the paradox of a universal feature (quality) the suspension of which maintains its field—the paradox which is ultimately that of identity itself: the identity of a state resides in the monarch, this "irrational" supplement which "sticks out" and suspends its essential quality (its rational character); the identity of a dialectical analysis resides in the "vulgar" lapses which suspend its essential quality (the delicacy of dialectical stratagems) . . . Therein consists the crucial shift that has to be made with reference to the "deconstructionist" commonplaces about identity: indeed, identity is impossible, inherently hindered, its constitutive gap is always already sutured by some supplementary feature—yet one should add that identity "itself" is ultimately nothing but a name for such a supplementary feature which "sticks out" and suspends the essential quality of the domain whose identity it constitutes. It is therefore not sufficient to present "identity of the opposites" as a paradoxical kind or species of identity: identity as such is ultimately always already "identity of the opposites."

And is not the same paradox of identity at work in the way *fantasy* guarantees the consistency of a socio ideological edifice? That is to say, "fantasy" designates an element which "sticks out," which cannot be integrated into the given symbolic structure, yet which, precisely as such, constitutes its identity. The psychoanalytic clinic detects its fundamental matrix in the so-called "pregenital" (anal) object: according to Freudian orthodoxy, the fixation on it prevents the emergence of the "normal" (genital) sexual relationship; in the Lacanian theory, however, the "object is not what hinders the advent of the sexual relationship, as a kind of perspective error makes us believe. The object is on the contrary a filler, that which fills in the relationship which does not exist and bestows on it its fantasmatic consistency."[27] Sexual relationship is in itself impossible, hindered, and the object does nothing but materialize this "original" impossibility, this inherent hindrance; the "perspective error" consists in conceiving it as a stumbling block to the emergence of the "full" sexual relationship—as if, without this troublesome intruder, the sexual relationship would be possible in its intact fullness. What we encounter here is the paradox of the *sacrifice* in its purest: the illusion of the sacrifice is that renunciation of the object will render accessible the intact whole. In the ideological field, this paradox finds its clearest articulation in the anti-Semitic concept of the Jew: the Nazi has to sacrifice the Jew in order to be able to maintain the illusion that it is only the "Jewish plot" which prevents the establishment of the "class relationship," of society as a harmonious, organic whole. Which is why, in the last pages of *Seminar XI*, Lacan is fully justified to designate the Holocaust as a "gift of reconciliation": is not the Jew the anal object *par excellence*, i.e., the partial object-stain which disturbs the harmony of the class relationship? One is tempted, here, to paraphrase the above-quoted Jacques-Alain Miller's proposition: "The Jew is not what hinders the advent of the class relationship, as the anti-Semitic perspective error makes us believe. The Jew is on the contrary a filler, that which fills in the relationship which does not exist and bestows on it its fantasmatic consistency."[28] In other words, what appears as the hindrance to society's full identity with itself is actually its positive condition: by transposing onto the Jew the role of the foreign body which introduces in the social organism disintegration and antagonism, the fantasy-image of society *qua* consistent, harmonious whole is rendered possible.

One of the lessons to be drawn from this notion of antagonism is that the concept of ideology must be disengaged from the "representationalist" problematic: *ideology has nothing to do with "illusion,"* with a wrong, distorted representation of its social content. To put it succinctly: a political standpoint can be quite accurate ("true") as to its objective content and yet thoroughly ideological, and *vice versa*, the idea it gives of its social content can prove totally wrong, and yet there is absolutely nothing "ideological" about it. Let us take the case of the "vanishing mediator" of the process of democratization in the former East Germany, *Neues Forum*. *Neues Forum* consisted of groups of passionate intellectuals who "took socialism seriously" and were prepared to put all at stake in order to destroy the compromised system and replace it with the utopian "third way" beyond capitalism and "really existing" socialism. Their sincere belief and insistence that they were not working for the restoration of Western capitalism, of course, proved to be nothing but an insubstantial illusion: with regard to the "factual truth," the position of *Neues Forum*—the position of conceiving the disintegration of the Communist regime as the opening up of a possibility to invent some new form of social space that would reach beyond the confines of capitalism—was doubtless illusory; however, we could say that precisely as such (as a thorough illusion without substance) it was *stricto sensu nonidelogical. Neues Forum* was opposed by the forces who put all their bets on the quickest possible annexation to West Germany, i.e., on the inclusion of their country into the world capitalist system; for them, the people around *Neues Forum* were nothing but a bunch of heroic daydreamers. This position proved accurate—*yet it is nonetheless thoroughly ideological*. Why? The conformist adoption of the West German model implied the ideological belief in the unproblematic, nonantagonistic functioning of late-capitalist "social state," whereas the first stance, although illusionary as to its factual content (its "enunciated"), by means of its "scandalous" and exorbitant position of enunication attested to an awareness of the antagonism that pertains to late capitalism. This is one of the ways to conceive the Lacanian thesis according to which truth has the structure of a fiction: in those confused months of the passage of "really existing socialism" into capitalism, *the fiction of a "third way" was the only point at which social antagonism was not obliterated*. Therein consists one of the tasks of the "postmodern" criticism of ideology: to designate the elements within an existing social order which—in the guise of "fiction," i.e., of the "utopian" narratives of possible but failed alternative histories—point toward its antagonistic character and thus "estrange" us to the self-evidence of its established identity.

What we have to be attentive to is the inherently *authoritarian* character of this feature, that is to say, the inherent link of identity with authority: the monarch performs his role as a figure of pure authority, as the one who, by means of his "Such is my will!" i.e., of his abysmal decision, cuts through the endless series of *pro et contra*. And does not the same hold for Adorno's "vulgar-sociological" outbursts, do they not perform the same authoritarian gesture of reference to the Marxist dogma which breaks the endless thread of dialectical argumentation? It is by no means accidental that tautologies—statements which purport the identity with itself of its subject—are the clearest example of ascertaining authority: "Law is law!" "It is so because I say so!" etc.—identity becomes "authoritarian" the moment we overlook, in a kind of illusory perspective, that it is nothing but the inscription of pure difference, of a lack.[29] In this sense, authority is far from being a kind of leftover of the pre-Enlightenment: it is inscribed in the very heart of the Enlightenment project. Not till the Enlightenment did the structure of authority come into sight as such, against the background of rational argumentation as the foundation of enlightened knowledge. It is a symptomatic fact that the first to render visible the outlines of "pure" authority was precisely Kierkegaard, one of the great critics of Hegel.

What one should bear in mind here is that, according to Lacan,[30] Antigone's defense against Creon's accusations ultimately consists in precisely such an "authoritarian" tautology: she does not counter Creon's arguments with the arguments of her own (she does *not* oppose to Creon's law of *polis* the subterranean divine law protecting the right of the deceased, as Hegel wrongly assumed), she simply interrupts his flow of argumentation by insisting that "It is so because it is so!" that "My brother is my brother!" . . . The best way to render visible the logic of her defense is perhaps to evoke Saul Kripke's notion of the "rigid designator," of a signifier which designates the same object "in all possible worlds," i.e., even if all of its positive properties were changed.[31] The "rigid designator" thus fixes the real kernel of the designated object, what, in it, "always returns to its place" (Lacan's definition of the real)—in the case of Polynices, it designates his absolute individuality that remains the same beyond the changing properties that characterize his person (his good or evil deeds). The "law" in the name of which Antigone insists on Polynices's right to burial is this law of the "pure" signifier, prior to every positive law that judges our deeds: it is the law of the Name which fixes our identity beyond the eternal flow of generation and corruption.[32]

Socrates versus Christ

The crucial text in which Kierkegaard delineates the break between the traditional and the "modern" (i.e., for him, Christian) status of knowledge is his *Philosophical Fragments*. At first sight, this text does not belong to philosophy but rather to an intermediate domain between philosophy proper and theology: it endeavors to delimitate the Christian religious position from the Socratic philosophical one. Yet its externality to philosophy is of the same kind as that of Plato's *Symposion*: it circumscribes the discourse's frame, i.e., the intersubjective constellation, the relationship toward the teacher, toward authority, which renders possible the philosophical (or Christian) discourse. In this sense, the *Fragments* are to be read as the *repetition* of Plato's *Symposion* (repetition in the precise meaning this term receives with Kierkegaard): their aim is to perform Plato's gesture in new circumstances, within the new status that knowledge acquired with the advent of Christianity. Both texts, *Symposion* as well as *Philosophical Fragments*, are texts on *love* and *transference* which form the basis of every relationship with the teacher *qua* "subject supposed to know." Kierkegaard's starting point is that all of philosophy from Plato to Hegel is "pagan," i.e., embedded in the pagan (pre-Christian) logic of knowledge and remembrance: our life as that of finite individuals by definition takes place in an aftermath, since all that really matters has always already happened; up till the Hegelian *Er-Innerung*, knowledge is therefore always conceived as a retrospective remembrance/internalization, a return to the "timelessly past being," "*das zeitlos gewesene Sein*" (Hegel's determination of essence). True, the transient, finite subjects attain eternal truth at some determinate instant in the time of their lives; once the subject enters the truth, however, this instant is abrogated, cast away like a useless ladder. Which is why Socrates is quite justified in comparing himself with a midwife: his job is just to enable the subject to give birth to the knowledge already present in him, so the supreme recognition one can grant to Socrates is to say he was forgotten the moment we found ourselves face to face with truth. With Christ, it is just the opposite which holds: the Christian truth, no less eternal than the Socratic one, is indelibly branded with an historical event, the moment of God's incarnation. Consequently, the object of Christian faith is not the teaching, but the teacher: a Christian believes in Christ as a person, not immediately in the content of his statements; Christ is not divine because He uttered such deep truths, His words are true because they were spoken by Him. The paradox of Christianity consists in this bond linking the eternal truth to an historical event: I can *know* eternal truth only insofar as I *believe* that the miserable creature who two thousand years ago walked around Palestine was God.

Motifs which, according to the philosophical common knowledge, define the post-Hegelian reversal—the affirmation of the event, of the instant, as opposed to the timeless, immovable truth; the priority of existence (of the fact *that* a thing exists) over essence (over *what* this thing is); etc.—acquire here their ultimate background. That which is "eternal" in a statement is its meaning, abstracted from the event of its enunciation, from its enunciation *qua* event: within the Socratic perspective, the truth of a statement resides in its universal meaning; as such, it is in no way affected by its position of enunciation, by the place from which it was enunciated. The Christian perspective, on the other hand, makes the truth of a statement dependent on the event of its enunciation: the ultimate guarantee of the truth of Christ's words is their utterer's authority, i.e., the fact *that* they were uttered by Christ, not the profundity of their content, i.e., *what* they say:

> When Christ says, "There is an eternal life"; and when a theological student says, "There is an eternal life"; both say the same thing, and there is no more deduction, development, profundity, or thoughtfulness in the first expression than in the second; both statements are, judged aesthetically, equally good. And yet there is an eternal qualitative difference between them! Christ, as God-Man, is in possession of the specific quality of authority.[33]

Kierkegaard develops this "qualitative difference" apropos of the abyss that separates a "genius" from an "apostle": "genius" represents the highest intensification of the immanent human capacities (wisdom, creativity, and so forth), whereas an "apostle" is sustained by a transcendent authority which a genius lacks. This abyss is best exemplified by the very case where it seems to disappear, namely the poetic exploitation of religious motifs: Richard Wagner, for example, in his *Parsifal*, used Christian motifs as means to invigorate his artistic vision; he thereby *estheticized* them in the strict Kierkegaardian sense of the term, i.e., made use of them with their "artistic efficacy" in mind—religious rituals like the uncovering of the Grail fascinate us with their breathtaking beauty, yet their religious authority is suspended, bracketed.[34]

The paradoxes of authority

If, however, the truth claim of a statement cannot be authorized by means of its inherent content, what is then the foundation of its authority? Kierkegaard is here quite outspoken: *the ultimate and only support of a statement of authority is its own act of enunciation*: "But now how can an Apostle prove that he has authority? If he could prove it *physically*, then he would not be an Apostle. He has no other proof than his own statement. That has to be so; for otherwise the believer's relationship to him would be direct instead of being paradoxical."[35] When authority is backed up by an immediate physical compulsion, what we are dealing with is not authority proper (i.e., symbolic authority), but simply an agency of brute force: authority proper is at its most radical level always *powerless*, it is a certain "call" which "cannot effectively force us into anything," and yet, by a kind of inner compulsion, we feel obliged to follow it unconditionally. As such, authority is inherently paradoxical; first, as we have just seen, authority is vested in a certain statement insofar as the immanent value of its content is suspended—we obey a statement of authority because it has authority, not because its content is wise, profound, etc.:

> *Authority is a specific quality which, coming from elsewhere, becomes qualitatively apparent when the content of the message or of the action is posited as indifferent*. . . . To be prepared to obey a government department if it can be clever is really to make a fool of it. To honor one's father because he is intelligent is impiety.[36]

Yet at the same time Kierkegaard seems to purport the exact opposite of this priority of the teacher over the teaching: an apostle—a person in whom God's authority is vested—is reduced to his role of a carrier of some *foreign* message, he is totally abrogated as a person, all that matters is the content of the message:

> Just as a man, sent into the town with a letter, has nothing to do with its contents, but has only to deliver it; just as a minister who is sent to a foreign court is not responsible for the content of the message, but has only to convey it correctly: so, too, an Apostle has really only to be faithful in his service, and to carry out his task. Therein lies the essence of an Apostle's life of self-sacrifice, even if he were never persecuted, in the fact that he is "poor, yet making many rich."[37]

An apostle therefore corresponds perfectly to the function of the signifying *Repräsentanz*; the invalidation of all "pathological" features (his psychological propensities, etc.) makes out of him a pure representative whose clearest case is a diplomat:

> We mean by representatives what we understand when we use the phrase, for example, the representative of France. What do diplomats do when they address one another? They simply exercise, in relation to one another, that function of being pure representatives and, above all, their own signification must not intervene. When diplomats are addressing one another, they are supposed to represent something whose signification, while constantly changing, is, beyond their own persons, France, Britain, etc. In the very exchange of views, each must record only what the other transmits in his pure function as signifier, he must not take into account what the other is, *qua* presence, as a man who is likable to a greater or lesser degree. Interpsychology is an impurity in this exchange. The term *Repräsentanz* is to be taken in this sense. The signifier has to be understood in this way, it is at the opposite pole from signification.[38]

Therein consists the paradox of authority: we obey a person in whom authority is vested irrespective of the content of his statements (authority ceases to be what it is the moment we make it dependent on the quality of its content), yet this person retains authority only insofar as he is reduced to a neutral carrier, bearer of some transcendent message—in opposition to a genius where the abundance of his work's content expresses the inner wealth of its creator's personality. The same double suspension defines the supreme case of authority, that of Christ: in his *Philosophical Fragments*, Kierkegaard points out how it is not enough to know all the details of the teacher's (Christ's) life, all he has done and all his personal features, in order to be entitled to consider oneself his pupil—such a description of Christ's features and deeds, even if truly complete, still misses what makes Him an authority; no better is the fare of those who leave out of consideration Christ *qua* person and concentrate on His teaching, endeavoring to grasp the meaning of every word he ever uttered—this way, Christ is simply reduced to Socrates, to a simple middleman enabling us the access to the eternal truth. If, consequently, Christ's authority is contained neither in his personal qualities nor in the content of his teaching, in what *does* it reside? The only possible answer is: in the empty space of *intersection* between the two sets, that of his personal features and that of his teaching, in the unfathomable X which is "in Christ more than Himself"—in this intersection which corresponds exactly to what Lacan called *objet petit a*.

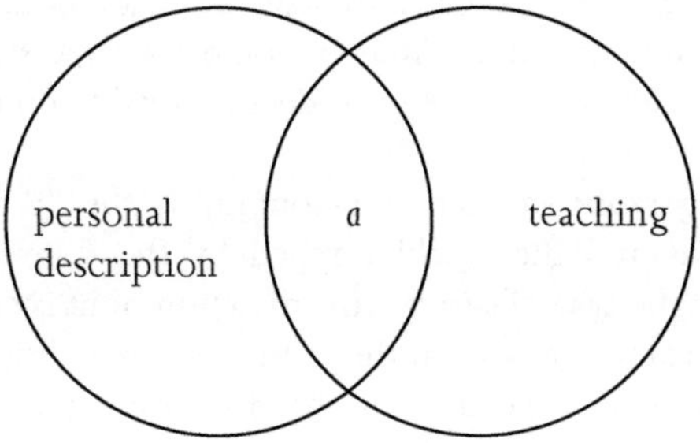

The "impossible" performative

As it is clear from the quoted passage from Lacan's *Four Fundamental Concepts*, the paradox of this double suspension is ultimately the paradox of the signifier itself. A signifier is by definition a pure representative which "has nothing to do with its signified content, but has only to deliver it" (to conceive the meaning of the word "fish," one has to obliterate all its immediate physical features); the necessary reverse of this is, however, the signifier's constitutive authority: in the symbolic order, the purely formal network of differential features has priority over the content (the "signified") of its individual components, i.e., its "signified" is ultimately posited as secondary and indifferent. To refer to the terms of speech-acts theory, this paradox is the "impossible" point of intersection between constative and performative—the true stumbling block of this theory. That is to say, already in John Austin's *How to Do Things with Words*, the passage from the opposition performative/constative to the triad locution/illocution/perlocution and to the subsequent classification of illocutionary acts betrays a fundamental theoretical deadlock. Far from being a simple elaboration of the original insight into how one can "do things with words," the transposal of performative into illocutionary act entails a certain radical loss: already at the level of an immediate, "naive" approach, one cannot avoid the impression that, in the course of this passage, what was truly subversive in the notion of performative somehow gets lost. On the other hand, it is clear that Austin was impelled to accomplish this passage from performative to illocutionary act by an insufficiency of the couple performative/constative itself. The taxonomy of illocutionary acts proposed by John Searle[39] has the advantage of enabling us to locate this lack by producing the point of intersection between Austin I and Austin II: one of the species of illocution ("declarations") coincides with the "pure" performative.

The starting point of Searle's taxonomy is the "direction of fit" between words and the world implied by the different species of speech acts: in the case of *assertives*, the direction of fit is words to world (when I say "There is a table in the room next door," the condition of satisfaction of this proposition is that the content of the utterance corresponds to the designated state of things, i.e., that there really is a table in the room next door); in the case of *directives*, the direction of fit is world to words (when I say "Shut the door!" the condition of satisfaction of this proposition is that the act in the world follows, realizes, the uttered command, i.e., that the addressee effectively shuts the door and that he does it because of my command and not for other reasons). The "trickiest case," as Searle puts it, is, however, *declarations*: their direction of fit is double, world to words as well as words to world. Let us take the proposition "The meeting is closed"—what does the speaker accomplish by pronouncing it? He brings about a new state of things in the world (the fact that the meeting is closed), the direction of fit is therefore world to words—yet how, precisely, does he effectuate it? By stating that the meeting is closed, i.e., *by presenting, in his utterance, this state of things as already accomplished*—in short, he effectuates the act by describing it as effectuated. In the declarations, the speaker "is trying to cause something to be the case by representing it as being the case. . . . [I]f he succeeds he will have changed the world by representing it as having been so changed."[40]

Every utterance, to be sure, accomplishes the act defined by the illocutionary force that pertains to it; there is, however, a crucial difference between declarations and, say, directives. By saying "Shut the door!" I accomplish the act of command, but it remains to the addressee to carry it out and effectuate the new state of things (to shut the door), whereas by saying "The meeting is closed" I effectively close the meeting—only declarations contain this "magical power" of effectuating their propositional content. The direction of fit world to words is here not limited to the fact that a new state of things in the world has to follow the utterance, since the causality is so to speak immediate: utterance itself brings about the new state of things. Yet, as we have just seen, the price to be paid for this "magic of the verb" is its "repression": one closes the meeting by *stating* that it is closed, i.e., one pretends to describe an already-given state of things—in order to be effective, the "pure" performative (the speech act which brings about its own propositional content) has to endure an inner split and assume the form of its opposite, of a constative.

It is in the light of this split that one has to interpret Searle's theory of "indirect speech acts," i.e., of the propositions of the type "Can you pass the salt?" where the primary illocutionary act (the directive, the demand to the addressee to pass the salt) is accomplished by means of a secondary illocutionary act (the interrogation concerning the addressee's ability to comply with the demand). Searle conceives such propositions as "parasitic": their nature is secondary, they presuppose some logically prior illocutionary act (in the case of "Can you pass the salt?" the direct command "Pass the salt!"). Yet do not "declarations" denote the case where "parasitism" is in a way *original*? Their primary illocutionary dimension (the "magical power" to bring about the propositional content) can manifest itself only under the guise of the assertive, of a statement that "it is like that." This paradox offers us a clue to Lacan's thesis according to which ontology pertains to the "discourse of the Master": the (philosophical) discourse of being

> is simply being on thrust [*à la botte*], being on order, what will have been if you have understood what I have ordered you. The entire dimension of being is produced within the movement of the discourse of the Master, of the one who, uttering a signifier, expects from it what is one of its effects of link not to be neglected, namely that the signifier commands. The signifier is first of all imperative.[41]

The discourse of ontology is thus sustained by an "indirect speech act": its assertive surface, its stating that the world "is like that," conceals a performative dimension, i.e., ontology is constituted by the misrecognition of how its enunciation brings about its propositional content. The only way to account for this "magical power" of declarations is by having recourse to the Lacanian hypotheses of the "big Other": Searle himself has a presentiment of it when he points out that "it is only given such institutions as the church, the law, private property, the state and a special position of the speaker and hearer within these institutions"[42] that one can accomplish a declaration. In Hans Christian Andersen's *Emperor's New Clothes*, all the world knows that the emperor has no clothes, and everybody knows that all the world knows it—why, then, does a simple public statement that "the emperor has no clothes" blow up the entire established network of intersubjective relations? In other words: if everybody knew it, *who did not know it?* The Lacanian answer is, of course: the big Other (in the sense of the field of socially recognized knowledge). Declarations imply the same logic: the meeting is closed when, by means of the utterance, "The meeting is closed," this fact *comes to the big Other's knowledge*.

When, in his *Four Fundamental Concepts*, Lacan specifies the Freudian "primordial repression" as the "fall of the binary signifier,"[43] he seems to allude precisely to this inherent split of the "pure" performative (of the declaration), i.e., to the fact that it can actualize itself only under the guise of its opposite. What is "originally repressed," what, in accordance with a structural necessity, has to disappear in order that the symbolic network can establish itself, is a signifier of the "pure" performative, i.e., of a performative which would *not* assume the form of its opposite, of a constative. In this split, in this impossibility of a "pure" performative, the subject of the signifier emerges: his place is the void opened up by the fall of the "impossible" binary signifier. That is to say, the gesture which constitutes the subject is the empty gesture of a forced choice: reality is "subjectivized" when the subject posits as his free choice what is forced upon him, i.e., what he encounters as given, positive reality. This formal act of conversion of reality *qua* given into reality *qua* produced is founded precisely in the above-described coincidence of "pure" performative with its opposite (constative): the performative production of reality necessarily assumes the form of stating that "it is so." Because of this split, the Lacanian mathem for the subject is $: an empty gesture of consenting to what is given as if to one's free choice.[44]

The Lacanian S_1, the "Master signifier" which represents the subject for other signifiers, is therefore the point of intersection between performative and constative, i.e., the point at which the "pure" performative coincides with (assumes the form of) its opposite. We can see, now, what is lacking to Austin I (that of the "performative") as well as to Austin II (that of the "illocutionary force"): a kind of paradoxical, inward-inverted topological model where the extreme interior of the "pure" performative coincides with the exterior of the constative. This "extimate" point of intersection is of course that of authority; its immanent split is best rendered by the ambiguity of the verb "to establish": authority is ultimately the name of a gesture which "establishes (constitutes, creates, sets up)" a certain state of things in the very act of "establishing (certifying, stating, ascertaining)" that "things are thus."

Kierkegaard's "materialist reversal of Hegel"

Such an assertion of authority seems to be the very opposite of the Enlightenment whose fundamental aim is precisely to render truth independent of authority: truth is arrived at by means of the critical procedure which questions the *pro et contra* of a proposition irrespective of the authority that pertains to its place of enunciation . . . To undermine the false evidence of this incompatibility between authority and Enlightenment, it suffices to recall how the two supreme achievements of the unmasking of ideological prejudices that grew out of the project of the Enlightenment, Marxism and psychoanalysis, both refer to the authority of their respective founders (Marx, Freud). Their structure is inherently "authoritarian": since Marx and Freud opened up a new theoretical field which sets the very criteria of veracity, their words cannot be put to the test the same way one is allowed to question the statements of their followers; if there is something to be refuted in their texts, these are simply statements which precede the "epistemological break," i.e., which do not belong under the field opened up by the founder's discovery (Freud's writings prior to the discovery of the unconscious, for example). Their texts are thus to be read the way one should read the text of a dream, according to Lacan: as "sacred" texts which are in a radical sense "beyond criticism" since they constitute the very horizon of veracity. For that reason, every "further development" of Marxism or psychoanalysis necessarily assumes the form of a "return" to Marx or Freud: the form of a (re)discovery of some hitherto overlooked layer of their work, i.e., of bringing to light what the founders "produced without knowing what they produced," to invoke Althusser's formula. In his article on Chaplin's *Limelight*, André Bazin recommends the same attitude as the only one which befits Chaplin's genius: even when some details in *Limelight* appear to us aborted and dull (the tedious first hour of the film; Calvero's pathetic vulgar-philosophical outbursts; etc.), we have to put the blame on us and ask ourselves what was wrong with our approach to the film—such an attitude clearly articulates the *transferential* relationship of the pupil to the teacher: the teacher is by definition "supposed to know," the fault is always ours . . . The disturbing scandal authenticated by the history of psychoanalysis and Marxism is that such a "dogmatic" approach proved far more productive than the "open," critical dealing with the founder's text: how much more fecund was Lacan's "dogmatic" return to Freud than the American academic machinery which transformed Freud's oeuvre into a collection of positive scientific hypotheses to be tested, refuted, combined, developed, and so on! Lacan's scandal, the dimension of his work which resists incorporation into the academic machinery, can be ultimately pinned down to the fact that he openly and shamelessly posited himself as such an authority, i.e., that he repeated the Kierkegaardian gesture in relationship to his followers: what he demanded of them was not fidelity to some general theoretical propositions, but precisely fidelity to his person—which is why, in the circular letter announcing the foundation of *La Cause freudienne*, he addresses them as "those who love me." This unbreakable link connecting the doctrine to the contingent person of the teacher, i.e., to the teacher *qua* material surplus that sticks out from the neutral edifice of knowledge, is the scandal everybody who considers himself Lacanian has to assume: Lacan was not a Socratic master obliterating himself in front of the attained knowledge, his theory sustains itself only through the transferential relationship to its founder. In this precise sense, Marx, Freud, and Lacan are not "geniuses," but "apostles": when somebody says "I follow Lacan because his reading of Freud is the most intelligent and persuasive," he immediately exposes himself as non-Lacanian.[45]

This "scandal" of the spot of contingent individuality which smears over the neutral field of knowledge points toward what we could designate as Kierkegaard's "materialist reversal of Hegel." Hegel ultimately stays within the boundary of the "Socratic" universe: in his *Phenomenology of Spirit*, consciousness arrives at the Truth, recollects it and internalizes it, *via* its own effort, by comparing itself with its own immanent Notion, by confronting the positive content of its statements with its own place of enunciation, by working through its own split, without any external support or point of reference. The standpoint of dialectical truth (the "for us") is not added to the consciousness as a kind of external standard by which the consciousness' progress is then measured: "we," dialecticians, are nothing but passive observers who retroactively reconstruct the way consciousness itself arrived at the Truth (i.e., the "absolute" standpoint without presuppositions). When, at some point of the consciousness' journey, Truth effectively appears as a positive entity possessing an independent existence, as an "in itself" assuming the role of the external measure of the consciousness's "working through," this is simply a necessary self-deception "sublated" in the further succession of the "experiences of consciousness." In other words—in the words of the relationship between belief and knowledge: the subject's belief in an (external) authority which is to be accepted unconditionally and "irrationally," is nothing but a transitional stage "sublated" by the passage into reflected knowledge. For Kierkegaard, on the contrary, our belief in the person of the Savior is the absolute, not abolishable condition of our access to truth: eternal truth itself clings to this contingent material externality—the moment we lose this "little piece of the real" (the historical fact of Incarnation), the moment we cut our link with this material fragment (reinterpreting it as a parable of man's affinity with God, for example), the entire edifice of Christian knowledge crumbles.[46] On another level, the same goes for psychoanalysis: in the psychoanalytic cure, there is no knowledge without the "presence of the analyst," without the impact of his dumb material weight. Here we encounter the inherent limitation of all attempts to conceive psychoanalytic cure on the model of the

Hegelian reflective movement in the course of which the subject becomes conscious of his own "substantial" content, i.e., arrives at the repressed truth which dwells deep in him.[47] If such were the case, psychoanalysis would be the ultimate stage of the Socratic "Know thyself!" and the psychoanalyst's role would be that of an *accoucheur*, a kind of "vanishing mediator" enabling the subject to achieve communication with himself by finding access to its repressed traumas.

This dilemma comes forth at its clearest apropos of the role of *transference* in psychoanalytic cure. Insofar as we remain within the domain of the Socratic logic of remembrance, transference is not an "effective" repetition but rather a means of recollection: the analysand "projects" past traumas which unconsciously determine his present behavior (the repressed and unresolved conflicts with his father, for example) onto his relationship to the analyst; by means of the deft manipulation of the transferential situation, the analyst then enables the analysand to recall the traumas which were hitherto "acted out" blindly—in other words, the task of the analyst is to make evident to the analysand how "he (the analyst) is not really the father," i.e., how the analysand, caught in the transference, used his relationship to the analyst to stage the past traumas . . . Lacan's emphasis is, on the contrary, throughout Kierkegaardian: transferential repetition cannot be reduced to remembrance, transference is not a kind of "theater of shadows" where we settle with past traumas *in effigia*, it is repetition in the full meaning of the term, i.e., in it, the past trauma is literally repeated, "actualized." The analyst is not father's "shadow," he is a presence in front of which the past battle has to be fought out "for real."

Lacan versus Habermas

The point of the preceding argumentation, of course, is not to defend blind submission to authority, but the fact that *discourse itself is in its fundamental structure "authoritarian"* (for that reason, the "discourse of the Master" is the first, "founding" discourse in the Lacanian matrix of the four discourses; or, as Derrida would say in his writings of the last years, every discursive field is founded on some "violent" ethicopolitical decision). Out of the free-floating dispersion of signifiers, a consistent field of meaning emerges through the intervention of a Master

Signifier—why? The answer is contained in the paradox of the "finite infinity/totality" which, as one knows from Claude Lévi-Strauss onward, pertains to the very notion of the signifier: the symbolic order in which the subject is embedded is simultaneously "finite" (it consists in a limited and ultimately contingent network which never overlaps with the Real) and "infinite," or, to use a Sartrean term, "totalizing" (in any given language, "everything can be told," there is no external standpoint from which one can judge its limitations). Because of this inherent tension, every language contains a paradoxical element which, within its field, stands in for what eludes it—in Lacanese, in every set of signifiers, there is always "at least one" which functions as the signifier of the very lack of the signifier. This signifier is the Master Signifier: the "empty" signifier which totalizes ("quilts") the dispersed field—in it, the infinite chain of causes ("knowledge") is interrupted with an abyssal, nonfounded, founding act of violence.

The philosophical term for this inversion of the impotence into a constitutive power is, of course, the notion of the *transcendental* with all its inherent paradoxes: the subject experiences as his constitutive power the very horizon which frames his vision due to his finitude. For that reason, it is precisely the notion of the transcendental which enables us to distinguish Lacan from, say, Habermas. With Habermas, the status of the "disturbances" which vitiate the course of "rational argumentation" by way of a nonreflected constraint is ultimately contingent/empirical, these "disturbances" emerge as empirical impediments on the path of the gradual realization of the transcendental regulative Idea. Whereas with Lacan, the status of the Master Signifier, the signifier of the symbolic authority founded only in itself (in its own act of enunciation), is strictly transcendental: the gesture which "distorts" a symbolic field, which "curves" its space by introducing in it a nonfounded violence, is *stricto sensu* correlative to its very establishment—in other words, the moment we subtract from a discursive field its "distortion," the field itself disintegrates ("dequilts"). Lacan's position is therefore the very opposite of that of Habermas according to whom the inherent pragmatic presuppositions of a discourse are "nonauthoritarian" (the notion of discourse implies the idea of a communication free of constraint where only rational argumentation counts, etc.).

Lacan's fundamental thesis is that the Master is by definition an *impostor*: the Master is somebody who, upon finding himself at the place of the constitutive lack in the structure, acts as if he holds the reins of that surplus, of the mysterious X which eludes the grasp of the structure. This accounts for the difference between Habermas and Lacan as to the role of the Master: with Lacan, the Master is an impostor, yet the *place* occupied by him—the place of the lack in the structure—cannot be abolished, since the very finitude of every discursive field imposes its structural necessity. The unmasking of the Master's imposture does not abolish the place he occupies, it just renders it visible in its original emptiness, i.e., as preceding the element which fills it out. Therefrom the Lacanian notion of the analyst *qua envers* (reverse) of the Master: of somebody who holds the place of the Master, yet who, by means of his (non)activity, undermines the Master's charisma, suspends the effect of "quilting," and thus renders visible the distance that separates the Master from the place it occupies, i.e., the radical *contingency* of the subject who occupies this place.

For that reason, their strategy of subverting symbolic authority is also fundamentally different. Habermas simply relies on the gradual reflective elucidation of the implicit, nonreflected, prejudices which distort communication, i.e., on the asymptotic approaching to the regulative ideal of free, unconstrained communication. Lacan is also "antiauthoritarian," he is as far as possible from any kind of obscurantism of the "ineffable," he too remains thoroughly attached to the space of "public communication"—this unexpected proximity of Lacan to Habermas is corroborated by a procedure, proposed by Lacan, which caused a great amount of resistance even among some of his closest followers: *la passe*, the "passage," of an analysand into the place of the analyst. Its crux is the intermediate role of the so-called *passeurs*: the analysand (the *passant*) narrates the results of his analysis, the insights he arrived at, to the two *passeurs*, his peers, who thereupon report on it to the committee (*comité de la passe*)—the committee then decides on the analysand's "passage" into the place of the analyst. The idea of these two middlemen who channel every contact between the *passant* and the committee is very "Habermasian" indeed: they are here to prevent any kind of "initiatic" relationship between the *passant* and the committee, i.e., to prevent *la passe* from functioning as the transmission of an initiatic knowledge, after the model of secret cults: the analysand must be able to formulate the results of his analysis in such a way that the two *passeurs*, these two average men who stand in for the common knowledge, are able to transmit it integrally to the committee—in other words, the detour through the field of public knowledge must not affect the "message" in any way.

The contrast between Habermas and Lacan finds its clearest expression apropos of the notion of the "ideal speech situation": Habermas conceives it as the asymptotic ideal of intersubjective communication free of constraint, where the participants arrive at consensus by means of rational argumentation. Contrary to the common opinion, Lacan also knows of an "ideal speech situation" which undermines the imposture of the Master Signifier: it is none other than the *analytic situation* itself—here, the abyss that separates Lacan from Habermas strikes the eyes. In the process of psychoanalysis, we also have two subjects speaking to each other; yet instead of facing each other and exchanging arguments, one of them lies on the couch, stares into thin air and throws out disconnected prattle, whereas the other mostly stays silent and terrorizes the first by the weight of his oppressive mute presence . . . This situation is "free of constraint" in the precise meaning of suspending the structural role of the Master Signifier: the analytic discourse *qua envers* of the discourse of the Master transposes us into a state of undecidability, previous to the "quilting" of the discursive field by a Master Signifier, i.e., in the state of the "free floating" of signifiers—what is "repeated" in it is ultimately the very contingency which engendered the analysand's symbolic space.

And, to conclude by uniting the two slopes of our argumentative edifice, is not "exception reconciled in the universal" the most succinct definition of *act*? In this precise sense, an act is always "beyond good and evil": it suspends the given ethical standards of good, yet it does so in a way that is inherent to the very maintenance of good. In other words, an act does not only apply the given ethical standards but redefines them. As to the problem of choice, this means that *choice becomes an act when its effectuation changes the value of its terms*. In a long note to the first chapter of *Philosophical Fragments*, Kierkegaard exemplifies it by means of the choice between freedom and nonfreedom (fall into sin): at the beginning, it is possible for me to choose equally between the two terms; however, as soon as I choose nonfreedom (sin), I am no longer in a position to exchange it for freedom, i.e., I lose the very freedom of choice.[48] The same goes for all ethical acts: once the decision is taken, the very field of choice is transformed. Is it necessary to add how it is precisely this paradox of an act of choice changing the value of its terms which escapes distributive justice?

NOTES

1 *Raymond Chandler's Unknown Thriller* (New York: The Mysterious Press, 1987), p. XIX.

2 A homologous repetition of the forced choice is found in a series of Hollywood films, from *Now, Voyager* to *Deerhunter*: in a primordial scene, the hero is forced to choose, and this choice, although forced, marks his existence with a permanent brand of guilt which is erased when, in a repeated scene of choice, he "chooses the impossible" *via* a gesture of suicidal renunciation (Christopher Walken in *Deerhunter* confronts DeNiro again in Russian roulette in the last days of pre-Communist Saigon and pays off his debt by his death; Bette Davis in *Now, Voyager* renounces her great love when she finds herself occupying the place that was once her mother's, since this is for her the only way to repay the maternal debt).

3 Cf. John Rawls, *A Theory of Justice* (Cambridge, Mass.: Harvard University Press, 1971).

4 What Rawls does here is simply to give theoretical expression to the everyday intuition according to which it is not ethical to change one's judgment when one perceives that one's particular interest is affected by it.

5 Cf. Jean-Pierre Dupuy, "*La Theorie de la justice*. Une Machine anti-sacrificielle," in *Critique* 505–6 (Paris: Editions de Minuit, 1989).

6 What we have here are, of course, paradoxes of the Lacanian logic of "not all (*pas-tout*)": the antisacrificial argument is founded upon principles which—when taken as positive determinations and applied to all possible situations—in a sacrificial situation justify the sacrifice.

7 Cf. René Girard, *Violence and the Sacred* (Baltimore: Johns Hopkins University Press, 1977).

8 The argument that Kantian ethics can offer as to its actual consequences is a new version of the logic of "by-products": the short-term costs of the radical refusal of scapegoating may appear exuberant, yet they are outweighed by the long-term benefits, since *the essential by-product of this refusal is that it prevents the advent of situations which call for a sacrificial solution*.

9 Cf. Joan Copjec, "The Sartorial Superego," in *October* 50 (Cambridge, Mass.: MIT Press, 1989).

10 Consequently, the obscene superego agency is the necessary reverse of the

choice of the Name of the Father: it was Freud who said that the superego draws its energy from the renounced drive.

11 As to this mechanism, cf. Slavoj Žižek, *The Sublime Subject of Ideology* (London: Verso Books, 1989), chapters 5 and 6.

12 Cf. Jacques-Alain Miller, "Die Lektion der Psychosen," in *Wo es war* 5–6 (Vienna: Hora Verlag, 1989).

13 This congruity of the religious with the Real attests anew Lacan's thesis that gods appertain to the Real.

14 Cf. "Interlude" in *Philosophical Fragments*, Kierkegaard's Writings VII (Princeton, N.J.: Princeton University Press, 1985), pp. 73–88.

15 With regard to the notion of the "vanishing mediator" which becomes invisible (i.e., a "missing link") once the change it set in motion reverses into a new equilibrium, we could say that repetition in the Kierkegaardian-Benjaminian sense *renders visible again the "missing link."* For the notions of "vanishing mediator" and "missing link," cf. chapter 5 of Slavoj Žižek, *For They Know Not What They Do* (London and New York: Verso Books, 1991).

16 The same goes also for the Lacanian triad Imaginary—Symbolic, Real: the choice is always between the two, i.e., we either have to choose between Imaginary and Symbolic (captivation by the imaginary form versus the empty symbolic structure: one of the great motifs of the Lacan of the 1950s) or between Symbolic and Real (the symbolic network versus the traumatic kernel of the Real which eludes its grasp: the focus of the late Lacan).

17 G. K. Chesterton, "A Defence of Detective Stories," in H. Haycraft, ed. *The Art of the Mystery Story* (New York: Universal Library, 1946), p. 6.

18 On another level, the same reversal is to be accomplished apropos of ancient Greece, this object of nostalgia *par excellence*, the originating moment of what we call "Western civilization." Classical hermeneutics in its different forms, from the Renaissance through the Classicist ideal of Greek harmony and temperate beauty up to the Heideggerian themata of Greece as the place of original disclosure of the truth of being, treats Greeks as part of our own historical continuum, as the starting point of the tradition out of which grew the very place from which we speak—in opposition to, let us say. Eskimos or Polynesians, who are to be dealt with from an "anthropological" perspective, as cultures which are not part of our tradition, as foreign lands to which bridges are yet to be constructed. Here, recent French historiography performed a true revolution when it assumed toward ancient Greeks the "anthropological" attitude and started to treat them as part of a foreign tradition, the same way one treats Eskimos or Polynesians. The results of such a new reading of Greek sources have been fascinating: instead of the "classical" Greece of the *polis*, of the harmony between individual and community, of the tragic but well-tempered organic unity of life as opposed to Oriental barbarism, we have obtained an "extraneated" image of Greece fully integrated into its Mediterranean context, a Greece of wild rituals, sacrifices, violence, and myths . . . In short, ancient Greeks did not know they were starting a new epoch of reason,

they did not become the "dawn of Western civilization" until later—until when? To locate this moment, one has to draw into the account the opposition between Athens and Rome; their respective positions within theoretical mythology are easy to determine by means of the Derridean opposition of voice and writing: Greece exemplifies the experience of origins, the harmony and tragic authenticity of the *polis*, whereas Rome stands for its disintegration, external understanding as opposed to inherent reason, etc. Yet it is crucial that the universal language of Western civilization became Latin, the language of oblivion, *not* Greek, the language of authentic roots and origins—why? There is only one answer possible: because Greece *qua* the image of authentic origins *came to be in the very moment of its loss*. In other words, "ancient Greeks" never existed: there were Mediterranean "barbarians" who retrospectively, for the Roman gaze, became "ancient Greeks." To be sure, Greeks were not "barbarians" like the rest, there *was* a radical break accomplished by them—yet this break is *not* the break between "barbarians" and our nostalgic figure of "ancient Greeks" inherited from Rome: if we are to conceive Greeks "in their becoming," "in their possibility," we have to unearth the contours of an unprecedented act which is the hidden reverse of the figure of "ancient Greeks" inherent to our historical tradition.

19 S. Kierkegaard, *Repetition*, Kierkegaard's Writings VI (Princeton, N.J.: Princeton University Press, 1983), p. 227.

20 Cf. Chapter 6 of Žižek, *For They Know Not What They Do*.

21 Fredric Jameson, *Late Marxism. Adorno, or, The Persistence of the Dialectic* (London: Verso Books, 1990), p. 30.

22 Cf. Žižek, *The Sublime Object of Ideology*, chapters 5 and 6.

23 Cf. Dieter Henrich, "Hegel's Grundoperation: Eine Einleitung in die 'Wissenschaft der Logik,' " in *Der Idealismus uns seine Gegenwart: Festschrift fuer Werner Marx*, ed. Ute Guzzoni (Hamburg: Felix Meiner Verlag, 1976); as well as Dieter Henrich, "Fichte's 'Ich,' " in *Selbstverhaeltnisse* (Stuttgart: Philipp Reclam Verlag, 1982). For a condensed recapitulation of Henrich's commentary in English cf. chapter 17 of Manfred Frank, *What Is Neostructuralism?* (Minneapolis: University of Minnesota Press, 1989), where this critique is extended also to Derrida's notion of *différance*.

24 The same deadlock as that encountered in Fichte, the not-yet-Hegel, is at work in Marx, the not-anymore-Hegel, i.e., the point at which the Hegelian identity of subject and substance begins to break up. That is to say, in his endeavor to delineate the capital universe by means of the categories of Hegel's logic, Marx continually and in a systematic way oscillates between two possibilities:

1) the qualification of capital as the alienated substance of the historical process which reigns over the atomized subjects (cf. the famous formulae from *Grundrisse* on the proletariat *qua* "substanceless subjectivity" which posits capital as its own nonbeing); within this perspective, revolution necessarily appears as an act by means of which the historical subject appropriates to himself his alienated substantial content, i.e., recognizes in it his own

product—the motif given its ultimate expression in Georg Lukacs's *History and Class Consciousness*;

2) the opposite qualification of capital as substance which is already in itself subject, i.e., which is not anymore an empty, abstract universality but a universality reproducing itself through the circular process of its self-mediation and self-positing (cf. the definition of capital as "money which begets more money": money → commodity → money)—in short, capital is money which became subject. This theme of "Hegel's logic as the notional structure of the movement of capital" was given its ultimate expression in the Hegelian reading of the "critique of political economy" that flourished in West Germany in the early 1970s; cf. Helmut Reichelt, *Zur logischen Struktur des Kapitalbegriffs bei Karl Marx* (Frankfurt: Suhrkamp Verlag, 1970).

25 Henrich articulated the detailed criticism of the Hegelian "absolute reflection" in his famous article "Hegel's Logik der Reflexion" (cf. Dieter Henrich, *Hegel im Kontext* (Frankfurt: Suhrkamp Verlag, 1971). What he has in mind is above all the nonthematized ambiguous status of the Hegelian "Immediate," the incessant shift in the meaning of this term between (1) the presupposition of the movement of reflection, its "immediate," external starting point, and (2) the result of the self-referring movement of reflection, i.e., the "sublation" (*Aufhebung*) of mediation by way of the double negation.

26 The Marxian version of this speculative identity is "the proletariat is money": the equation of the proletariat—the pure, substanceless working-force capacity, freed of all substantial bonds—with the inert objective presence of money. The proletariat establishes itself as pure, substanceless subjectivity only through its radical "reification," i.e., its identification with its opposite, its exchangeability for money, for this piece of dead metal I can hold in my hand and manipulate freely . . . For a more detailed account of the paradoxical proposition "Spirit is a bone," cf. chapter 6 of Žižek, *The Sublime Object of Ideology*.

27 Jacques-Alain Miller, "D'un autre Lacan," *Ornicar?* 28 (Paris: Navarin Editeur, 1984), p. 55.

28 The notion of fantasy again points toward the inherent limitation of Rawls's trial by the "veil of ignorance": the "veil of ignorance" *a priori* leaves out of consideration fantasy as the absolutely particular (i.e., nonuniversalizable) structure of enjoyment. In the "original situation," I identify with the other, yet not with the other *qua* bearer of fantasy, but with the other *qua* empty symbolic subject; for that reason, although his interests are taken into account, *his fantasy is wronged*. In other words, when the trial by "veil of ignorance" tells me that, even if I were to occupy the lowest place in the community, I would still accept my ethical choice, I move within my own fantasy frame—*what if the other reasons within the frame of an absolutely incompatible fantasy?*

29 Cf. chapter 2 of Žižek, *For They Know Not What They Do* (London: Verso Books 1991).

30 Cf. Jacques Lacan, *Le Seminaire, livre VII: L'Ethique de la psychanalyse* (Paris: Editions du Seuil, 1986).

31 Cf. Saul Kripke, *Naming and Necessity* (Cambridge, Mass.: Cambridge University Press, 1980). As to a Lacanian reading of Kripke, cf. Žižek, *The Sublime Object of Ideology*, chapter 3.

32 Now, we can also locate the mistake of Plato's idealism: Plato wrongly transposes this "congealment" of the flow of events—which is an effect of the *signifier*—onto the level of the *signified*, and endeavors to determine the positive content of eternal, immovable Ideas.

33 Soren Kierkegaard, "Of the Difference between a Genius and an Apostle," in *The Present Age* (New York: Harper Torchbooks, 1962), pp. 100–1. The immediate content of Christ's statements can be utterly insipid, yet as soon as we take into consideration the fact that they were pronounced by Christ, God's son, the same statements acquire unfathomable profundity—their very insipidity turns miraculously into an index of its opposite . . . What we encounter here is yet another way to conceive the Hegelian "coincidence of the opposites": a statement turns into its opposite the moment we take into account its place of enunciation. Today, in the "postmodern" era, such a reversal is easily detectable in the way different political parties proclaim their goals to reach "beyond narrow party interests" and to be "nonideological": uttered by a *political party*, the reference to a "nonpartisan" content is nothing but a form of appearance of its opposite, i.e., a way to score points in the political struggle; the same goes for the self-proclaimed "nonideological" or "postideological" attitude which is nothing but a strategy to assume hegemony in the ideological struggle. In other words, the elementary rule here is "the cleaner you are, the dirtier you are": the more the content (the enunciated) of our goals is "really" nonpartisan, nonideological, etc., the more our position of enunciation is that of an agent in the ideological struggle.

34 Such an esthetic attitude toward religion is of course characteristic of romanticism as such; the very title of Chateaubriand's *Genie du Christianisme* (1802) is indicative in this respect: what interests him is not the inherent truth and authority of Christian religion but the poetic power of Christian mythology . . .

35 Kierkegaard, "Of the Difference between a Genius and an Apostle", p. 105.

36 Ibid., pp. 96 and 100.

37 Ibid., p. 106.

38 Jacques Lacan, *The Four Fundamental Concepts of Psycho-Analysis* (London: Tavistock Publications, 1979), p. 220.

39 Cf. John Searle, "A taxonomy of Illocutionary Acts," in *Expression and Meaning* (Cambridge: Cambridge University Press, 1979).

40 John Searle, *Intentionality* (Cambridge: Cambridge University Press, 1983), p. 172.

41 Jacques Lacan, *Le Séminaire de Jacques Lacan, livre XX: Encore* (Paris: Editions du Seuil, 1975), p. 33.

42 Searle, *Expression and Meaning*, p. 18.

43 Cf. Lacan, *The Four Fundamental Concepts of Psycho-Analysis*, chapter 17.

44 As to this notion of the "empty gesture" constitutive of the subject, cf. Žižek, *The Sublime Object of Ideology*, chapter 5 and 6.

45 To avoid a fatal misunderstanding: Lacan, of course, locates himself *within* Enlightenment and conceives the psychoanalytic process precisely as an attempt to get rid of the authority—yet he also points out the terrible price to be paid for this "liberation": since the very structure of the "big Other" (of the symbolic order, the space of intersubjectivity) is ultimately authoritarian, the subject is effectively "free" only when he *assumes the nonexistence of the big Other*, i.e., when, in a quasi-psychotic gesture, he suspends its functioning. Cf. the Habermas-Lacan section of the present chapter.

46 As to the philosophical weight of this notion of contingency and its roots in the Christian tradition, cf. Ernesto Laclau, *New Reflections On the Revolution of Our Time* (London: Verso Books, 1990).

47 The two most elaborate versions of this approach are to be found in Juergen Habermas, *Knowledge and Human Interests* (Cambridge, Mass.: MIT Press, 1971), and in Helmut Dahmer, *Libido und Gesellschaft* (Frankfurt: Suhrkamp Verlag, 1972).

48 Kierkegaard, *Philosophical Fragments*, Kierkegaard's Writings VII (Princeton, N.J.: Princeton University Press, 1985), pp. 16–17.

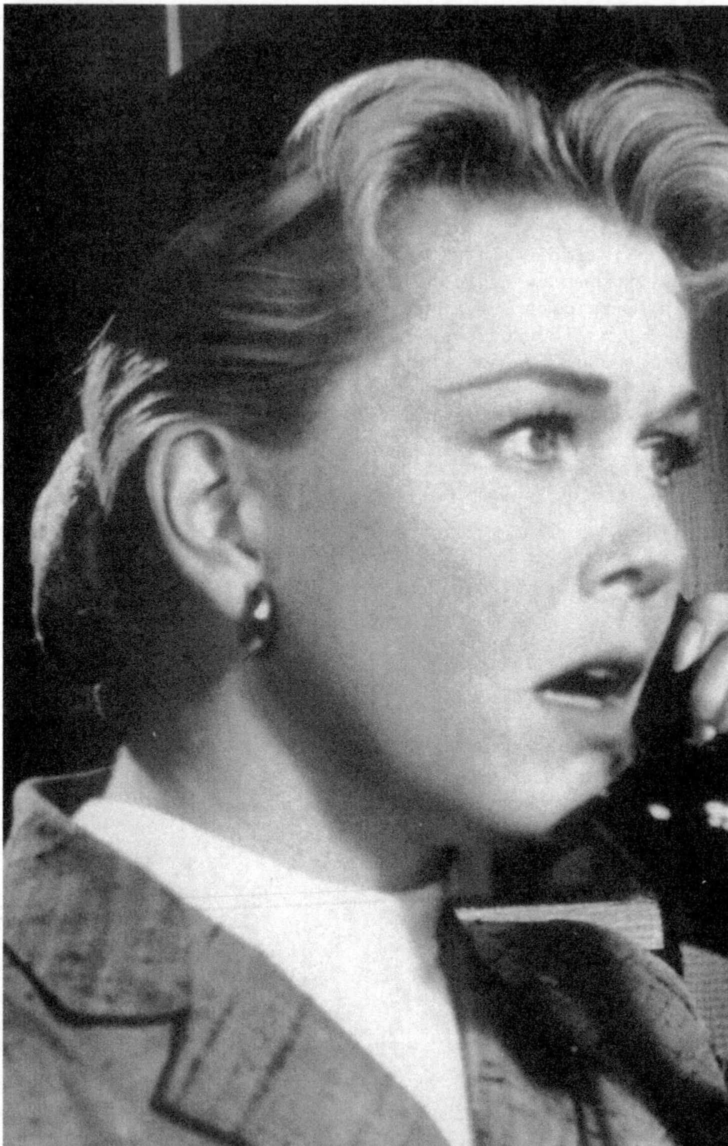

4

WHY DOES THE *PHALLUS* APPEAR?

4.1 GRIMACES OF THE REAL

The "phantom of the opera": A spectroscopy

The coincidence of motifs between high art (and theory) and mass culture is today a theoretical commonplace: is not the clearest figuration of the famous *je est un autre* to be found in the mass-culture tradition of vampires and living dead who "decenter" the subject, undermining from within his consistency and self-control?[1] The main problem with this resonance, which is a constant from the outset of the modern to the relationship between postmodern theory and today's popular culture, is how to elude the notion of some common *Zeitgeist* as its interpretive device. One way to avoid this deadlock is to take into account the antagonism which makes it possible to play high art and mass culture against each other, i.e., to interpret alternately one with the help of the other, as in Lévi-Straus's *mythologiques* in which myths interpret one another. Let us take the "phantom of the opera," undoubtedly mass culture's most renowned specter, which has kept the popular imagination occupied from Gaston Leroux's novel at the turn of the century through a series of movie and television versions up to the recent triumphant musical: in what consists, on a closer look, the repulsive horror of his face? The features which define it are four:

1) the *eyes*: "His eyes are so deep that you can hardly see the fixed pupils. All you can see is two big black holes, as in a dead man's skull."[2] To a connoisseur of Alfred Hitchcock, this image instantly recalls *The Birds*, namely the corpse with the pecked-out eyes upon which Mitch's mother (Jessica Tandy) stumbles in a lonely farmhouse, its sight causing her to emit a silent scream. When, occasionally, we do catch the sparkle of these eyes, they seem like two candles lit deep within the head perceivable only in the dark: these two lights somehow at odds with the head's surface, like lanterns burning at night in a lonely, abandoned house, are responsible for the uncanny effect of the "living dead." The first "free association" from the domain of high culture is here Edvard Munch's paintings from the same period, primarily his *Spring Evening on Karl Johan* (1892) where the stream of ghostlike pedestrians move toward the spectator, their goggling eyes at odds with the death-mask faces.

2) the *nose*: "His nose is so little worth talking about that you can't see it side-face: and *the absence* of that nose is a horrible thing *to look at*."[3] Is it necessary to recall how Freud, in his article on fetishism, uses exactly the same words to describe the horror of castration: what horrifies the child is the very *absence* of the penis, i.e., the fact that there is nothing to see where the gaze expects something? (The corresponding feature in Munch's paintings—if we are to continue the homology—is the absence of nose and ears from the homunculus's head in his most famous painting *Scream* (1893).) As to this point, there is an interesting divergence between Leroux's novel and the recent television mini-series on the "phantom": in the novel, the phantom's primordial trauma was that, as a child, he was so ugly that even his own mother found him repulsive (when he approached her for an embrace, she pushed him aside with disgust and asked him to put on his mask),[4] whereas in the television series, nobody could stand his distorted face—*with the exception of his mother* to whom he seemed nice and normal and who constantly caressed his face, while entertaining him with her heavenly voice (this is why he is later obsessed with opera: he is desperately seeking the repetition of his mother's voice among the singers). Here, one has to avoid the pseudo problem of

which version is "proper": they are to be read in the Lévi-Straussian manner, as two complementary versions of the same myth which interpret each other. That is to say, what did his mother see on his face (in the second, television version) that she found so irresistibly attractive, while the same feature was so repugnant to all others? There is only one answer possible: *the exact opposite of the first version*, i.e., an excessive phallic protuberance, repulsive to a "normal" gaze, in place of the nose—so to speak, the accomplishment of her (maternal) desire to obtain in the child her missing phallus, something resembling a famous case of the eighteenth-century monster analyzed by Alain Grosrichard.[5]

3) the *amorphous distortion of the face*: the flesh has not yet assumed definite features, it dwells in a kind of preontological state, as if "melted," as if having undergone an anamorphotic deformation; the horror lies not in his death mask, but rather in what is concealed beneath it, in the palpitating skinned flesh—everyone who catches sight of this amorphous life substance has entered the forbidden domain and must therefore be excluded from the community . . . Therein consists the ultimate paradox of the "living dead": as if death, the death-stench it spreads, is a mask sheltering a life far more "alive" than our ordinary daily life. The place of the "living dead" is not somewhere between the dead and the living: precisely as dead, they are in a way "more alive than life itself," having access to the life substance prior to its symbolic mortification.[6] Lacanian psychoanalysis locates the cause of this deformity in the anamorphotic gaze, i.e., the gaze sustained by an incestuous enjoyment: the anamorphotic distortion of reality is the way the gaze is inscribed onto the object's surface. One should recall here another case from the same period, that of the "elephant man" immortalized by David Lynch in the film of the same name: according to the mythology surrounding this figure, the grotesque protophallic protuberance on his forehead (the "elephant's nose"), as well as the general deformity of his body, designates the inscription of the maternal gaze onto the bodily surface. The myth of the "elephant man" goes as follows: during a circus parade watched by his pregnant mother, an elephant went berserk and almost trampled her down; this "view from below" on the mad elephant affected the mother and caused the elephant-like distortion of the embryo.[7] Again,

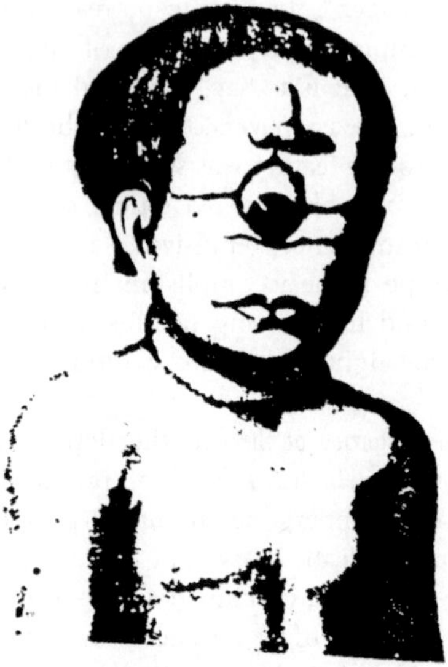

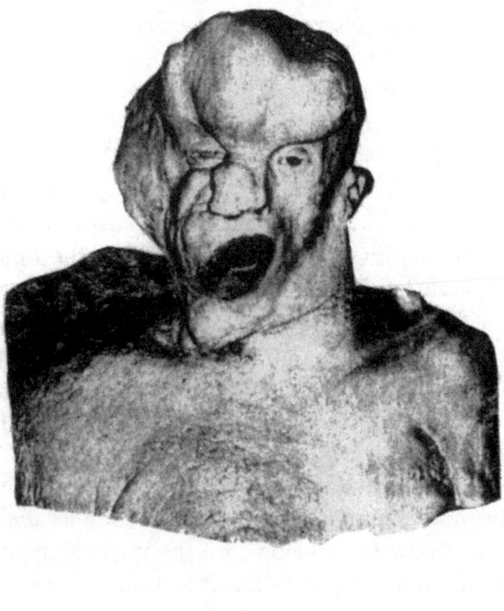

we encounter the same anamorphotic deformity of the face in a series of Munch's paintings where the face seems to lose its contours and "melt down" into a whitish slime (let it suffice to mention *Ashes, Vampire* and *The Kiss*, three drawings in which, during sexual intercourse or in its aftermath, the man literally "loses his face").

4) the exceptional status of his *voice*: the phantom of the opera is first of all a being of voice, in the novel he is regularily addressed as "the man's voice," as if the "normal" relationship of voice and its bearer (its source) were inverted: instead of the voice appertaining to the body as one of its properties, it is the body itself which, in its distortion, materializes an "impossible," originally bodiless and as such all-powerful (all-present) voice baptized by Michel Chion as "*la voix acousmatique*".[8] The first association here is, of course, again Munch's *Scream*: in it, the energy of the hindered scream—which cannot burst out and release itself in sound—finds an outlet (one is almost tempted to say: "is acted out") in the anamorphotic distortion of the body, in its "unnatural" serpentine windings, and of the coast and water beyond the bridge—as if these spiral lines are here to materialize sound vibrations, in a kind of effect of *conversion* of the hindered sound into a distortion of matter.

The voice *qua* object

In his seminar on *anxiety* (1960–1961, unpublished), Lacan referred to Munch's *Scream* in order to exemplify the status of the voice *qua* object. That is to say, the crucial feature of the painting is the fact that *the scream is not heard*. What we aim at here is not the obvious fact that "paintings do not speak": there are paintings which are definitely "resonant" and "call to mind sounds"—the paintings of street scenes bursting with life, of dancing, of stormy nature, etc.; whereas here, it pertains to the very essence of the depicted content that the scream we perceive is mute, since the anxiety is too stringent for it to find an outlet in vocalization (August Strindberg totally missed the point when he prattled on about how, in order to enjoy properly Munch's paintings, one should imagine appropriate music to accompany them). As we have already pointed out, this structural muteness is indexed within the painting itself by the absence of ears in the desperate homunculus's head: as if these ears, foreclosed from the (symbolic) reality of the face, return in the Real of the anamorphotic stain the form of which recalls a gigantic ear . . . In everyday language, one could say that the scream "got stuck in the throat": the voice *qua* object is precisely what is "stuck in the throat," what cannot burst out, unchain itself and thus enter the dimension of subjectivity. It is by no accident that, in his *Four Fundamental Concepts*, Lacan determines the *object small a* as the bone which got stuck in the subject's throat: if the exemplary case of the gaze *qua* object is a blind man's eyes, i.e., eyes which *do not see* (we experience the gaze *qua* object when a partner in conversation suddenly takes off his black glasses, exposing us to the uneasy depthless white of his eyes), then the exemplary case of the voice *qua* object is a voice which remains silent, i.e., which we *do not hear*.[9]

It should be of no surprise, then, that the most famous scream in the history of cinema is also silent: the scream of a mother who watches powerlessly her son being shot down by soldiers, in the scene at Odessa's staircase from Eisenstein's *Battleship Potemkin*. When, in a tracking shot, the camera approaches the mother who desperately grasps her head, and almost enters the black hole of her open mouth, its entire effect is again based on the fact that we do not hear her scream, i.e., that it "gets stuck in her throat"—as in the above-mentioned scene from Hitchcock's *Birds* where Mitch's mother, upon encountering the corpse with pecked-out eyes, utters her silent scream. To this silent scream which bears out the horror-stricken encounter with the real of enjoyment, one has to oppose the scream of release, of decision, of *choice*, the scream by means of which the unbearable tension finds an outlet: we so to speak "spit out the bone" in the relief of vocalization; in Hitchcock's *oeuvre*, its most famous case is Doris Day's scream from his second version of *The Man Who Knew Too Much* which, at the last moment, prevents the murder in Albert Hall. What one has to bear in mind here is the contrast between this scream and the silent mother's scream from *Potemkin*: they are both placed within the mother-son relationship; the silent scream manifests her resistance to cutting the umbilical cord that links her with the son, whereas the scream from *The Man Who Knew Too Much* signals that the mother, driven into the corner by a forced choice between her son and the community, renounced the child and chose the community—this scream is therefore in its very coarseness "an act of civilization." In other words, the opposition of silent and vocalized screams coincides with that of enjoyment and Other: the silent scream attests to the subject's clinging to enjoyment, to his/her unreadiness to exchange enjoyment (i.e., the object which gives body to it) for the Other, for the Law, for the paternal metaphor, whereas the vocalization as such corroborates that the choice is already made and that the subject finds himself/herself within the community.[10]

The voice which obsesses the phantom is, however, not a scream, but a hypnotic operatic air: he falls in love with Christine after he recognizes in her seductive singing the resonance of the lost maternal voice. In *The Man Who Knew Too Much*, this incestuous song which links the subject to the Thing (the maternal body), i.e., by means of which the Thing catches him with its tentacles, is, of course, none other than the notorious "Che sara, sara" sung by Doris Day in the embassy where her son is kept prisoner. It is, as said above, a song through which *the mother reaches, "catches," her son*, that is to say, a song which expressly establishes the incestuous umbilical link (here, Hitchcock makes use of a formal procedure whose audacity has not yet been fully perceived: the camera directly "tracks" the voice, "shows" its resonance on the staircase and its climb to the attic room where the son is locked up). Another crucial feature of this scene is the accentuated vulgarity and obscenity of Doris Day's singing: her voice is far too noisy, so that the distinguished guests in the reception room avoid each other's gaze and stare down, as if embarrassed by such an obscene exhibition. The third and final feature not to be missed is the song's content itself which directly exhibits its *superego* status: "Che sara, sara," what will be, will be—how could one avoid noticing, in this answer to the child's question as to what will become of him when he grows up, the malevolent indifference that pertains to the very notion of superego. This superego status is further confirmed if one locates "Che sara, sara" in the context of other Hitchcock films, as the middle term between *Rear Window* and *Psycho*. What we have in mind is, of course, a peculiarity of the *Rear Window*'s soundtrack:[11] when, late in the evening, Grace Kelly approaches James Stewart who is taking a nap on his wheelchair (first as an ominous shadow which overflows his face, then as "herself"), the background sounds—the rich texture of everyday noises—are suddenly suspended, and all we hear is the voice of an unknown soprano practicing scales, as if mother is yet learning to sing (which is why she still tolerates the exchange of kisses between Stewart and Kelly). In *The Man Who Knew Too Much* mother already knows how to sing, her voice finally reaches the son—the ultimate result of which is then shown in *Psycho*: a son dominated by the mother's voice, so that one is tempted to risk the thesis that the boy from *The Man Who Knew Too Much* is none other than Norman Bates in his childhood. In other words, the answer to the question "what will be," what will become of the boy from *The Man Who Knew Too Much*, is contained in *Psycho*. In order to avoid the danger of the so-called "psychoanalytic interpretation of art" which lurks here (maternal superego as the "secret" of the voice-stain . . .), one has to accomplish the properly dialectical *reversal of the explanans into explanandum*: the point is not to interpret the unfathomable "*acousmatique*" voice as the maternal superego, but rather its opposite, i.e., to explain the very logic of the maternal superego by means of this vocal stain—what we call "maternal superego" is *nothing but* such a voice which smears the picture and disturbs its transparency. Our procedure is therefore strictly allegorical: the "mother" *qua* a diegetic personality is ultimately an agency which, within the narrative content of Hitchcock's films, stands in for, holds the place of, a certain formal disturbance, a stain which blurs the field of vision.

The scream and the song thus form an opposition: the status of the song is that of a stain which materializes incestuous enjoyment, whereas the scream is—to put it simply—a horrified reaction to this stain. A cursory glance at Munch's *Scream* reveals how its surface is "drawn": the right half is far more anamorphotically distorted than the left half, i.e., the painting is "sucked" toward its center of gravity somewhere around two-thirds the height of its right side—the homunculus is seized with horror at being drawn into this whirlpool. The spiral lines of the distorted reality form a new shape vaguely remindful of a gigantic ear or eye, a kind of paranoiac agency which "sees all and hears all"—how not to recall here Syberberg's *Parsifal* where the depth of the visual field (the background) is often filled out by a flat *rear projection* which deliberately destroys the effect of perspective and sometimes directly figures a gigantic eye (like the eye frescos from Eisenstein's *Ivan the Terrible*—or, of course, the background with painted eyes in Salvador Dali's dream sequence from Hitchcock's *Spellbound*).[12] In Hitchcock's *Marnie*, the same role of a fantasy element which patches up the hole (the blank) in reality is played by the gigantic black hulk at the end of the street where Marnie's mother lives: it is evidently drawn and thus destroys the depth effect. Therein consists the most elementary formal definition of psychosis: the massive presence of some Real which fills out and blocks the perspective openness constitutive of "reality."[13] This magnetic force which distorts the linear perspective on reality is of course enjoyment: Munch's *Scream* depicts the intrusion of enjoyment into reality. The more we approach its vortex, the more the painting loses its "realist" character, i.e., the more its spiral lines of color strike us with the weight of their material presence; the illusion of "reality" of the depicted content is thereby not simply undermined—it is far more appropriate to say that the depicted reality loses its free-floating, ethereal character and becomes loaded with a kind of substantial density (considering that, according to Lacan, the only substance ascertained by psychoanalysis is enjoyment, it is thus not difficult to conceive how the material weight of Munch's stains bears out the density of enjoyment).

From the modernist *sinthome* . . .

The standard designation by which *Scream* conveys anxiety is therefore appropriate—provided that we conceive the notion of anxiety in its strict Lacanian sense, i.e., as the affect which registers the subject's panic reaction to the *overproximity* of the object cause of desire: the little man's features clearly recall a homunculus or a fetus, that is to say, a subject not yet torn from the mother's body (the same homunculus is depicted in the lower left corner of Munch's *Madonna* (1895/1902), as part of the frame otherwise ornamented by spermatic trickles).[14] The general conclusion to be drawn from it is that the stain as such has the status of the *objet petit a* (surplus enjoyment). Aside from *Starlit Night* (1893) where the substantial mass of dark earth in the foreground directly evokes a blurred stain, the same effect occurs at its clearest in two paintings from the turn of the century, *Girls on the Bridge* (1899) and *The Dance of Life* (1900): the background earth and trees in the first case, the contours of the dancing bodies in the second, transmute into extended sperm-like stains which encumber reality with the substance of enjoyment. As to their status, these stains present therefore a kind of visual correlate to the "*voix acousmatique*" in the cinema, the voice which transgresses the boundary outside/inside, since it belongs neither to diegetic reality nor to the external vocal accompaniment, but lurks in the in-between space, like a mysterious foreign body which disintegrates from within the consistency of "reality."

On this basis, one could risk some passing general remarks concerning the relationship between modernism and postmodernism. The modernist procedure is that of a "symptomal reading": confronted with the totality, modernism endeavors to subvert it by detecting the traces of its hidden truth in the details which "stick out" and belie its "official" truth, in the margins which point toward what has to be "repressed" so that the "official" totality could establish itself—modernism's elementary axiom is that details always contain some surplus which undermines the universal frame of the "official" Truth. What characterizes a typical modernist film is therefore the fact that its material texture ("writing") in a way tells another story which, by means of its lateral links and resonances, redoubles and undermines the "official" story. An exemplary case of it is to be found in the excellent early Blake Edwards thriller *Experiment In Terror*, the story of a young bank teller (Lee Remick), victim of an asthmatic blackmailer. One of a multitude of motifs which resound in it beneath the "official" narrative line is the melancholic, inanimate gaze: first the gaze of the hanged woman hidden between the dolls, then the doll of a tiger with a sad face, a gift from the blackmailer to his lover's son—although these elements have nothing whatsoever in common on the level of the "official" narrative, they nonetheless constitute the same *sinthome*, the uncanny gaze which subverts the border between life and death, since it belongs to a "dead" object (corpse, doll), which nonetheless possesses a gaze of melancholic expressiveness. This gaze of a "living dead" is of course a metonymy of the status of the blackmailer himself, who functions as an "*acousmatique*" entity in Chion's meaning of the term: the horror of an all-present voice whose body all of a sudden emerges "out of nothing." When, at the very end of the film, the police shoot him down in the empty, illuminated stadium, it is by no accident that the blackmailer, with his asthmatic wheeze, recalls a fish choking on dry land, out of its "natural element": he is effectively like an octopus who, once out of water, loses its terrifying fascination and changes into a powerless slime—this is the fate which befalls the phantom-like, "*acousmatique*" being as soon as it is reduced to its ordinary corporeity.

How, then, does postmodernism subvert this modernist frame? Let us take a novel which, although still modernist, approaches the very border of postmodernism: *The Handmaid's Tale* by Margaret Atwood, a dystopian vision of the near future when, in the USA, the Moral Majority takes over and establishes a new state, the "Republic Gilead," based on severe patriarchal order (women are not allowed to read or write, etc.). What we have here is, ostensibly, an extrapolation and thereby a clear condemnation of tendencies which are detectable in today's late capitalism, i.e., a kind of feminist version of 1984. Such a reading, obvious as it may seem, nevertheless misses the crucial point of the novel: the extraordinary libidinal cathexis of the scenes where the heroine—"Offred," Fred's girl—alone in the room allotted to her in the master's house, gradually discovers material details of the objects around her, looks for the traces of past experiences inscribed in them, learns how to notice microscopic features of her body which have previously gone unnoticed . . . One is tempted to say that the novel was written in order to put in words this experience of discovering the material weight and density of our immediate surroundings: the ultimate function of the plot of the Moral Majority's *coup d'état* is simply to serve as a narrative frame which impels the heroine toward such a microscopic experience (the same as with "space operas" whose intermingled plots of planetary battles ultimately serve as a pretext for rendering the experience of floating freely in empty space without gravitation). The true "feminine" subject position thus comes forth not so much in the novel's "official" ideological content (the condemnation of Moral Majority rule) as in this attitude of microscopic probing, and the ambiguity of the novel is that, in order to give expression to the "feminine" position, it must construct a grandiose fantasy of patriarchal totalitarianism.

Here we have again the difference between *meaning* and what Lacan calls *sinthome*: on the level of meaning, *The Handmaid's Tale* is a straightforward case of dystopia depicting a possible new form of "closed society," yet this level is underpinned with the traces of feminine enjoyment. What is crucial here, however, is that this feminine "writing" cannot be staged directly, bypassing the circuitous route of meaning: it can be rendered only as a by-product of the story whose "official" content is the totalitarian universe of the Moral Majority. The same dialectic is at work in Chandler's hard-boiled novels: the insipid view that Chandler took advantage of the detective narrative, using it as a frame that he filled out with a wealth of detailed observations and insights about the corruption of California-style wild capitalism and its psychic impact, overlooks the crucial fact that such detailed observations are artistically "effective" only as marginal by-products of a text which "officially" purports to be a detective story centered on revealing the mystery of who-dunit, etc. This, precisely, is the reason why *The Handmaid's Tale* remains a *modernist* novel: it would become "postmodern" the moment it posited an undercurrent of paradoxical codependence, complicity even, between this feminine "writing" and the totalitarian universe of the Moral Majority, introducing thereby a moment of ambiguity into its univocal condemnation—the step accomplished, among others, by Kafka whose great novels are haunted with the secret complicity that links the bureaucratic Thing (castle, court) to feminine enjoyment.

. . . to the postmodernist Thing

What characterizes postmodernism is therefore an obsession with Thing, with a foreign body within the social texture, in all its dimensions that range from woman *qua* the unfathomable element that undermines the rule of the "reality principle" (*Blue Velvet*), through science-fiction monsters (*Alien*) and autistic aliens (*Elephant Man*), up to the paranoiac vision of social totality itself as the ultimate fascinating Thing, a vampire-like specter which marks even the most idyllic everyday surface with signs of latent corruption. (In this sense, one could say that, today more than ever, capital is the Thing *par excellence*: a chimeric apparition which, although it can nowhere be spotted as a positive, clearly delimited entity, nonetheless functions as the ultimate Thing regulating our lives.) The ambiguity of the postmodern relationship to the Thing pertains to the fact that the Thing is not simply a foreign body, an intruder which disturbs the harmony of the social bond: precisely as such, the Thing is what "holds together" the social edifice by means of guaranteeing its fantasmatic consistency. Within modernism, the Thing assumes either the form of "remnants of the past," of the inertia of prejudices to be cast away, or the form of the repressed life power to be unchained (as in the naive psychoanalytical ideology of the liberation of drive potentials from the constraints of social repression); we enter postmodernism when our relationship to the Thing becomes *antagonistic*: we abjure and disown the Thing, yet it exerts an irresistible attraction on us; its proximity exposes us to a mortal danger, yet it is simultaneously a source of power . . . One is even tempted to propose a reading of Schopenhauer and Marx as postmodern philosophers, insofar as perhaps the most distinctive feature of their thought is a radical hatred for its object—the will (interpreted by Schopenhauer as the "secret" of the Kantian *Ding-an-sich*), capital.

Postmodernism thus accomplishes a kind of shift of perspective in relation to modernism: what in modernism appeared as the subversive margin—symptoms in which the repressed truth of the "false" totality emerges—is now displaced into the very heart, as the hard core of the Real that different attempts of symbolization endeavor in vain to integrate and to "gentrify." In short, it is as if the universal and the particular paradoxically *exchange places*: what one encounters in the center instead of the universal is a kind of "particular absolute" (to use Jacques-Alain Miller's term), a particular traumatic kernel, while the various universals are all of a sudden reduced to the role of species of an impossible-un-fathomable genus, i.e., they start to function as a series of specific, ultimately failed attempts to symbolize (transpose into the medium of symbolic universality) and thus to "neutralize" the traumatic core of the Real. The theoretical antagonism thus shifts from the axis Imaginary-Symbolic to the axis Symbolic-Real: the aim of the modernist "symptomal reading" is to ferret out the texture of discursive (symbolic) practices whose imaginary effect is the substantial totality, whereas postmodernism focuses on the traumatic Thing which resists symbolization (symbolic practices).

This shift comes forth exemplarily apropos of Foucault's profoundly *modernist* treatment of the relation between sexuality and sex—in what consisted the reversal in their relation that exerted such fascination on the theoretical public? Instead of reducing sexuality (i.e., the series of discursive—legal, medical, ethical, economical, etc.—practices in which sex is "actualized") to the external secondary effect of a unique cause ("sex" *qua* substantial entity), Foucault conceived sex as the effect of this series of practices. "Sex" is not an object given in advance, prior to its discursive actualizations and guaranteeing their consistency: it comes to be as a constructed unique reference of these practices, as a result of their hegemonic articulation: "The notion of 'sex' made it possible to group together, in an artificial unity, anatomical elements, biological functions, conducts, sensations, pleasures, and it enabled the use of this fictitious unity as a causal principle."[15] From the Lacanian perspective, however, Foucault overlooks here the inherently "antagonistic" status of sex, the "antagonistic" relation between sex and sexuality *qua* plurality of discursive practices: these practices endeavor again and again to integrate, to dominate, to neutralize, "sex" *qua* traumatic core which eludes their grasp. "Sex" is therefore not the universality, the neutral common ground of discursive practices which constitute "sexuality," but rather *their common stumbling block*, their common point of failure. In other words, "sex" pertains to the register of the Real: it is an "effect" of sexuality (of symbolic practices), but its *antagonistic* effect—there is no sex prior to sexuality, sexuality itself produces ("secrets" in all the meanings of the term) sex as its inherent stumbling block (the same as with the notion of trauma in psychoanalysis, which is a retroactive effect of its failed symbolization). Therein consists the ultimate paradox of the Lacanian notion of the cause *qua* real: it is produced ("secreted") by its own effects.[16]

4.2 PHALLOPHANY OF THE ANAL FATHER

The anal father

This postmodern shift affects radically the status of paternal authority: modernism endeavors to assert the subversive potential of the margins which undermine the Father's authority, of the enjoyments which elude the Father's grasp, whereas postmodernism *focuses on the father himself and conceives him as "alive," in his obscene dimension*. The phantom-like object which hinders a "normal" sexual relationship therefore is a paternal figure, yet not the father who was sublated [*aufgehoben*] in his Name, i.e., the dead-symbolic father, but the father who is *still alive*—father insofar as he is not yet "transubstantiated" into a symbolic function and remains what psychoanalysis calls a "partial object." That is to say, the father *qua* Name of the Father, reduced to a figure of symbolic authority, is "dead" (also) in the sense that *he does not know anything about enjoyment*, about life substance: the symbolic order (the big Other) and enjoyment are radically incompatible.[17] Which is why the famous Freudian dream of a son who appears to his father and reproaches him with "Father, can't you see I'm burning?" could be simply translated into "*Father, can't you see I'm enjoying?*"—can't you see I'm alive, burning with enjoyment? Father cannot see it since he is dead, whereby the possibility is open to me to enjoy not only *outside* his knowledge, i.e., unbeknownst to him, but also *in his very ignorance*. The other, no less known Freudian dream, that about the father who does not know he is dead, could thus be supplemented with "(*I, the dreamer, enjoy the fact that*) father does not know he is dead."[18] What emerges under the guise of the phantom-like "living dead"—of the specter which hinders "normal" sexual relationship—is, however, the reverse of the Name of the Father, namely the "anal father" who definitely *does* enjoy: the obscene little man who is the clearest embodiment of the phenomenon of the "uncanny" (*Unheimliche*). He is the subject's double who accompanies him like a shadow and gives body to a certain surplus, to what is "in the subject more than subject himself"; this surplus represents what the subject must renounce, sacrifice even, the part in himself that the subject must murder in order to start to live as a "normal" member of the community. The crucial point here is therefore that this "anal father" is Father-Enjoyment (*le Père-Jouissance*, as Michel Silvestre calls it):[19] it is not the agency of symbolic Law, its "repression," which hinders the sexual relationship (according to a Lacanian commonplace, the role of the Name of the Father is precisely to *enable* the semblance of a sexual relationship), its stumbling block is on the contrary a certain excessive "sprout of enjoyment" materialized in the obscene figure of the "anal father."[20] A whole series of Munch's paintings are to be conceived as variations on this motif, first of all the two *Mephistopheles* from 1935. *Mephistopheles I: The Duel* depicts a dark figure in the act of killing his white, shadow-like double, whereas in *Mephistopheles II: Split Personality* the same dark figure walks down the same street arm in arm with his almost transparent double and ignores a girl who turns round to cast a seductive glance at him. Here, one has to go beyond the standard "Lacanian" reduction of the motif of a double to imaginary mirror relationship: at its most fundamental, the double embodies the phantom-like Thing in me; that is to say, the dissymmetry between me and my double is ultimately that between the (ordinary) object and the (sublime) Thing. In my double, I don't simply encounter myself (my mirror image), but first of all what is "in me more than myself": the double is "myself," yet—to put it in Spinozian terms—conceived under another modality, under the modality of the other, sublime, ethereal body, a pure substance of enjoyment exempted from the circuit of generation and corruption. Prior to his being "sublated" in his Name, "father" designates such a Thing which is "in me more than myself."[21]

It would be, however, wrong to draw the conclusion that the relationship to the double *qua* Thing has nothing whatsoever to do with the imaginary relationship between ego and ideal ego, its mirror image, i.e., with the axis *m—i(a)* or, as Lacan writes it down in his "scheme L," *a-a'*. What one should render problematic in this mirror relationship is the apostrophe which distinguishes the image of a double (*a'*) from "myself" (*a*): this apostrophe later (i.e., when *a* is no longer conceived as an imaginary other, but as the real object-cause of desire) becomes the *objet petit a*. In other words, *objet petit a* is the *unheimliches* surplus forever missing in the mirror image, i.e., "unspecularizable," yet precisely as such present in it in the shape of that unfathomable X on account of which the mirror image obtains its *unheimliches* character—the double is "the same as me," yet totally strange; his sameness all the more accentuates his uncanniness. This is why the image of a double so easily turns into its opposite, so that, instead of experiencing the radical otherness of his similar, the subject recognizes *himself* in the image of radical otherness, i.e., he recognizes his equivalent in the amorphous mass of the Real whose literary and cinematic versions reach from Maupassant's *Horla* to the "alien" from Scott Ridley's film of the same name. In this sense, one could say that the Lacanian formula of fantasy, $ *a*, the confrontation of the empty subject with the amorphous presence of the real, displays the "truth" of the mirror relationship *a—a'*, i.e., what confers on this relationship its antagonistic tension—another confirmation of how the Real persists in the very heart of the Imaginary. It is therefore clear why vampires are invisible in the mirror: because they have read Lacan and, consequently, know how to behave—they materialize *objet a* which, by definition, *cannot be mirrored*.

What is crucial here is therefore the radical assymmetry in the relationship *a—a'*, i.e., a Dorian Gray-like imbalance between myself and my mirror image: the price to be paid for my image to retain its harmonious consistency is that the entire horror of its amorphous leftover falls into me. This amorphous left over is the material correlative of the gaze; that is to say, when I find myself face to face with with my double, when I "encounter myself" among the objects, when "I myself" *qua* subject appear "out there," what am I at that precise moment as the one who looks at it, as a witness to myself? Precisely the gaze *qua* object: the horror of coming face to face with my double is that this encounter reduces me to the object-gaze. In other words, the part missing in the mirror image of myself (the " "' of the axis *a-a'*) is my own gaze, the object-gaze which sees me out there . . . As a rule, one focuses on the horror of being the object of some invisible, unfathomable, panoptical gaze (the "someone-is-watching me" motif)—yet it is a far more unbearable experience to find oneself at this very point of a pure gaze. The lesson of the dialectic of the double is therefore the discordance between eye and gaze: there certainly is in the mirror image "more than meets the eye," yet this surplus that eludes the eye, the point in the image which eludes my eye's grasp, is none other than *the gaze itself*: as Lacan put it, "you can never see me at the point from which I gaze at you."

This is the way psychoanalysis subverts the usual opposition of the paternal and the maternal: it brings out what this opposition has to repress, to exclude, in order to establish itself, namely the *reverse* of the father, the "anal father" who lurks behind the Name of the Father *qua* bearer of the symbolic Law. This "anal father" is the third element which disturbs the familiar narrative of the gradual prevalence of the paternal over the maternal in history as well as in the subject's ontogenesis, the narrative which even Freud seems to follow in his *Moses and Monotheism*, at least upon a superficial reading of it. The mad "anal father" is the nauseous debauchee, threatening yet ridiculously impotent, who simply does not fit the frame of the "complementary relationship between *yin* and *yang*" and the like. A new light is thus shed on the Cartesian *cogito*, on its inherent link with the God which guarantees its consistency. The Cartesian God—the correlate of the *cogito*—is, of course, none other than Lacan's "big Other," the place of the supposed symbolic knowledge (*le sujet supposé savoir*) which supplants the primordial Thing, i.e., Father-Enjoyment *qua* presymbolic Other. *Cogito ergo sum* is thus to be translated as: I think where enjoyment was evacuated; or, to give a deontological twist to it: if I am to think, the Other's enjoyment has to be suspended.

One can detect this subjective attitude in those moments in Raymond Chandler's novels when, exhausted by his activity, Philip Marlowe disconnects from the frenetic run of things, lies down and takes a rest. Through the luminescence of advertisements, through the stench of alcohol and garbage, through the intrusive noise of a big city, all the rot and decay from which he has tried to escape by means of activity—in short: the substance of enjoyment—return to strike him in the face. There is nothing calming or reassuring in these moments; passive thought, confronted with the nausea of existence, is, on the contrary, pervaded by paranoia. Marlowe "thinks," yet his thought is not a free-floating, calming reflection, but rather a sneaking, crawling under the watchful eye of a cruel superego: "I thought, and thought in my mind moved with a kind of sluggish stealthiness, as if it was being watched by bitter and sadistic eyes" (*Farewell, My Lovely*). This would be, then, Marlowe's *cogito*: I think, therefore an obscene, sadistic superego specter is watching me. And what is the "phantom" if not such a stumbling block of the "normal" sexual relationship (in Leroux's novel, the relationship between Christine Daae and Vicomte de Chagny)? If not the so-called "pregenital" (anal) object which must disappear, pass away, for the "normal" sexual relationship to realize itself? Yet one must avoid here the trap into which Freudian orthodoxy fell, i.e., the fallacy according to which fixation on this object prevents the emergence of the "normal" (genital) sexual relationship: the "phantom" *qua* object does nothing but materialize the inherent hindrance, the "original" impossibility that pertains to the sexual relationship.[22]

The ambiguous role of this object-impediment which, at the same time, guarantees fantasmatic consistency,[23] enables us to delineate the logic of the sublime reversal in *Phantom of the Opera*, i.e., of its supreme melodramatic moment when the phantom who has hitherto *prevented* the fulfillment of the sexual relationship, suddenly emerges as the one who, by means of his sacrifice, *enables* it;[24] what we have in mind is, of course, the final moment when the phantom Eric sacrifices himself in order to make possible for Christine a happy life with Vicomte de Chagny. In terms of Propp's narrative analysis, one could say that in this final reversal the agent previously identified as malefactor suddenly changes into donator, i.e., into a "mediator" who, by means of his sacrifice, enables the hero's salvation. And it is perhaps the very experience of this reversal of the "condition of impossibility" into a "condition of possibility"—the experience of how "only the spear that smote you/can heal your wound" (to quote from Wagner's *Parsifal*)—which constitutes the core of what we call "dialectics."[25]

Phallophany versus phallic signifier

It should be clear, now, what is the name of the "secret" beneath the mask, so terrible that anyone who sees it is not allowed to survive: as Lacan recalls it apropos of the Greek mysteries, this "secret" is the *revealed phallus*, the phallus which is not yet "sublated" (*aufgehoben*) in the signifier: the *maternal* phallus, the phallus *qua* sign of the incestuous link. As Gilles Deleuze puts it: *"Si vous êtes pris dans le rêve de l'autre, vous êtes foutu"* ("If you are caught in another's dream, you are done for"). The revealed phallus, the phallic-anamorphotic distortion of the face, is a kind of brand attesting that the subject is caught in the desire of the other (mother), entrapped in her dream. In this precise sense, phallus "appears" in the obscene protuberance on the "elephant man" 's forehead and marks it with the brand of mother's desire, as if striking it with the whip of her gaze. What Lacan calls "phallic identification" is, on the contrary, the exact opposite of this "revelation of the phallus": it is the identification with the phallus *qua* signifier of desire, i.e., the paradox of *identification with nonidentity*, with the gap which maintains the desire. In the phallic identification proper, we identify with the element which functions as the signifier of its own opposite (in short, as signifier *tout court*). Let us just recall the Hitchcockian blonde (Grace Kelly, e.g.): in her figure, the external opposition of frigid blonde and hot brunette is surmounted ("sublated," *aufgehoben*, in the precise Hegelian sense), so that the very surface coldness functions as a sign of its opposite—the more calm she is, the more this restraint attests to an underlying passion . . . It is the same with fury: we enter the phallic dimension when we surmount the external opposition of outbursts of noisy rage and of restrained silence, so that cold silence itself starts to function as something infinitely more threatening than violent roars. On another level, it is the same with the dialectic of the leader: political hagiographers know very well that the leader is to be depicted as fundamentally *alone* in his heights, since it is precisely in these moments of absolute solitude that, in a "deeper" sense, "he is with us all": the leader is "us all" precisely as absolutely alone, as one. This is what Hegel calls "self-relating negation": the way effectively to negate and surmount frigidity is not to *supplant* it by its external opposite (passion), but to make it *designate* this opposite. Therein consists the ultimate paradox of what Lacan calls "the *dialectic* of desire"—the renunciation of desire as the very form of appearance of its fulfillment—the paradox which gets lost as soon as the phallus begins to "appear."

In postmodernism, this "apparition" of the phallus is *universalized*. David Lynch, whose *Elephant Man* features the above-mentioned historical case of the phallophany at the onset of modernism, developed in *Blue Velvet* and *Wild at Heart* a style whose underlying premise is the expanse of the anamorphotic distortion, still localized in the case of the "elephant man," into the ontological condition of reality as such: at the very beginning of *Blue Velvet*, the suspension of the paternal function (epitomized by the father's heart attack) is immediately followed by the intrusion of the Real in the shape of a fragment of reality (a cut-off ear) which, as soon as one approaches it too closely, turns into a nauseating, crawling life substance (ants swarming in the ear). In Lynch's "ontology," the universe is a palpitating slime that continually threatens to blow up the settled frame of everyday reality. The counterpart to the cut-off ear in *Wild at Heart* is a repeated close shot of lighting a cigarette which then dissolves into raging fire—through this opening in reality the substance of the Real breaks in. All that remains of diegetic "reality" in *Wild at Heart* is narrative fragments from old cinematic genres (*film noir*, soft porn, musical comedy, etc.)—a patchwork designed to prevent us from "burning our fingers" too much on the Real.

Therein consists the fundamental ambiguity of the image in postmodernism: it is a kind of barrier enabling the subject to maintain distance from the Real, protecting him/her against its irruption, yet its very obtrusive "hyperrealism" evokes the nausea of the Real. Some of today's commonplaces are phrases on the postmodern "society of the spectacle" whose reality is supplanted by an image of itself, and where, consequently, individuals more and more lose the character of agents, embedded in social reality, and are reduced to external observers of the spectacle. Yet the reverse of this "derealization" is the hypersensitivity to reality as something that can be hurt, for the inherently painful dimension of our contact with reality even at the most microscopic level—as if the subject is reduced to a pure receptive gaze precisely because he is aware of how every encroachment upon the world, even the most benevolent, *cuts into* the world, hurts it. "Edward Scissorhands" from Tim Burton's film of the same name, a failed, aborted, Frankensteinian monster with scissor-like hands, epitomizes the postmodern subject: a melancholic subject condemned to pure gaze since he knows that touching the beloved one equals causing him/her unbearable pain. This inherent link between "scopic drive" and violence characterizes also the figure of Norman Bates from *Psycho*: the reverse of his "voyeurism" is that the only proper "act" of which he is capable is slaughtering his neighbor.[26]

In the Lacanian notion of the Real, the hard kernel which resists symbolization coincides with its opposite, the so-called "inner," "psychic" reality;[27] within postmodernism, the same ambiguity is reproduced in the shape of the tension between the obtrusive bodily density (one is tempted to say: the Heideggerian "earth") which overshadows the narrative frame, and the opposite attitude which, *vulgari eloquentia*, reduces reality itself to "something that exists only in our heads," a "product of the delirium of our brain": "The most prudent and effective method of dealing with the world around us is to assume that it is a complete fiction—conversely, the one small node of reality left to us is inside our own heads."[28] One should recall here the series of great "postmodern" *mise-en-scènes* of Wagner's operas which transpose part of the action or even all of it into the "head" of one of its protagonists: in Jean-Pierre Ponelle's *Tristan*, the action following Tristan's death (Isolde's return, etc.) is staged as the delusion of the dying Tristan; at the end of Hans-Juergen Syberberg's film version of *Parsifal*, the entire content is twice "subjectivized," located first in Kundry's head, then in the head of Wagner himself.[29] The most indicative is here, however, Harry Kupfer's staging of *Fliegende Hollaender* (Bayreuth 1977–1985): the Dutchman is presented as Senta's hysterical delusion, as the mode by which Senta "does not give way as to her desire" and refuses the poor and faithful Eric, the sexual partner at her disposal in "reality." Her final suicidal gesture is thus reinterpreted as a kind of reflective redoubling: Senta does not sacrifice herself for the Dutchman, she sacrifices herself to keep alive the fantasy of the Dutchman which gives consistency to her desire—she chooses death rather than accepting the dreadful reality of the provincial town where she "really" lives. The screen onto which Senta's fantasy is projected consists of a big black hulk strangely resembling the hulk in the above-mentioned shot from Hitchcock's *Marnie*; this hulk is located at the back of the stage, in the very place where the viewer's eye expects to meet the imaginary point of the infinite axis of perspective, i.e., the Other's gaze which confers on the field of vision its depth: the specter of the Dutchman appears when the gigantic hands that form the hulk spread and allow a view to its interior, the folded vividly red Real, the space of enjoyment not yet "colonized" by the sociosymbolic order.[30]

Class struggle in the opera

Is not then the Flying Dutchman—again, like Leroux's phantom, an intruder preventing the "normal" sexual relationship between Senta and her poor Eric—literally a "phantom in the opera," a phantom-like apparition on the stage? The fantasy screen in the background holds the space open for the "ghosts of the past" for whom there is no place in the grey utilitarian bourgeois everyday life which forecloses the very possibility of a heroic sacrifice: Senta yearns for a world in which something akin to the Dutchman's tragedy is still conceivable. Yet if one is to avoid the historicist trap, one must learn the materialist lesson of the antievolutionist creationism which resolves the contradiction between literal meaning of the Scripture (according to which the universe was created ca. 5000 years ago) and irrefutable proofs of its greater age (million-years-old fossils, etc.) not *via* the usual indulging in the delicacies of the allegorical reading of the Scripture ("Adam and Eve are not really the first couple but a metaphor for the early stages of humanity . . .") but by sticking to the literal truth of the Scripture: the universe was created recently, i.e., only 5000 years ago, *yet with inbuilt false traces of the past* (God directly created fossils, e.g.).[31] The past is always strictly "synchronous," with the present, it is *the way the synchronous universe thinks its antagonism*—it suffices to recall the infamous role of the "remnants of the past" in accounting for the difficulties of the "construction of socialism."

In this sense, the Phantom and his sexual rival, Vicomte de Changy, form a kind of Kleinian opposition of "bad" and "good" aristocratic object: the Phantom embodies the excess aristocracy has to renounce in order to become integrated into bourgeois society. In other words, he is a kind of "fossil" created by the Enlightenment itself as a distorted index of its inherent antagonism: what was, prior to the advent of Enlightenment, a sovereign expenditure, a glitter of those in power, an inherent moment of their symbolic status, now undergoes a kind of anamorphotic distortion, falls out from the social space whose contours are defined by utilitarian ideology, and is perceived as decadent debauchery epitomized in the bourgeois myth of a corrupted demonic aristocrat.[32] The notion of "decadence" acquires here its full weight as the concept which "fantasizes the return of all the weirdest religious sects and cults, after the triumph of the secular, of *homo oeconomicus* and of utilitarianism: it is thus the ghost of the superstructure, of cultural autonomy itself, that haunts the omnipotence of the base."[33] This superego side of the Phantom *qua* return of an archaic enjoyment is, however, supplemented by its opposite which is inscribed into Leroux's novel by means of its very topography—although "apolitical," the novel nevertheless establishes a mysterious link between the Phantom and the Paris Commune, this ultimate trauma of the French bourgeois society of the late nineteenth-century: deep under the Opera, where the Phantom has his premises, there were the secret torture chambers of the Communards . . . The political topography of *Phantom of the Opera* thus consists of an extimate field, a field whose innermost center meets its radical exterior: the very heart of the Parisian high society, the building of the Opera with its luxurious staircases, reveals—the moment we dive into its foundations—the traces of the traumatic "repressed" past, i.e., of the historical moment which shook the foundations of the bourgeois state.

Such is then the social-ideological topography of the Phantom: his figure constitutes an impossible "point of passage" at which the subversive power of the new (the working class) rejoins the return of the old (aristocratic decadence). In this precise sense, the Phantom is *a fetishistic representative of (a stand-in for) the class struggle*: it disavows it by condensing into one both of its extremes which undermine the established bourgeois order, aristocratic decadence as well as the coming proletarian subversion. It is therefore wrong to ask directly "which is the class equivalent of the Phantom?": its "class meaning" is contained in the very distortion that results from the "impossible" conjunction of opposites (as in fascist anti-Semitism where the "Jew" condenses in a unique figure the excessive nature of capitalism—its wild profiteering, etc.—and its proletarian subversion, i.e., the "Jewish-Communist plot"). This distortion betrays the work of "class desire," its effort to render invisible the actual contours of social antagonism and thereby pave the way for its "imaginary solution": by means of his transformation from malefactor to donator, the Phantom becomes the "vanishing mediator" rendering possible the final reconciliation.

Convincing as it may appear, such a direct analysis of "ideological content" is nevertheless marked by a brand of ultimate arbitrariness; and the same goes for all analyses of this kind: Dr. Frankenstein's creature can be a metaphor for the monstrous results of man's manipulation with nature, for the horrors of the French revolution, etc.; Kaspar Hauser can epitomize the catastrophic results of the lack of family education; the elephant man can be cathexed by the ideological problematic of the body-soul relationship ("Such a horrible body, and yet such a great soul!"); the killer shark in *Jaws* can signify anything from repressed sexuality to unbriddled capitalism and the threat of the Third World to America . . . The way out of this deadlock is not *via* deciding which of the multiple meanings is "true" ("Is the shark a representative of the repressed drives of the late-capitalist subject, or does it epitomize the destructive nature of capitalism itself?"); what one should do is rather to conceive the monster as a kind of fantasy screen where this very multiplicity of meanings can appear and fight for hegemony. In other words, the error of direct content analysis is to proceed too quickly and to presuppose as self-evident the fantasy surface itself, the empty form/frame which offers space for the appearance of monstrous content: the crucial question is not "What does the Phantom signify?" but "How is the very space constituted where entities like the Phantom can emerge?" Or, to return to Kupfer's *Fliegende Holländer*, the crucial question is not the meaning of Senta's fantasies but rather "Where does the black hulk at the background of the stage come from, so that Senta has a surface onto which she can project her fantasies?" What we have here is the same disjunction as that of the well-known visual paradox of the vase/two faces: as we perceive meaning(s), the form *qua* place of their inscription becomes invisible—and the fundamental gesture of a dialectical analysis is precisely a step back from content to form, i.e., a suspension of content which renders visible anew form as such. The elementary ideological operation consists in this very "conversion of the form" by means of which the possible space for ideological meanings emerges—or, as Fredric Jameson put it apropos of *Jaws*:

> . . . the vocation of the symbol—the killer shark—lies less in any single message or meaning than in its very capacity to absorb and organize all of these quite distinct anxieties together. As a symbolic vehicle, then, the shark must be understood in terms of its essentially polysemous function rather than any particular content attributable to it by this or that spectator. Yet it is precisely this polysemousness which is profoundly ideological, insofar as it allows essentially social and historical anxieties to be folded back into apparently "natural" ones, both to express and to be recontained in what looks like a conflict with other forms of biological existence.[34]

This "folding back" is what Lacan calls a "*point de capiton*": the emergence of the shark as symbol does not add any new meaning, it simply reorganizes meanings which were already there by binding them to the same signifier—ideology is at work in this purely symbolic gesture, in the addition of a signifier which "quilts" the floating plurality of anxieties.[35] What remains outside this formal symbolic gesture, what resists absorption into meaning, is, however, the horrifying power of fascination that pertains to the presence of the shark—its *enjoyment*, to use the Lacanian term for it. One should therefore reformulate the above-mentioned disjunction between content and form: *you cannot have both meaning and enjoyment*. The analysis focused on the "ideological meaning" of monsters overlooks the fact that, previous to signifying something, previous even to serving as an empty vessel of meaning, monsters embody enjoyment *qua* the limit of interpretation, that is to say, *nonmeaning as such*.

The subject of the enlightenment

This empty form, this black stain in the very heart of reality, is ultimately the "objective correlative" of the subject himself (if one is allowed to transplant T. S. Eliot's term into another context): *by means of anamorphotic stains, "reality" indexes the presence of the subject*. The emergence of the empty surface on which phantasmagorical monsters appear is therefore strictly correlative to what Heidegger calls "the advent of the Modern-Age subjectivity," i.e., to the epoch in which the symbolic "substance" (the "big Other" *qua* texture of symbolic tradition) can no longer contain the subject, can no longer bind him to his symbolic mandate. This cutting off of substantial tradition is the constitutive gesture of Enlightenment; in this sense, *the "monster" is the subject of the Enlightenment*, that is to say, the mode in which the subject of the Enlightenment acquires his impossible positive existence. A new light is thus shed on the ill-famed problem of the "death of the subject": the "eclipse" of the subject in front of the Thing—what one (mis)perceives as his "death"—is strictly equal to his emergence, i.e., *the "subject" is precisely the void which remains after the entire substantial content is taken away*. The source of this customary confounding of the "death of the subject" with its very emergence lies in the fact that the motif of the "death of the subject" stands in for another motif, that of the "death of man": "subject" and "human person" are strictly opposed, i.e., "subjectivization" entails a radical "evacuation," emptying, of "man" *qua* substantial "person."

To exemplify this split between "subject" and "person," one has only to evoke one further figure in the series of legendary "monsters":

Kaspar Hauser. On 26 May 1828, a young man appeared in the central square of Nuremberg, singularily dressed, of stiff, unnatural gestures; his entire language consisted of a few fragments of the Lord's prayer learned by heart and pronounced with grammatical errors, and of the enigmatic phrase "I want to become such a knight as was my father," the design of an identification with the Ego Ideal; in his left hand, he carried a paper with his name—Kaspar Hauser—and the address of a captain in the Nuremberg cavalry. Later, when he learned to speak "properly," Kaspar told his story: he had spent all his life alone in a "dark cave" where a mysterious "black man" procured food and drink for him, until the very day when he dressed him and took him to Nuremberg, teaching him on the way a few phrases . . . He was confided to the Daumer family, quickly "humanized" himself and became a celebrity: an object of philosophical, psychological, pedagogical, and medical researches, even the object of political speculation about his origin (was he the missing Prince of Baden?). After a couple of quiet years, on the afternoon of 14 December 1833, he was found mortally wounded with a knife; on his deathbed, he announced that his murderer was the same "black man" who had brought him to the central square of Nuremberg five years ago . . .[36]

Although the sudden apparition of Kaspar Hauser provoked a shock that pertains to this kind of brutal encounter with a real/impossible which seems to interrupt the symbolic circuit of cause and effect, the most surprising thing about it was that, in a sense, *his arrival was awaited*: precisely as a surprise, he arrived in time. It is not only that Kaspar realized the millenary myth of a child of royal origins abandoned in a wild place and then found at the age of adolescence (cf. the rumor that he was the Prince of Baden), or that the fact that the only objects in his "dark cave" were a couple of figures of wooden animals pathetically realizes the myth of a hero saved by the animals who take care of him. The point is rather that toward the end of the eighteenth-century, the theme of a child living excluded from human community became the object of numerous literary and scientific texts: it staged in a pure, "experimental" way the theoretical question of how to distinguish in man the part of culture from the part of nature. (A couple of decades earlier, Frederick, the "enlightened" king of Prussia, was directly involved in a similar experiment: on a fenced country estate, he and his assistants isolated a couple of children and secretly observed how they found their way without any help from educated adults.) What is therefore crucial about the figure of Kaspar Hauser is that he appeared as the subject of the Enlightenment at its purest: as the very embodiment of the ideological problematic that pertains to the Enlightenment project. This "Thing which speaks" with its "mechanical," abrupt, doll-like gestures, lacking the "depth" that defines someone as a person, was the pure subject ($) prior to subjectivization, freed from all imaginary lures. (Even the "black man," Kaspar's paternal substitute, was devoid of any positive features.) Its most succinct Lacanian diagnosis is therefore that Kaspar Hauser was the subject lacking the mirror captivation, in other words, *the subject without the ego*: he was directly thrown into the symbolic network, bypassing the imaginary (mis)recognition which enables one to experience oneself as a "person." (As it is known from his story, Kaspar Hauser was not able to relate to his mirror image, i.e., he did not recognize "himself" in it—the same as with all monster figures, real or "fictitious," from Dr. Frankenstein's creature to the elephant man, who could not stand their mirror images.)

This is the way the Enlightenment project has gone wrong: the Enlightenment philosophers wanted to pour out of the bathtub the dirty water of corrupted civilization and to retain only the healthy, unspoiled, natural child-ego, yet what they inadvertently threw out in the process was precisely the ego, so that they were left with the dirty water of a monster.[37] In short: the pure "subject of the Enlightenment" is a monster which gives body to the surplus that escapes the vicious circle of the mirror relationship. In this sense, monsters can be defined precisely as the fantasmatic appearance of the "missing link" between nature and culture: as a kind of "answer of the real" to the Enlightenment's endeavor to find the bridge that links culture to nature, to produce a "man/woman of culture" who would simultaneously conserve his/her unspoiled nature. Therein consists the ambiguity of the Enlightenment: the question of "origins" (origins of language, of culture, of society) which emerged in all its stringency with it, is nothing but the reverse of a fundamental prohibition, the prohibition to probe too deeply into the obscure origins, which betrays a fear that by doing so, one might uncover something monstrous . . .[38]

If, consequently, one bears in mind the fact that, according to Lacan, the ego is an *object*, a substantial "res," one can easily grasp the ultimate sens of Kant's transcendental turn: it desubstantializes the subject (which, with Descartes, still remained "*res* cogitans," i.e., a substantial "piece of reality")—*and it is this very desubstantialization which opens up the empty space (the "blank surface") onto which fantasies are projected, where monsters emerge.* To put it in Kantian terms: because of the inaccessibility of the Thing in itself, there is always a gaping hole in (constituted, phenomenal) reality, reality is never "all," its circle is never closed, and this void of the inaccessible Thing is filled out with phantasmagorias through which the transphenomenal Thing enters the stage of phenomenal presence—in short, prior to the Kantian turn, there can be no black hulk at the background of the stage. It was, of course, well before Kant that philosophers doubted the capacity of man to know the Infinite and affirmed that we can only conjecture the Infinite by means of improper metaphors. Yet Kant adds to it the crucial twist: man's finitude is not the simple finitude of an inner-worldly entity lost in the overwhelming totality of the universe. The knowing subject is a substanceless point of pure self-relating (the "I think") which is *not* "part of the world" but is, on the contrary, correlative to "world" as such and therefore *ontologically constitutive*: "world," "reality," as we know them, can appear only within the horizon of the subject's finitude. The black space of the Thing in itself is therefore something extremely dangerous to approach—if one gets too close to it, "world" itself loses its ontological consistency, like the anamorphotic stain on Holbein's *Ambassadors*: when we shift our perspective and perceive it "as it is" (as a skull), *all remaining reality loses its consistency and turns into an amorphous stain.*

The subject is the nonsubstance, he exists only as nonsubstantial self-relating which maintains its distance from inner-worldly objects; yet in monsters, this subject encounters the Thing which is his impossible equivalent—*the monster is the subject himself, conceived as Thing.* Therein consists the paradox of the Lacanian mathem $ *a*: what we have here is not the relationship of two entities but rather the two sides, the two "slopes," of one and the same entity. The subject is "the same" as the Thing, he is so to speak its negative (the trace of its absence) within the symbolic network—Lacan's obsession with topological models of the "folded" space in the last years of his teaching (the Moebius band, the inverted 8, etc.) attests to his effort to articulate clearly this folding back wherein the subject encounters its own reverse. Hegel radicalized Kant by conceiving the void of the Thing (its inaccessibility) as equivalent to the very negativity that defines the subject; the place where phantasmagorical monsters emerge is thus identified as the void of the pure Self: "This night, the inner of nature, that exists here—pure self—in phantasmagorical presentations, is night all around it, here shoots a bloody head—there another white shape, suddenly before it, and just so disappears."[39]

From here, one can return to *Scream* for the last time: the standard modernist reading which conceives it as the manifestation of a monadic subject, desperate at his inability to establish contact with the world, condemned to solipsistic void, etc., falls short insofar as it continues to conceive the subject as substance, as a positive entity whose adequate expression is hindered. We enter postmodernism the moment we get rid of this perspective illusion: what appears, within modernism, as the limit impeding the subject's self-expression, is actually *the subject himself*.[40] In other words, we enter postmodernism when we pass from the "emptied subject" to the subject *qua* the emptiness of substance (homologous to the reversal from the matter *qua* substance which curves space into matter *qua* the curvature of space in the theory of relativity): in its most radical dimension, the "subject" is *nothing but* this dreaded "void"—in *horror vacui*, the subject simply fears himself, his constitutive void.[41] Far from displaying the subject's horror at the prospect of losing himself, the scream is therefore the very gesture by means of which the dimension of subjectivity is inaugurated—(what, through the scream, will become) the subject shrinks from what is "in him more than himself," from the Thing in himself, i.e., he assumes a minimal distance from it.

In this precise sense, subject and object are correlative in Lacanian theory, but in a way which is the reverse of their epistemological correlation in transcendental philosophy. According to the worn-out commonplace, the Lacanian subject is $, a barred and barren, crossed-out subject, its hindrance, its failed status, is constitutive, etc.—what one should add to it is just that *"object" in the Lacanian sense is a name for this inherent impediment, for the "bone in the throat" which hinders the subject's full realization—therefore $ a*. In other words: object is "correlative" to the

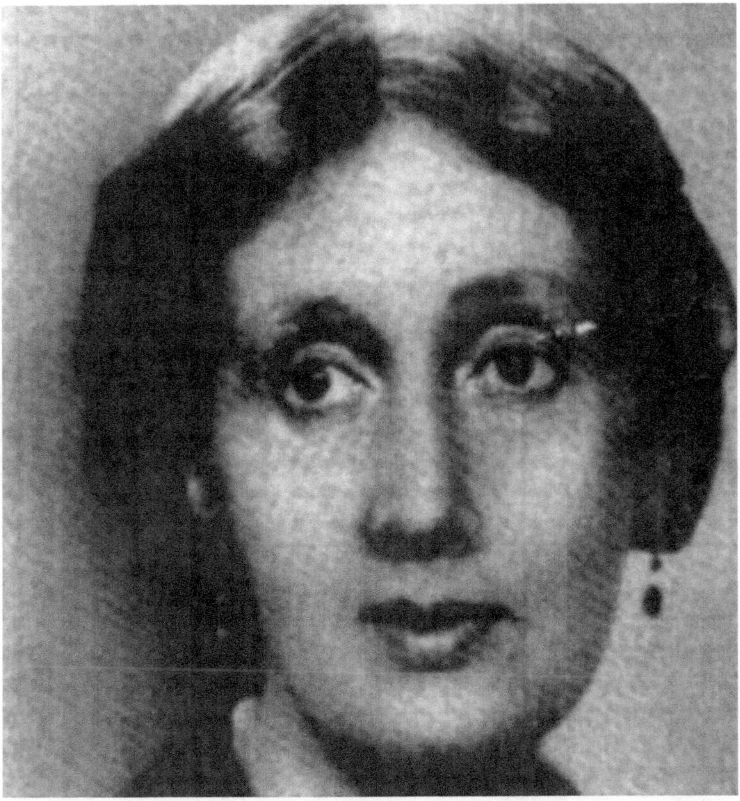

subject *qua* barred, to the very bar that prevents its realization. It is for that reason that, in his Seminar on *Transference* (1960–1961), Lacan renounced the motif of intersubjectivity: what is lost in it is the fact that, to a subject, another subject is first and foremost an *object (a)*, that which prevents him from fully realizing himself, or (the reverse of the same) that which possesses what the subject constitutively lacks—a *Master*, in short. The aim of the analysis is to undermine this illusion: the analyst occupies the place of the Master, but does not "play his role," thereby rendering visible the Master's imposture—the lack always already pertains to the Other itself.[42]

The ultimate "social mediation" of the monster figure is therefore to be sought in the social impact of capital, this terrifying force of "deterritorialization" which dissolves all traditional ("substantial") symbolic links and marks the entire social edifice with an irreducible structural imbalance—it is by no accident that "monsters" appear at every break which announces a new epoch of capital: its rise (Frankenstein, Kaspar Hauser); its transformation into imperialism (the elephant man, the phantom of the opera); today's emergence of the "postindustrial" society (the revival of the motif of the "living dead"). This structural imbalance is inscribed into the very form of anamorphosis, namely in its radical ambiguity: anamorphotic distortions of reality may function as repellent horror, like the forehead protuberance of the "elephant man," yet phallophany may also occasion an effect of sublime beauty. Let us just recall the face of Virginia Woolf: its ethereal, refined sublimity pertains to its anamorphotic extension, as if the reality of her face itself were protracted by a crooked mirror. To ascertain this link between anamorphosis and sublimity, it suffices to "retrench" this face to its "normal" measure by means of a simple computer treatment, i.e., to accomplish an operation homologous to that of reshaping the soft, "melted" watches from Dali's famous painting back into their "normal" contours—what we get is, of course, a "healthy," chubby face without any trace of the unretouched photo's sublimity. The status of sublimity is therefore ultimately that of a "grimace of reality" (as Lacan puts it in *Television*); Lacan's definition of the sublime ("an object elevated to the level of the Thing") could be rendered as "the sublime is an object, a piece of reality, upon which the Real of desire is inscribed by means of an anamorphotic grimace." The boundary that separates beauty from disgust is for that reason far more unstable than it may seem, since it is always contingent on a specific cultural space: the "anamorphotic" torture of the body which can exert such a fascination within some cultural spaces (from the bandaging of female feet in China, the Indo-Chinese tribe whose women put tight rings on their necks in order to protract them, etc., up to *erection* itself, the paradigm of anamorphotic protraction of a piece of reality), can evoke nothing but disgust in a foreign gaze. Have we not thus also delineated the contours of a *postmodern* critique of ideology which instructs us to assume such a foreign gaze upon one's own ideological field, whereby the ideological anamorphosis loses its power of fascination and changes into a disgusting protuberance?

NOTES

1 For a detailed account of this parallel, cf. James Donald, "The Fantastic, the Sublime and the Popular; or, What's at Stake in Vampire Films?" in *Fantasy and the Cinema*, ed. J. Donald (London: British Film Institute, 1989), pp. 233–52.

2 Gaston Leroux, *The Phantom of the Opera* (New York: Hippocrene Books Inc., 1990), p. 12.

3 Ibid.

4 According to Lacan's classical definition, the function of the mask is "to dominate the identifications through which refusals of love are resolved" ("The Meaning of the Phallus," in *Feminine Sexuality: Jacques Lacan and the Ecole Freudienne*, ed. Juliet Mitchell and Jacqueline Rose (New York: Norton, 1985), p. 85; it is therefore not difficult to conceive the Phantom's compulsive mask wearing—another of his features—as a strategy to counter the refusal of maternal love.

5 Cf. Alain Grosrichard, "Le Cas Polyphème ou Un Monstre et sa mère," in *Ornicar?* 11 (pp. 19–36) and 12–13 (pp. 45–57) (Paris: Navarin Editeur, 1977).

6 We allude here to the difference between the two deaths, the real (biological) death and the symbolic death (erasure of symbolic traces). In his seminar on *The Ethic of Psychoanalysis*, Lacan elaborated the notion of the "second (symbolic) death" apropos of the Sadean distinction between the ordinary

crime, which is still a part of the natural cycle of generation and corruption, and the absolute crime, the destruction, the eradication, of this cycle itself. (Cf. chapter 4 of Slavoj Žižek, *The Sublime Object of Ideology* (London and New York: Verso Books, 1989).) The ultimate identity of the second (symbolic) death and the Sadean absolute crime can be exemplified by Immanuel Kant's obsession with the trauma of a judicial process against the king, his sentencing to death (in contrast to the simple regicide in the act of rebellion). That is to say, why is the legal action against the king, his execution, a Sadean absolute crime that no punishment or penitence can recompense? The murder of the king in the act of rebellion undermines the existing legal power, but only at the level of reality—it is simply a part of the process of (social) corruption and generation which leaves intact the symbolic legality. If, on the contrary, after the successful overthrow of the king, we organize a judicial process against him, i.e., against the embodiment and ultimate guarantee of the legal power, we commit the absolute crime: we undermine the legal power, the rule of law, *qua* symbolic institution—which is why, as Kant puts it, legal execution of the king is a "suicide of the state." Or, in Hegelese: this crime cannot be measured by the standards of legality anymore, it is not a simple external negation of legality but its "negation of negation"—it undermines the very standpoint from which one can conceive of an act as "illegal." As to the Kantian notion of the "suicide of the state," cf. chapter 5 of Slavoj Žižek, *For They Know Not What They Do* (London and New York: Verso Books, 1991).

7 There is a piquant detail as to the elephant man's "true story": when the historians examined the sources, they discovered that the myth of his origins has surprising foundations in fact: a local newspaper from his native town contains a small note according to which—precisely in the time of his mother's pregnancy—during a circus parade an elephant went mad and almost trampled down a pregnant woman!

8 As for the concept of the "*voix acousmatique*," cf. Michel Chion, *La Voix au cinema* (Paris: Cahiers du Cinéma, 1982).

9 The opposition of voice and gaze as objects corresponds to the antagonism of the life drive and the death drive: voice vivifies, whereas gaze mortifies.

10 There is, however, a third type of scream which is neither silent nor vocal, but *vocalized with deferral*. We find it, among other examples, toward the end of Coppola's *Godfather* III: it is uttered by Michael Corleone (Al Pacino) on the staircase of Palermo's opera, after a mafia killer shoots his beloved daughter: at first, the scream is silent, in complete silence we witness the desperate opening of his mouth; after a couple of seconds, the sound strikes us with all its force—what is at work here is a kind of self-reflectivity, as if the scream is vocalized at the very moment when the subject perceives, becomes aware of, its silence. As long as the scream remains silent, we float in a kind of "stasis" of time (in the sense this term obtained with Walter Benjamin), the movement is suspended, the hero's entire life is condensed in three images superimposed in the timeless "now" (the murdered daughter; the murdered bride long years ago; the

lost wife); when the scream resounds, Michael finds himself in the place homologous to that of Oedipus at Colonnus: by way of the scream, his "life force" evaporates, Michael is "emptied," his symbolic destiny is fulfilled—what remains of him is an empty shell, a burst soap bubble, a pure leftover of the Real. It is therefore quite consistent that this scream is followed by a kind of reverse flashback, a jump into the unspecified future when Michael, a lonely old man on a garden chair, suddenly falls down and drops dead: this utterly void figure drained of life is all that remains of him after the scream . . .

11 Cf. Michel Chion, "Le Quatrième Côte," in *Cahiers du Cinéma* 309 (1980), pp. 5–7.

12 Such a gigantic eye living its own life—i.e., a particular *organ* which mysteriously coincides with the *entire body (organism)*—is perhaps the ultimate psychotic object and at the same time the purest embodiment of the *objet petit a*. Therein consists the uncanny effect of Amfortas' wound in Syberberg's *Parsifal*, of this bleeding piece of human flesh which is carried on a pillow *outside* Amfortas himself, as an external, autonomous, partial object. Roald Dahl's story "William and Mary" relies on the same fantasy matrix: a terminally ill patient accepts to undergo an experimental operation—if the operation succeeds, his brain alone will survive, floating in a special liquid and connected with the outside world through one eye . . .

13 What constitutes "reality" is therefore precisely the *extraction* of this stain of the real which covers up the void of the infinite axis of perspective. This (Lacan's third and last) determination of psychosis supplements the preceeding two—captivation by the image of the double, paradigm of the paranoiac agency; foreclosure of the Name of the Father—and thus closes the series the inherent logic of which follows the triad Imaginary, Symbolic, Real. That is to say, each of these two subsequent determinations retroactively grounds the previous one: the subject is captivated by the image of its double insofar as he lacks the efficiency of the central signifier, the Name of the Father, which enables him to gain distance from imaginary relationship, i.e., to mediate it by its symbolic context; the Name of the Father is ultimately nothing but a designation of the central lack around which the symbolic order is structured, the lack which is opened by the extraction of the surplus stain from the frame of "reality."

14 At this point, one should recall that "The Silent Scream" is also the title of the famous antiabortion pseudodocumentary depicting the fetus's desperate struggle for survival against the abortionist's scissors. Munch's *Scream* provides a kind of advance answer to it: the true horror is not to be plucked out from the maternal womb but to be imprisoned in it.

15 Michel Foucault, *The History of Sexuality, Volume I: An Introduction* (New York: Vintage, 1980), p. 154.

16 What one should do here is "allegorize" Jameson himself, i.e., read his theory of the break between modernism and postmodernism as an allegorical indexing of his own theoretical strategy: on the one hand, his procedure remains within the modern confines of an abstract theoretical scheme (ultimately the

very triad realism, modernism, postmodernism) the function of which is to serve as the frame and pretext for a wealth of particular observations; on the other hand, Jameson's "last horizon" is the postmodern notion of History as Real/Impossible, i.e., the implacable necessity undercutting every attempt to master it, to reduce its contingency to a coherent symbolic narrative.

17 Cf. Abraham Lincoln's famous answer to a request for a special favor: "As President, I have no eyes but constitutional eyes; I cannot see you."

18 Therein consists, according to Lacan, the dissymmetry between Oedipus and Jocaste: Oedipus did not know what he was doing, whereas his mother knew all the time who her sexual partner was—the source of her enjoyment was precisely Oedipus's ignorance. The notorius thesis on the intimate link between feminine enjoyment and ignorance acquires thereby a new, intersubjective dimension: woman enjoys insofar as her *other* (man) does not know.

19 Cf. Michel Silvestre, "Le Père, sa fonction dans la psychanalyse," in *Demain la psychanalyse* (Paris: Navarin Editeur, 1987), pp. 84–111.

20 One is tempted to propose a reading of Charles Vidor's *Gilda* (1946) along these lines: the fundamental libidinal axis of the film is the latent homosexual relationship between Glenn Ford and his corrupted, obscene, paternal double, whereas the role of Gilda, the *femme fatale*, is precisely to induce him to renounce this "sprout of enjoyment" and assume "normal" sexual relationship. In other words, the obscene surplus that derails the "normal" circuit pertains to the "anal father," *not* to the *femme fatale* who is actually an agent of normalization—the title of the famous song from the film should be "Put the Blame on the Anal Father" instead of "Put the Blame on Mame!" Cf. Greg Foster, "Going Straight with *Gilda*," *Qui Parle* 2, vol. 4 (Berkeley: University of California, 1991).

21 The father *qua* Thing is what is originally prohibited, i.e., the part of himself that the subject must renounce in order to become "himself," to attain his symbolic identity. This symbolic universe is, on the other hand, "held together" by the Name of the Father *qua* the agency of prohibition—the agent of the symbolic *prohibition* is therefore precisely the object which was originally *prohibited*.

22 Which is why we prefer the term "anal father" to the usual "primordial father": although they both designate the same entity, "anal father" points in a more appropriate way toward the obscene nature of the father *qua* presymbolic "partial object."

23 As to this ambiguity of the "anal" object, see chapter 3.2 of the present book.

24 The same reversal characterizes the popular-culture figure of the "malefactor," from the ambiguous status of the Hitchcockian malefactor up to Darth Vader in the *Star Wars* trilogy (who, one should not forget it, also wears a mask concealing a distorted, amorphous face, i.e., who also plays the role of "anal father").

25 It is interesting to note how Aldous Huxley (in his screenplay for William Wyler's version of *Pride and Prejudice*) changed the figure of Lady Catherine de Bourgh, adding to it a kind of reflective twist: Lady de Bourgh who, in the novel,

is mocked as thoroughly "evil" and plays the role of the "mediator" enabling the final reunion of Darcy and Elizabeth quite unknowingly, in the film consciously assumes the role of a mischievous old woman in order to test Elizabeth's love for Darcy—in short, she is a donator who purposely assumes the role of a malefactor.

26 Yet one does not need to have recourse to cinematic fiction in order to epitomize this split attitude of the "postmodern" subject—it suffices to recall the mode of presence of the West in Baghdad during the Gulf War: on the one hand, Peter Arnett from CNN reporting live, reduced to a pure gaze, as if he did not speak from down there, i.e., as if he himself were watching the bombing on television; on the other hand the total physical destruction of the country on which more bombs were dropped than on Vietnam . . .

27 Cf. chapter 5 of Žižek, *The Sublime Object of Ideology*.

28 James G. Ballard, *Crash*, "Introduction to the French Edition" (London: Triad/Panther Books, 1975), p. 8. This attitude finds its clearest expression in a series of recent films which stage the paradox of Zhuang Zi and his butterfly: what at first seems to be a dream (or a flashback memory), is retroactively shown to be "reality" itself, and *vice versa*, as in Adrian Lyne's *Jacob's Ladder* at the very end of which the perspective of its hero, a Vietnam veteran persecuted by old war nightmares, is reversed: the only "present" is Vietnam itself, scenes from America are nothing but the hero's deathbed delusions . . .

29 On a more general level, the very succession of three modalities in the staging of Wagner's musical dramas in Bayreuth epitomizes the Jamesonian triad *realism, modernism, postmodernism*. Modernism is of course the mark of the so-called "neo-Bayreuth" in the early 1950s when Wieland Wagner threw off "realistic" swords, helms, and similar "Nordic" *bric-à-brac*, and imposed abstract ascetism: the empty stage with just some barren symbols on it, singers in white tunics, the interplay of light and darkness as the main generator of visual dramatic tensions (the use of strong reflectors). Post-modernism's main exponent was, on the other hand, Patrice Chereau in his legendary staging of the *Ring* in 1976–1980: the return to the wealth of "realistic" details (including live horses in the first year of *Walküre*), yet within the "hyperrealist" frame which suspends their "veracity" and posits them as moments of a nightmarish "psychic reality."

30 This background also enables us to locate the fantasy power of the image of a "ghost ship" roving alone in the sea like a black stain, as in Alistair Maclean's adventure thriller *The Wreck of Mary Deare*: is not the captain found by the rescuers in the abandoned ship a new figuration of the Flying Dutchman?

31 Cf. Stephen Jay Gould, "Adam's Navel," in *The Flamingo's Smile* (Harmondsworth: Penguin Books, 1985). Incidentally, therein consisted Friedrich Engels's mistake in his *Origins of the Family, State and Private Property*: he mistook the "punalua" family (all brothers in clan A married to all sisters in clan B, its counterpart), an ideological "fossil" fabricated by the recent Indian society, for an effective past form of family.

32 Georg Lukacs articulated a homologous shift apropos of Walter Scott's *Waverly*: from the perspective of "civil society," the romantic outcast is suddenly perceived as a common criminal.

33 Fredric Jameson, *Postmodernism, or, The Cultural Logic of Late Capitalism* (Durham: Duke University Press, 1991), p. 382. Let us just recall how he exerts his power within the Opera: he takes revenge on the new director for giving preference to commercial over artistic considerations, i.e., he endeavors to impede the Opera's utilitarian commercialization.

34 Fredric Jameson, *Signatures of the Visible* (New York: Routledge, 1990), pp. 26–27.

35 Let us just recall, from the ideological domain proper, the way Juan Péron "held together" the movement that bears his name: Péronism was a profoundly heterogeneous movement, there was place in it for leftist trade unionism as well as for aristocratic militarism; Péron functioned as a Name which did not reduce this heterogeneity but simply contained it as in an empty vessel—the unity of Péronism was rendered possible by the fact that all its currents recognized themselves in a common *signifier*.

36 Cf. *Ich möchte ein solcher werden wie . . . Materialien zur Sprachlosigkeit des Kaspar Hauser*, ed. Jochen Hoerisch (Frankfurt: Suhrkamp Verlag, 1979).

37 This inversion of the metaphor of the child and the dirty water enables us also to determine succinctly the opposition between Lacanian psychoanalysis and its ego-psychology version. In the latter, the aim of the analytical cure is to get rid of the dirty water (symptoms, pathological tics, etc., i.e., everything that appears as a disturbance) in order to keep the child (ego) as unspoiled as possible, cleansed of all dark spots, whereas the aim of the Lacanian cure is to throw out the child (to suspend the analysand's ego), so that the analysand is confronted with his "dirty water," with symptoms and fantasies which organize his/her enjoyment. In other words, is not the strategy of the so-called "free associations" in the psychoanalytical cure precisely to suspend the function of the ego, so that, once its control diminishes, the "dirt" of the analysand's enjoyment comes to light?

38 As to this prohibition, cf. chapter 5 of Žiěk, *For They Know Not What They Do*.

39 Quoted from D. Ph. Verene, *Hegel's Recollection* (Albany: State University of New York Press, 1985), pp. 7–8.

40 As to this notion of the subject, cf. Joan Copjec, "The Orthopsychic Subject: Film Theory and the Reception of Lacan," in *October* 49 (Cambridge, Mass.: MIT Press, 1989), pp. 53–72.

41 When the borderline theorists (Otto Kernberg *et al.*) deplore the notorious "feeling of emptiness" as the major complaint of today's patients, a Lacanian should therefore recognize in this "emptiness" *another name for the subject*: we encounter the subject at the very point at which the "self" is cleared of its content.

42 The Master's illusion is therefore *stricto sensu* "transcendental": a Master is somebody who feigns to possess the unfathomable *je ne sais quoi*, the

noumenal Thing beyond positive phenomenal qualities. The fundamental gesture of Kant's transcendental turn is precisely to forbid to whomever to act in this way: the Thing remains inaccessible forever. If, as Lacan puts it, philosophy is the reappropriation of knowledge by the Master and as such a version of the discourse of the Master (cf. his *Séminaire XVII: L'envers de la psychanalyse* (Paris: Editions du Seuil, 1991)), Kant's "transcendental turn" cuts this link between philosophy and the discourse of the Master: transcendental philosophy "changes the register" to the discourse of the hysteric.

5

WHY ARE THERE ALWAYS TWO *FATHERS*?

5.1 AT THE ORIGINS OF *NOIR*: THE HUMILIATED FATHER

The paranoiac Other

In today's popular culture, there are two phenomena which exert an everlasting power of fascination on so-called "postmodern" theory: Alfred Hitchcock and *film noir*. Yet in the two cases, the fascination works in a wholly different way: Hitchcock's *oeuvre* unleashes a flood of interpretations, for the most part mutually exclusive (psychoanalytic, hermeneutic, deconstructivist, feminist, religious, semiotic, and so on), a wealth of ingenious interpretive moves which endeavor to turn into successes even his obvious failures,[1] whereas the first feature that strikes the eye apropos of the texts on *film noir* is their unusual theoretical poverty and uniformity. That is to say, the bulk of what is being written on *film noir* consists of cliché-ridden variations on its visual style (the influence of German expressionism: the interplay of lights and shadows, the unusual angles, and so on); on its narrative procedures (flashback, voiceover, etc.); on its social background (the corruption of the American megalopolis; the social impact of the Second World War; the emancipation of women as the basis of the *femme fatale* figure which gives expression to the instability of the male identity); on the *noir* existential vision (inexorable fate and its paradoxical interconnection with freedom, e.g.); etc.[2] The will to put into words the obvious fascination with *film noir*, to translate it into positive theoretical accomplishments, seems somehow inherently hindered, doomed to fail: as if the opposition Hitchcock/*film noir* repeats the classic Lacanian opposition of the symptom which gives rise to interpretations and the fantasy which blocks them. Instead of deploring the weaknesses of writings on *film noir*, instead of directly trying to supplant them with a new, better theory, our first step should therefore be a kind of "metacommentary" which elucidates the very opposition of Hitchcock and *film noir*.

One of the quintessential Hitchcockian scenes is the hero's "solitude in the crowd": the hero and his adversary exchange blows in full view of an ignorant public which does not (and should not) know the true stakes of the confrontation; both have to confine their moves to what fits the frame of the publicly admissible. The three versions of this scene are, of course, the political rally in *The Thirty-Nine Steps* (1934), the charity ball in *Saboteur* (1942), and the auction in *North by Northwest* (1959): in the latter, Cary Grant causes a public scandal in order to be taken away by the police and thus elude the grasp of Russian spies who control the building; the spies can only observe the spectacle passively, since any open action of theirs would alert the ignorant public. We have here three gazes, three subjective positions: the actant who makes a move; his opponent against whom this move is intended, who clearly recognizes its meaning, yet who can only observe it helplessly; and the ignorant Other, the public present.[3] The crucial feature, the structural condition, of this interplay is the *benevolent ignorance of the Other*: the Other epitomizes public opinion in its inherent innocence, and it is due to this innocence that the three scenes function as comic interludes.

Yet let us recall the final scene of *Notorious* (1946): Devlin elopes with the poisoned Alicia from Sebastian's house in full view of the latter's Nazi collaborators. What we have here is a homologous underlying structure of the three gazes, of the three subjective positions: the ignorant Other is here the members of the Nazi ring who do not know that Alicia is an American spy and that Sebastian knows it (the reason why he is slowly poisoning her with his mother's help); the actants are Devlin and Alicia—Devlin escorts her down the staircase, posing as her friend who will take her to the hospital, with Sebastian's agreement; the helpless opponents are Sebastian and his mother, reduced to the role of passive observers—although Devlin's act is directed against them, any public countermove of theirs would instantly reveal to the members of the Nazi gang present that Alicia is an American spy and that Sebastian knows it, whereby Sebastian would sign his death warrant. What makes this scene different from the three above-mentioned comic interludes is the character of the third agency, the ignorant big Other, the public which witnesses the duel of the actant and his opponent: the Other loses here its benevolent innocence and assumes features of a threatening paranoiac agency. Those who range *Notorious* among the few Hitchcock's films which display *noir* sensibility are therefore in the right: one of the features which characterize the *noir* universe is precisely this mutation in the status of the big Other.

This changed vision of the universe enables us to define the gap that separates the classical (logic-and-deduction) detective novel from the hard-boiled novel.[4] That is to say, the logic-and-deduction novel still relies on the consistent big Other: the moment, at the novel's end, when the flow of events is integrated into the symbolic universe, narrativized, told in the form of a linear story (the last pages of the novel when, upon identifying the murderer, the detective reconstructs the true course of events), brings about an effect of pacification, order and consistency are reinstated, whereas the *noir* universe is characterized by a radical split, a kind of structural imbalance, as to the possibility of narrativization: the integration of the subject's position into the field of the big Other, the narrativization of his fate, becomes possible only when the subject is in a sense already dead, although still alive, when "the game is already over," in short: when the subject finds himself at the place baptized by Lacan "the in-between-two-deaths" (*l'entre-deux-morts*).[5] Here, we have only to recall Rudolph Mate's *DOA* (1949): the hero is notified by the doctor that he has been mortally poisoned and has only a day or two to live; he spends his remaining time in a frenetic search for his own murderer, i.e., in reconstructing the story which led to his murder.[6] Insofar as the subject does not assume this stature of the "living dead," every attempt at narrativization, at the integration of his fate into the symbolic texture, is by definition lethal: a deadly menace looms over his endeavor to "tell the entire story" about himself. The putting into words does not bring about pacification, reconciliation with one's symbolic community (as in the classical detective novel), but rather gives rise to a mortal danger. Among the numerous cases of it, here are the four most eloquent:

1) *The Big Clock* (1947, John Farrow). What confers on this story its *noir* character? Ray Milland, an investigative journalist, is hired by a corrupted press tycoon (Charles Laughton) to identify the unknown individual who secretly left the house of a murdered girl the previous evening and is thus the prime suspect; what only the journalist knows is that this unknown individual is none other than *himself*—he is thereby forced to set in motion the investigative machinery which, sooner or later, will point its finger at him. The *noir* flavor pertains to this position of the subject who can only observe helplessly how the trap set by the investigative—i.e., discursive—machinery, nominally led by himself, tightens around him . . .

2) *Sorry, Wrong Number* (1948, Anatole Litvak), is the story of an arrogant rich woman, tied to bed because of her paralytic legs, who accidentally overhears a phone conversation about a planned murder; she sets out to investigate the affair and, after a whole day of phoning, finally establishes that the victim of the intended murder is herself—too late, since the murderer is already on the way . . . The film is a textbook example of the Lacanian thesis on how the subject's truth is constituted by the discourse of the Other: the narratrice gradually puts all the pieces together and (re)constructs the events, realizing that she was unknowingly the central piece of an intricate plot—in short, she finds her truth outside herself, in the intersubjective network whose effects elude her grasp.

3) *The Window* (1949, Ted Tetzlaff). This is an exemplary case of what Gilles Deleuze calls "*le flagrant délit de légender*,"[7] the story of a boy, inclined to inventing stories, who one night witnesses an actual murder taking place in the neighboring apartment. When he reports on it to his parents, they naturally take it for another of his fantasies and, as a punishment, force him to tell the neighbors what lies he was divulging about them; the neighbors thus learn that the boy is a dangerous witness and set to kill him when the parents leave him alone in the apartment for a weekend . . .

4) Orson Welles's *Mr. Arkadin* (or *Confidential Report*, 1955), the story of

an immensely rich man who, feigning amnesia, hires a journalist to unearth details about his past. Step by step, the journalist reconstructs the truth, a dark story of murder, betrayal, and fraud, yet all witnesses of Arkadin's past whom the journalist contacted are soon afterward found dead. Finally, the journalist grasps the true aim of his research: Arkadin hired him to locate all remaining witnesses to his criminal past—by disposing of them and, in the end, of the journalist himself, his past would be buried forever . . . The irony of it, of course, is that remembrance (unearthing of the truth about the past) is here directly in the service of oblivion—and is not this story also a succinct metaphor of a capitalism characterized (as one knows from Marx onward) by a structural asymmetry between synchrony and diachrony: it can establish itself as a synchronous totality only by effacing the traces of its traumatic diachronous past?

What do these (as well as numerous other) examples have in common? The intersubjective, "public" symbolic space has lost its innocence: narrativization, integration into the symbolic order, into the big Other, opens up a mortal threat, far from leading to any kind of reconciliation.[8] What one should bear in mind here is that this *neutrality* of the symbolic order functions as the ultimate guarantee for the so-called "*sense of reality*": as soon as this neutrality is smeared, "external reality" itself loses the self-evident character of something present "out there" and begins to vacillate, i.e., is experienced as delimited by an invisible frame: the paranoia of the *noir* universe is primarily visual, based upon the suspicion that our vision of reality is always already distorted by some invisible frame behind our backs—which is why Edward Hopper should also be included among the *noir* auteurs. What we have in mind here is neither the fact that, prior to his fame, Hopper earned his living by drawing cover designs for hard-boiled pulp novels, nor the fact that a lot of his drawings, above all his etchings (*Night Shadows* (1921), for example), contain motifs which evoke the *noir* universe (the play of shadows, strange point-of-view angles, lone scenes from the nocturnal megalopolis, and so on). The case is somewhat more refined: it concerns primarily the way the *frame* operates in his paintings (taking into account the fundamental ambiguity of this term in the *noir* universe).

That is to say, it is as if, in his paintings, the frame "unglued," came off, extended, or contracted with regard to its actual boundaries. On the one hand, his paintings enforce the idea of spaces and elements beyond the limits of the scene itself, as if envisageing a wider field than the sphere the picture can surround. Apropos of Hopper's paintings, Pascal Bonitzer spoke about "a semblance of off-field" ("*un semblant de hors-champ*"): Hopper's paintings function as fragments in the interplay of *champ* and *hors-champ*, they always refer to an external, absent supplement; as Bonitzer points out, this effect of "contingent and nomadic framing" is possible only against the background of cinema, i.e., it presents the way painting reflected the advent of cinema, the fact that the "moving camera" captures a reality which is in itself contingent and ultimately meaningless.[9] On the other hand, there is the opposite effect of the contracted frame; what we have in mind here is the fact, noted by numerous art historians, that Hopper's paintings render visible the interior and the exterior of a building simultaneously (say, an illuminated room with a lonely person, seen from outside, through the window of an otherwise dark house)—far from being suspended, their antagonistic tension is thereby staged as such. Even when the "official" content of a painting is limited to the interior, it seems as if the depicted scene is viewed through an invisible window which enframes it. Suffice it to recall his *Office at Night* (1940): although the "official" point of view is internal to the illuminated office (close to its ceiling), one cannot elude the effect that an invisible (window) frame separates us from the interior of the office (an effect confirmed by the sketches for this painting where the traces of a window frame are clearly discernible). On a thematic level, the *hors-champ* effect manifests itself in Hopper's two constant motifs:

- a woman or a couple whose gaze is transfixed on some point external to the painting (in Hopper, the couple never looks straight into each other's eyes—a kind of visual equivalent to the "modernist" couples in Marguerite Duras's novels who can find love only by concentrating on some external task—the search for a third person, e.g.);
- the limitation of the depicted content to a fragmentary reflection of an external source of light (the illuminated part of the room close to the open window, for example).

The inscription of the frame into the picture, on the other hand, makes itself palpable in Hopper's obsession with the motif of the window *qua* boundary and link between the interior and the exterior. This surplus/lack of the frame with regard to the actual sphere of the painting introduces an inherent *instability of vision*: the effect obtained is that what we see is always a fragment—the crucial X always eludes us, our vision is always "framed," by definition, it implies a minimal "*Realitätsverlust*," "loss of reality."

"Woman as the symptom of man" revisited

Where are we to look for the key to this shift, to this disturbance in the "big Other" which causes the loss of reality? In the *noir* universe is evil not epitomized by the *femme fatale* who poses a threat not only to the hero's moral integrity, but to his very ontological identity? Is the axis of the *noir* universe not therefore to be sought in the relationship of the male detective to the woman *qua* his *symptom*?

"Woman is a symptom of man" seems to be one of the most notoriously "antifeminist" theses of the late Lacan. There is, however, a fundamental ambiguity as to how we are to read it: this ambiguity reflects the shift in the notion of the symptom within the Lacanian theory.[10] If we conceive the symptom as it was articulated by Lacan in the 1950s—namely as a *cyphered message*—then, of course, woman-symptom appears as the sign, the embodiment of man's fall, attesting to the fact that man "gave way as to his desire." For Freud, the symptom is a compromise formation: in the symptom, the subject gets back, in the form of a cyphered, unrecognized message, the truth about his desire, the truth that he was not able to confront, that he betrayed. So, if we read the thesis of "woman as a symptom of man" against this background, we inevitably approach the position that was most forcefully articulated by Otto Weininger, Freud's contemporary, a notorious Viennese antifeminist and anti-Semite from the turn of the century, who wrote the extremely influential bestseller *Sex and Character*[11] and then commited suicide at the age of twenty-four. Weininger's position is that, according to her very ontological status, woman is nothing but a materialization, an embodiment of man's sin: in herself, she doesn't exist, which is why the proper way to get rid of her is not to fight her actively or to destroy her—it is enough for man to purify his desire, to rise to pure spirituality, and, automatically, woman loses the ground under her feet, disintegrates. Note here Richard Wagner's *Parsifal*, the basic reference of Weininger: when Parsifal purifies his desire and rejects Kundry, she loses her speech, changes into a mute shadow and finally drops dead—she existed only insofar as she attracted the male gaze. Here, it would be possible to articulate a general theory of the "Wagnerian performative": when, at the end of *The Flying Dutchman*, the offended unknown captain publicly announces that he is the "flying Dutchman" wandering around oceans for centuries in search of a faithful wife, Senta throws herself from a cliff to her death; in *Lohengrin*, after the mysterious knight reveals his true identity in the Grail narrative (". . . *ich bin Lohengrin genannt!*"), the unfortunate Elsa collapses ("*Mir schwankt das Boden! Luft!*"); when, at the end of *Parsifal*, Parsifal takes over the ritual function of the king and reveals the Grail, Kundry drops dead . . . In all three cases, the performative gesture by means of which the hero openly assumes his symbolic mandate, reveals his symbolic identity, proves incompatible with the very being of woman.[12]

This tradition, which may appear extravagant and outdated, reemerges precisely in *film noir* where the *femme fatale* also changes into a formless, mucous slime without proper ontological consistency the moment the hard-boiled hero rejects her, i.e., breaks her spell upon him—witness the final confrontation of Sam Spade with Brigid O'Shaughnessy in Hammett's *Maltese Falcon*. We have thus the male world of pure spirituality and undistorted communication, communication without constraint (if we may be permitted to use this Habermasian syntagm), the universe of ideal intersubjectivity, and woman is *not* an external, active cause which lures man into a fall—she is just a *consequence*, a result, a materialization of man's fall. So, when man purifies his desire of the pathological remainders, woman disintegrates in precisely the same way a symptom dissolves after successful interpretation, after we have symbolized its repressed meaning. Does not Lacan's other notorious thesis—the claim that "woman doesn't exist"—point in the same direction? Woman doesn't exist in herself, as a positive entity with full ontological consistency, but only as a symptom of man. Weininger was also quite outspoken about the desire compromised, betrayed when man falls prey to a woman: the death drive; after all the talk about man's superior spirituality, inaccessible to woman, and so on, he proposes, in the last pages of *Sex and Character*, collective suicide as the only path of salvation for humanity.

If, however, we conceive the symptom as it was articulated in Lacan's last writings and seminars—as, for example, when he speaks about "Joyce the symptom"—namely as a particular signifying formation which confers on the subject its very ontological consistency, enabling it to structure its basic, constitutive relationship to *enjoyment* (*jouissance*), then the entire relationship is reversed: if the symptom is dissolved, the subject itself loses the ground under his feet, disintegrates. In this sense, "woman is a symptom of man" means that *man himself exists only through woman qua his symptom*: all his ontological consistency hangs on, is suspended from his symptom, is "externalized" in his symptom. In other words, man literally *ex-sists*: his entire being lies "out there," in woman. Woman, on the other hand, does *not* exist, she *insists*, which is why she does not come to be through man only—there is something in her that escapes the relation to man, the reference to the phallic signifier; and, as is well known, Lacan attempted to capture this excess by the notion of a "*not-all*" *feminine jouissance*. In this way, the relationship to the death drive is also reversed: woman, taken "in herself," outside the relation to man, embodies the death drive, apprehended as a radical, most elementary ethical attitude of uncompromising insistence, of "not giving way as to . . ." Woman is therefore no longer conceived as fundamentally "passive" in contrast to male activity: the act as such, in its most fundamental dimension, is "feminine." Is not the act *par excellence* Antigone's act, her act of defiance, of resistance? The suicidal dimension of this act is self-evident, so that when Lacan says, in another provocative statement, that the only act which is not a failure, the only act *stricto sensu*, is suicide, he thereby reconfirms the "feminine" nature of act as such: men are "active," they take refuge in relentless activity in order to escape the proper dimension of the act. The retreat of man from woman (the retreat of the hard-boiled detective from the *femme fatale* in *film noir*, for example), is thus effectively a retreat from the death drive as a radical ethical stance: we are now at the exact opposite of Weininger's image of woman as incapable of a proper ethical attitude.[13]

From Ned Beaumont to Philip Marlowe

This answer, however, cannot be considered satisfactory: the *femme fatale* *qua* embodiment of the universe's corruption is clearly a male fantasy, she materializes its inner antagonisms, which is why she cannot be made into the *cause* of the "loss of reality," of the paranoiac mutation of the Other. Consequently, we have to return to our initial question: "What change had to befall the symbolic order, so that woman finds herself occupying the place of a traumatic Thing?" As we know from Lacanian psychoanalysis, the ultimate guarantor of the "neutral" stature of the symbolic Law within the subjective economy is the father *qua* symbolic function, the Name of the Father, what Lacan calls the "paternal metaphor": Master Signifier, the "empty" signifier without a signified. The Law which is "in running order" is by definition "blind," ignorant, raised above particular passions: a community is ultimately held together through a signifier which "means everything" insofar as it does not mean anything in particular and thereby enables everyone to recognize himself/herself in it.[14] For that reason, our next step should be to look for eventual mutations in the stature of the paternal function. The proper place to begin is the very beginning, more precisely: the point just prior to it, the ultimate stage of the "prehistory" of the hard-boiled novel where things are still visible which, a moment later, will become invisible—not Chandler, but Hammett.

In the glare of Chandler's everlasting glory, Dashiell Hammett is today somehow forgotten: all attempts at a revival by way of pocket-book reprints of his novels, of new biographies, etc., seem doomed to fail. In view of this persistent failure, one is tempted to risk the hypothesis that its ultimate reason is not the lower quality of Hammett's writing but a structural break between his and a fully established *noir* universe. There is obviously something in the inherent logic of Hammett's work that resists serialization: his five novels are five *hapaxes*, each of them is unique. It did set off a series, but with *other* writers (*Red Harvest* opened up a series on a recluse detective who intervenes in a town devastated by the war of rival gangs; after cleansing the town by pitting one gang against another, he leaves alone as he came—a series which runs across genre boundaries from Akira Kurosawa's

Yojimbo to Sergio Leone's *For a Fistful of Dollars*; *The Dain Curse* opened up a series of detective novels in which the source of evil operates under the guise of obscure religious cults; *The Maltese Falcon* combined the detective novel with the formula of the "search for the lost treasure"; *The Glass Key* gave the detective story a flavor of "corrupted politics"; *The Thin Man* inscribed the detective novel into the tradition of high-circle "comedies of manners"). Upon exhausting this matrix of combinations, Hammett simply ceased to write—a gesture almost unique in its radicality.

For that reason, and in spite of the fact that in most of his stories and in two of his novels the same nameless private eye appears ("Continental Op"), Hammett's narrative universe is the very opposite of Chandler's, in which the private eye's subjective point of view offers to the reader a recurrent point of identification. This—as well as the fact that Hammett sticks to the third-person narrative, whereas Chandler's universe is unthinkable without the first-person narrative—indicates clearly the locus of their divergence: the status of the detective. Chandler himself, on praising Hammett for introducing into the detective novel the reality of "mean streets," qualifies his panegyric with "But all this (and Hammett too) is for me not quite enough": "But down these mean streets a man must go who is not himself mean, who is neither tarnished nor afraid. The detective in this kind of story must be such a man. He is the hero, he is everything. He must be a complete man and a common man and yet an unusual man. . . ."[15] In short, what Hammett's detective lacks is precisely the dimension of imaginary identification, of the ideal ego, of an image in which the detective can "see himself as likeable to himself" (a *bricolage* of contradictory features which define the impossible ideal: common, yet unusual; loser, yet successful; cynic, yet believing in justice).

Let us take Hammett's masterpiece, *The Glass Key*: in what consists the difference between Ned Beaumont, its principal character, and Philip Marlowe? Marlowe is a cynical romantic, full of wisecracks, inviting the reader to identify with his subjective perspective, whereas Beaumont is somehow "empty," a kind of blank page: his "inner self-experience" remains totally inaccessible. (The very style of *The Glass Key* is "ascetic," limited to a scarce designation of external objects and gestures, avoiding even evocative predicates.) The crucial point is, however, that this blank fulfills a precise and necessary function, since the novel's central libidinal tension hangs on it: Ned agrees to collaborate with the gang in conflict with Paul Madvig, his boss and paternal figure, yet he ultimately returns to Paul and organizes his victory, and *The Glass Key* in its entirety pivots on the following question: when Ned consented to collaborate with the enemy, did he really betray Paul or was it all a kind of squared double cross devised to obtain the much-needed information on the enemy plans? Because of Ned's "blank," this question remains forever without answer, undecided.

In contrast to Ned's "introverted," inhibited attitude, Paul Madvig epitomizes the obscene-licentious display of power.[16] Thereby, we have reached the looked-for mutation in the paternal figure: instead of the traditional father—guarantor of the rule of Law, i.e., the father who exerts his power as fundamentally *absent*, whose fundamental feature is not an open display of power but the threat of potential power—we obtain an excessively *present* father who, as such, cannot be reduced to the bearer of a symbolic function. Ned's "blank," his inhibitory attitude, is therefore *stricto sensu* a reaction to the excessive presence of the obscene father: this presence sets off a compulsion to forsake, even betray, the father, to turn against him by putting to trial his power. The betrayal of the father is a desperate attempt to test his (im)potence, sustained by a contradictory desire: a desire to catch him in his impotence, to denounce his imposture, yet simultaneously a desire to see him undergo successfully the ordeal and thus belie our doubt.[17]

This figure of the "other father"—the obscene, uncanny, shadowy double of the Name of the Father—emerged for the first time in all its force in the novels of Joseph Conrad; what we have in mind here, of course, are figures like Kurtz in *Heart of Darkness* or Mister Brown in *Lord Jim*. In the midst of the African jungle, in the very "heart of darkness," the hero—whose name is again Marlow, yet without the last *e*—encounters Kurtz, a kind of "master of enjoyment," a paternal figure which comes closest to the impossible representation of what Kant called "radical evil," evilness *qua* ethical attitude, *qua* pure spirituality. This father is distinguished by a series of features: he is all-powerful and cruel to the utmost, an absolute Master for whom there are no limits; yet, simultaneously, he possesses an insight into the very kernel of our (subject's) being, our desire has no secret for him, he knows we are here to kill him and is resigned to it (in Coppola's *Apocalypse Now*, based upon *The Heart of Darkness*, Kurtz (Brando) knows that Martin Sheen has come to kill him and, in effect, comes forward, submits himself to his fate). Perhaps, the contemporaneousness of these works with the moment when, in *Totem and Taboo*, Freud proposed his theory on the "primordial father," is not a mere external coincidence: one is tempted to say that Conrad depicted what remained hidden to Freud (insofar as we read him on the level of what he explicitly said, at least)—the fact, namely, that the "primordial father" is not a primitive figure of pure, presymbolic, brute force, but a *father who knows*. The ultimate secret of the parricide is that the father knows the son has come to kill him and accepts his death obediently. In his interpretation of *Hamlet*, Lacan pointed out the crucial fact that, in contrast to Oedipus (who does not know what he is doing), Hamlet's father *knows* what befell him and who is the murderer—it is precisely on account of this knowledge that the father returns in the guise of a ghost and charges Hamlet with revenge. This knowledge concerns a dark, licentious side of the father-king who is otherwise presented as an ideal figure: he was murdered in full blossom of his sins . . . It is therefore a very special kind of knowledge, a *knowledge of enjoyment*, i.e., the knowledge which is by definition excluded from the Law in its universal-neutral guise: it pertains to the very stature of Law that it is "blind" to this knowledge.

Now we can return to Wagner's *Parsifal*: here, also, the libidinal "center of gravity" of the action, its true axis, is not Parsifal-Kundry, but rather the relationship of Parsifal to Amfortas, the king unable to perform his symbolic-ritual function—he was wounded in the midst of sin and only wants to die (the two Amfortas "laments" are indubitably the opera's highlights). Amfortas, the humiliated, suffering king, and his counteragent, the evil magician Klingsor, himself impotent (castrated), though he dominates Kundry—does not their opposition form a matrix of figures which emerge later in the *noir* universe (Masters who are humiliated because of their attachment to the *femme fatale*; asexual-impotent masters who exert power over the *femme fatale*)? In other words, the allegedly archaic figure of the "primordial father" is actually a thoroughly *modern* entity, a result of the *decline* of the paternal metaphor.[18]

In the very last page of his *Seminar XI*, Lacan says that "any shelter in which may be established a viable, temperate relation of one sex to the other necessitates the intervention—this is what psychoanalysis teaches us—of that medium known as the paternal metaphor."[19] This is what is ultimately at stake in the *noir* universe: the failure of the paternal metaphor (i.e., the emergence of the obscene father who supplants the father living up to his symbolic function) renders impossible a viable, temperate relation with a woman; as a result, woman finds herself occupying the impossible place of the traumatic Thing. The *femme fatale* is nothing but a lure whose fascinating presence masks the true traumatic axis of the *noir* universe, the relationship to the obscene father, i.e., the default of the paternal metaphor—all the usual babble about "latent homosexuality" misses completely the primordial dimension of this relationship.[20]

The crucial point not to be missed here is that the *femme fatale* and the obscene-knowing father cannot appear simultaneously, within the same narrative space: as long as the obscene-knowing father is still present, the woman is not yet fatal, she remains an *object of exchange* between father and son—father *qua* "Master of Enjoyment" disposes of the woman. *The Glass Key* is unique insofar as it renders visible this hidden "genesis" of the *femme fatale*. That is to say, the *femme fatale* (Janet Henry, the senator's daughter, a woman torn between Paul and Ned, loved by both men) is already there, yet in a kind of prenatal state, as that which will become the *femme fatale*—like the hard-boiled detective himself who is also already there, yet lacking "it," his crucial feature, the form of subjectivization that defines him.[21] The last lines of *Glass Key*, after Ned announces to Paul his intention of leaving him together with Janet, are therefore a true antipode to the standard ending of a hard-boiled novel: in contrast to the standard dénouement of the hero's relationship to the *femme fatale* (either his definitive succumbing to her power which ends in a paroxysm of their common death—*Double Indemnity*, *Out of the Past*, etc.—or his repudiation of her which changes her into a mucous slime—*The Maltese Falcon*, e.g.), the (future) *femme fatale* serves here as an instrument to deal the final blow to the paternal figure, turning him into a living wreck:

> Ned Beaumont said: "Janet is going away with me."
>
> Madvig's lips parted. He looked dumbly at Ned Beaumont and as

> he looked the blood went out of his face again. When his face was quite bloodless he mumbled something of which only the word "luck" could be understood, turned clumsily around, went to the door, opened it, and went out, leaving it open behind him.
>
> Janet Henry looked at Ned Beaumont. He stared fixedly at the door.[22]

This interplay of gazes whereby—at the very moment of what, "officially" at least, purports to be a kind of happy ending—Ned does not return the loving gaze, since his gaze remains transfixed on the empty frame of the open door, throws the cards of the happy ending on the table:[23] the couple will "live happily forever," yet at the price of the broken, humiliated, removed father—all that remains after him is the empty frame, the trace of the retracted *objet a* which, by means of its withdrawal, renders possible the stabilization of reality. The price to be paid for the happy ending is thus the radical violation of the symbolic alliance which leaves the Other shattered and for which "betrayal" is all too kind a word. This broken word is the hidden truth concealed by the traditional hard-boiled detective's narcissistic claim for "authenticity." All this suggests the hypothesis that the Hammettian type of hero (whose clearest expression is Ned Beaumont, not Sam Spade or the nameless Continental Op) functions as a kind of *"vanishing mediator" between the classical and the hard-boiled detective*: what emerges for a brief moment in the interspace between the two narcissisms, between the two figures enamored of their own ideal ego (self-admiration of one's own "grey little cells" with the "logic-and deduction" detective; self-admiration of one's "authenticity" with the hard-boiled detective), is a unique figure, "empty" insofar as it lacks imaginary identification—the figure of the *noir* subject prior to his subjectivization.

From Philip Marlowe to Dale Cooper

The "blank," the staying out of imaginary identification, is constitutive for the Hammettian subject: he is able to confront his "repressed," to overcome his indecision and to accomplish the act destined to elucidate his ambiguous relationship with the obscene paternal figure, only at the price of his *aphanisis* (eclipse, blackout). This accounts for one of the fundamental motifs of the *noir* universe, the "loss of memory" which threatens the subject's self-identity: there is always a margin of uncertainty that sticks to the very ontological status of the *noir* subject—is he "truly himself"? Is he not the unconscious tool of an alien force which acts through him? An exemplary case of it is Cornell Woolrich's *Black Curtain*: following a minor street accident, the hero awakens from (what he assumes to have been) a brief spell of unconsciousness and learns that four years have passed; he is totally unaware of what he was doing during this time, yet he soon catches sight of policemen in civil clothes tailing him—he is suspected of murder; so he sets out to discover the truth about himself . . . There is a similar blackout in the very center of *Red Harvest*, Hammett's first novel: a dead-drunk Continental Op falls asleep in the apartment of the local *femme fatale*; on awakening, he finds her at his side with a knife in her back, and for a brief moment, a radical uncertainty springs up—did he himself kill her during his blackout?[24] What, then, is the precise nature of this *aphanisis*? Here, Richard Rorty's reading of Orwell's *1984* can perhaps be of some help: apropos of Winston's breakdown in the hands of O'Brien, his torturer, Rorty points out that people can experience

> the ultimate humiliation of saying to themselves, in retrospect, "Now that I have believed or desired *this*, I can never be what I hoped to be, what I thought I was. The story I have been telling myself about myself . . . no longer makes sense. I no longer have a self to make sense of. There is no world in which I can picture myself as living, because there is no vocabulary in which I can tell a coherent story about myself." For Winston, the sentence he could not utter sincerely and still be able to put himself back together was "Do It to Julia!" and the worst thing in the world happened to be rats. But presumably each of us stands in the same relations to some sentence, and to some thing.[25]

One of the fundamental propositions of Lacanian psychoanalysis is that this sentence or thing which encapsulates the kernel of the subject's being beyond imaginary identifications, is in an irreducible way decentered with regard to the symbolic texture which defines the subject's identity: the subject can confront this extimate kernel only at the price of his temporary *aphanisis*. This is what Lacan's formula of fantasy—$ *a*—designates: the subject's self-erasure in the face of this strange body (belief, desire, proposition) which forms the core of his/her being. In other words, *aphanisis* bears witness to the irreducible discord between the fantasmatic hard core and the texture of symbolic narrative: when I risk confrontation with this hard core, "the story I have been telling myself about myself no longer makes sense," "I no longer have a self to make sense of," or, as Lacan puts it in his *Seminar VIII*, the big Other (the symbolic order) collapses into the small other, *objet petit a*, the fantasy object. The extraction of *objet a* from the field of reality confers on this field its consistency: in *aphanisis*, the *objet a* is no longer extracted, it acquires full presence—in consequence of this, the symbolic texture which constituted my reality disintegrates.

Alan Parker's *Angel Heart*, centered upon this motif of *aphanisis*, is perhaps the key film of the postmodern *noir* renaissance in the 1980s. Its hero is also a pathologically split subject, a private eye (Mickey Rourke) hired by the mysterious Louis Cipher (Robert de Niro) to elucidate the fate of a jazz musician who disappeared years ago; all witnesses contacted by the detective are soon thereafter mysteriously and brutally murdered—the dénouement: Louis Cipher is actually the devil himself (Lucifer) who has hired the detective to "expose himself," since, years ago, the detective exchanged his identity for that of the jazz musician in an occult ritual and then disposed of the witnesses in a state of *aphanisis* . . . The theme of occult rituals which play with supernatural forces is of course a constant of the *noir* universe (first introduced by Hammett in *The Dain Curse*); however, with rare exceptions (among them Cornell Woolrich's *The Night Has a Thousand Eyes*), the supernatural reference turns out to be a mask concealing some mundane greedy plot. *Angel Heart* reverses this relationship: what at first purports to be the standard *noir* probing into a nest of corruption whose roots reach far into the past, suddenly mutates into a tale of the supernatural. The same mutation of the theme of "social corruption" into the "supernatural" is at work in *Twin Peaks*: in spite of periodic "supernatural" hints (whose exact status is unclear: are they ironic or to be taken seriously?), the first half of the series remains a variation (albeit a peculiar one) on the standard *noir* theme of unmasking the corruption that lurks behind the small-town idyllic surface; in the second half, it turns out that the murderer of Laura Palmer (her father) was an unconscious tool of "Bob," the evil spirit which dwells in "Red Lodge."[26]

One should recall here the reproach of Jean Renault, the ultimate embodiment of "mundane" evil, to Dale Cooper: "Before you arrived, life in Twin Peaks went on quietly and smoothly, we were selling drugs, we organized prostitution, everybody was content—once you were here, everything went wrong, the normal run of things was derailed . . ." In short, in Twin Peaks, the logic of unveiling the corruption which lurks under the idyllic surface no longer works, since corruption is already part of this idyllic everyday life. The only thing that can effectively derange the normal circuit is therefore an intervention of pure, saintly innocence (Cooper) whose counterpoint cannot any longer be mundane, social evil, but externalized "supernatural" evil. For that reason, the "human" counteragent to Cooper in the second half of the series, his ex-colleague Wyndom Earle, can only be somebody in search of a contact with the source of this supernatural evil (the "Red Lodge"), and who, furthermore, accomplishes his crimes in an artificial, estheticist way (e.g., clad in chess symbols)—in pure contrast with the brutal, impulsive violence of the hard-boiled novels. The circle is thus in a way closed—that is to say, we all remember Chandler's famous words by means of which he defined the way Hammett pulverized the universe of the classical logic-and-deduction novel: "Hammett gave murder back to the kind of people that commit it for reasons, not just to provide a corpse; and with the means at hand, not with handwrought duelling pistols, curare, and tropical fish."[27] In *Twin Peaks*, Lynch traversed the same path backward: he took murder back from the streets and returned it to the kind of people who do not commit it for (vulgar-acquisitive) reasons, but precisely to provide a corpse in an estheticist game; who do not commit it with the means at hand, but with ancient crossbows and venomous spiders in a cage above the victim's head . . .

In order to conceive the logic of this shift, one has to turn to Kant's *Critique of Judgment*, more precisely, to the difference between the beautiful and the sublime deployed in its first part. What concerns us here is their opposition as to the possibility of representation and/or symbolization: although the suprasensible Idea/Thing cannot be represented in a direct, immediate way, one can represent the Idea "symbolically," in the guise of beauty (in other words, the beautiful is a way to represent to ourselves "analogically" the good in the phenomenal world); what the chaotic shapelessness of sublime phenomena renders visible, on the contrary, is the very *impossibility* of representing the suprasensible Idea/Thing. The sublime thereby reveals itself as something uncannily close to evil: the dimension that announces itself in the sublime chaos (the rough sea, mountain rocks, and so forth) is the very dimension of radical evil, i.e., of an evil whose nature is purely "spiritual," suprasensible, not "pathological." What one should bear in mind here is the asymmetry between good and evil: the fact that "evil is not beautiful" means that it cannot be represented, not even symbolically, in an intermediate way, by means of an analogy, i.e., that it is in a sense more purely "spiritual," more suprasensible than good—radical evil is something so terrible that it is barely conceivable as a pure mental possibility and not in any way representable:

> . . . by means of the sentiment of beauty, we can represent to ourselves in an intermediate, symbolic way our freedom, our destiny which consists in our being free, whereas by means of the sentiment of the sublime, we experience the impossibility of representing to ourselves—although analogically—radical evil, the alterity and the conflict of freedom. Every symbolization of evil externalizes it in its relationship to the subject, while every sublimation of the good exposes us to the danger of mysticism, to the illusion of omnipotence which, in the practical domain, is called the delirium of holiness.[28]

Is not precisely this inversion of the symbolization of good and the sublimation of evil into the symbolization of evil and the sublimation of good which defines the ideological coordinates of the universe of *Twin Peaks*? In it, evil is externalized—it appears as a supernatural, external force which takes possession of the individuals—and, by the same token, symbolized, i.e., posited as an invisible entity which can be represented "analogically," in the guise of the possessed individuals. The reverse of the same operation is the sublimation of the good: the good is epitomized by the saintly Cooper, a mystical dream seer full of what Kant would call metaphysical *Schwärmereien*. In this sense, the figure of Dale Cooper is to be conceived as the final term in the series *Ned Beaumont, Philip Marlowe, Dale Cooper* which designates the three stages of the *noir* hero: the cold, distanced Ned, the romantic, cynical Philip, the "innocent," saintly Dale, to whom correspond the three figures of evil: the obscene-impotent father, the *femme fatale*, the supernatural/externalized impersonal Force.

5.2 DIE VERSAGUNG

The "sacrifice of the sacrifice"

How is our common ideological notion of man's division between profession and woman structured? An exemplary case of it is *Rhapsody* (1954, Charles Vidor), a melodrama about a rich girl (Elizabeth Taylor) who oscillates between her two loves, an arrogant violinist and an emotional pianist. She leaves the violinist when he lets her know that his career as a virtuoso has priority in his life and that she has to subordinate herself to its demands; she disdains the pianist whom she marries out of revenge and drives him to the brink of a breakdown precisely because he neglects his career on account of his blind devotion to her—she returns to him only after he stands the ordeal by proving that he is capable of surviving without her (he performs successfully on his debut although, immediately before it, she let him know she is leaving him for good). This is, then, what "a woman wants" (within this fantasy logic): neither a man to whom his profession means more than she, nor a man who neglects his profession because of her, but a man to whom she means most, more than his profession, yet who, for all that, is prepared to sacrifice her on account of allegiance to his profession.[29]

The point not to be missed here, again, is the necessity of the *repeated* choice. The pianist's first choice (of a woman against his career) is "pathological" in the Kantian sense: a choice between two worldly, contingent, empirical goods (and the same goes for the violinist's choice of career against woman). It is only when the pianist chooses for the second time—i.e., when he chooses to endure the ordeal, to assume the loss of the woman—that his object choice, the woman, loses her "pathological" character and becomes a sublime Thing. At the same time, his profession also acquires a non-"pathological" status: performing becomes for him a "duty for the sake of a duty" precisely insofar as it is *separated* from the Thing, insofar as it implies the integration of its loss. Cheaply melodramatic as it may seem, such an act of renunciation is eminently *modern*: it implies a split—the split between duty (responsibility to one's profession) and the supreme good (the beloved woman)—which defines the modern subject. That is to say, the renunciation assumed by the pianist has the structure of what Freud called *die Versagung*; as Lacan points out, this *Versagung* is not a simple "frustration" but an abjuration which announces a tragic dimension even more devastating than the antique *ate*.

The antique tragedy occurs against the background of fate in the guise of "family curse," i.e., a symbolic debt which, following an initial trespass, is carried over from one generation to another: Oedipus, Eteocles and Polynices, Antigone, etc., are nothing but links in the chain of the Labdaid family curse. This fate operates unconsciously, as a blind, "impulsive" force: individuals fly in the face of fate precisely insofar as it operates behind their backs—the only way for them to preserve their dignity is to assume unreservedly their assigned place in this succession. What we encounter here is the fundamental dimension of the subject's "alienation" in the signifier: without any active guilt or knowledge on his part, the subject contracts a debt which weighs down on him and outlines his fate. Is there anything more horrifying than this? Lacan's answer is: yes, the tragedy of the modern, "new-age" subject. Its presupposition is the Christian principle of the Word: the final outcome of its consummation is that the obscure, "underground," blind machinery of antique fate is expounded, unearthed, brought into the light of day.

What Lacan has in mind here is that Christianity is the religion of revelation. As Hegel points out, in the content revealed by Christ we look in vain for any new elements, for any elements not already contained in the preceding religious tradition—the only thing "revealed" is ultimately *the necessity of revelation itself*. Every religion purports to reveal to humanity the divine truth; yet it is only Christianity which repudiates the idea of some transcendent truth to be revealed—in it, the revealed truth coincides with the act of revelation. Ironically, one is tempted to conceive the Christian revelation as the first formulation of the Freudian maxim *Wo es war, soll ich werden*—where it was (the God-Father who still belongs to the Real), I (Christ) shall become . . . In a way, God *will have been*: he must reveal himself in order to become God. In other words, the inversion of Christianity with regard to Judaism consists in the "reflection into itself" of the split between God and man: this split is reflected into God himself as his own lack. A God which appears to humans as an inaccessible, transcendent Master, as an impenetrable enigma, is in himself a failed God, an enigma also to himself.

For that reason, Christ's death on the cross has quite another significance than the divine self-sacrifice in pagan religions where God's death designates a stage in the cyclic movement of divine expiration and rebirth. If this were also the case in Christianity, the role of the Holy Spirit would become totally incomprehensible: Christ's death would simply announce the insufficient, transitory, ephemeral character of the Incarnation, one would remain within the confines of the pagan notion of a God who, from time to time, incarnates himself and then strips off his incarnation, withdrawing again to his Beyond. In the case of Christianity, however, the death of Christ does not announce the return to the Father but the arrival of the Holy Spirit: God continues to live eternally after his death in the community of believers, in its symbolic ritual. Hegel is thus quite justified in saying that, paradoxically, what expires on the cross is not an ephemeral, transitory incarnation of God but the God of Beyond himself, i.e., the notion of God *qua* inaccessible, transcendent, nonrevealed entity—in other words, the God which belongs to the Real, the antique God. In Christianity, God ceases to be a transcendent entity who incarnates himself in a finite human figure, he becomes a name for this very movement of incarnation/revelation: his existence is purely "performative," an effect of his own relevation in the Word.

In this way, i.e., once fate is transformed into a revealed Word, the possibility is opened up for the subject to acquire a "reflected" distance from fate, to refuse to assume the place assigned to him in the texture of fate. And, according to Lacan, this is what the Freudian *Versagung* ultimately is about: by means of it, we renounce the very symbolic mandate for the sake of which we were prepared to put everything at stake. Therein consists the constitutive, fundamental guilt attested to by the neurotic symptoms which pertain to the very being of what we call "the modern man": the fact that, ultimately, there is no agency in the eyes of which he can be guilty weighs upon him as a redoubled guilt. The "death of God"—another name for this retreat of fate—makes our guilt absolute.

What Lacan says here seems a philosophical commonplace: by means of the reflective distance toward the substantial content, the modern subject disengages himself from the constraints of fate; in contrast to the traditional individual wholly determined by the blind circuit of fate, he "reflects," brings into the light of day, the implicit presuppositions that delineate the contours of his life behind his back—a motif varied by all proponents of modernity up to Habermas. This self-evidence, however, is deeply misleading: what Lacan renders visible is a radical, redoubled, self-referring renunciation by means of which the dimension of subjectivity emerges. The first level is the symbolic pact: the subject identifies the kernel of his being with a symbolic feature to which he is prepared to subordinate his entire life, for the sake of which he is prepared to sacrifice everything—in short, the alienation in the symbolic mandate. The second level consists in sacrificing this sacrifice itself: in a most radical sense, we "break the word," we renounce the symbolic alliance which defines the very kernel of our being—the abyss, the void in which we find ourselves thereby, is what we call "modern-age subjectivity." This void opens up only insofar as, prior to it, we subordinated the entire wealth of our being to the symbolic obligation affected by *Versagung*—in other words, our "betrayal" counts only insofar as we renounce the object of our highest love and devotion; otherwise our act of betrayal is not the "sacrifice of the sacrifice," but simply reinstates the primacy of "pathological" pleasures which we were not prepared to renounce, i.e., to sacrifice for the sake of the symbolic obligation. It is not difficult to discern in these two stages of renunication the duality of alienation and separation that Lacan elaborated later in his *Seminar XI*: the sacrifice of all "pathological" content for the Cause is the alienation in the signifier (in the symbolic mandate), whereas the sacrifice of this mandate itself involves a gesture of separation, of gaining a distance from the symbolic order.

The ultimate example of this sacrifice, of course, is the Stalinist monster trials (a phenomenon contemporary to the rise of the hard-boiled novel): the accused finds himself in an absolute void insofar as he is compelled to authenticate his devotion to the communist cause by confessing his betrayal. In this sense, one could say that the accused who confesses his betrayal of the communist cause is the Cartesian subject at its purest: at the end of the age of modernity, its truth comes to light, reduced to its bare essential. That is to say, Lacan's thesis is here very precise: the Cartesian subject, this substanceless void of the pure *cogito*, constitutes himself by way of such a dreadful "betrayal." It is the paternal metaphor, the Name of the Father, which determines the place of the subject within the symbolic network; consequently, the most elementary form of *Versagung* is the "betrayal of the father": withdrawal from the symbolic pact, from the most fundamental alliance that links us with the father's Name. The subject of psychoanalysis, as Lacan puts it, is the Cartesian subject.

This is, then, how we are to interpret Ned's "blank" in *The Glass Key*: in *Seminar VIII*,[30] Lacan himself conceives the subject-son's *Versagung* as the structural incidence of the emergence of the obscene-knowing father. And the shift from the Hammettian to the Chandlerian subject marks precisely the moment of subjectivization of this "blank" subject of renunciation: certainly, Philip Marlowe is also characterized by a fundamental renunciation (he can fulfill his ethical mission only in the guise of a "loser," i.e., in his corrupted environs, he can only be successful insofar as he remains socially *unrecognized*), yet this renunciation functions as a source of narcissistic satisfaction, as a sign of his "authenticity." The crucial point here, however, is that this shift from the "blank" subject to his subjectivization, to the imaginary identification which fills out the void of the Hammettian subject, is strictly correlative to the shift in the libidinal center of gravity from the obscene father to the *femme fatale*. The word *fatale* is to be taken here as literally as possible—we are again within the confines of destiny, of fate, from which the Hammettian hero disengaged himself. In the classical hard-boiled novel and *film noir*, the *femme fatale* is an agent of (evil) fate: the moment she appears (and these moments of her first appearance are perhaps the most sublime in *film noir*: the entry of Barbara Stanwyck in *Double Indemnity*, of Jane Greer in *Out of the Past*, of Lana Turner in *The Postman Always Rings Twice*, of Yvonne de Carlo in *Criss-Cross*

. . .), the hero's fate is sealed, events take their inexorable course. As a rule, the "blackness," the "*noir*" character of the *noir* universe, is affiliated to this inexorable fate epitomized by the woman-Thing: in her face, the hero can read the foreboding of his future doom. Our thesis, however, is here the exact opposite: the lowest ebb, the point of true horror, is the moment of *Versagung* when the subject finds himself face to face with the groundless abyss of his lack of being. With regard to this moment, the entry of the *femme fatale* already brings a kind of relief, we can take refuge again within "narrative closure": the subject eludes anew the confrontation with his lack of being. In this sense, Lacan's thesis on woman as "one of the Names of the Father" fully applies to the *femme fatale* in the *noir* universe: the function she performs is exactly homologous to that of the Name of the Father, i.e., she renders it possible for the subject to locate himself again within the texture of symbolic fate.

Die Versagung, castration, alienation

It is against the background of this notion of *Versagung* that one has to conceive also the *Verzicht* from the famous verses of Georg Trakl: "*So lern'ich traurig den Verzicht: Kein Ding sei wo das Wort gebricht*" (So sadly I learned renunciation: Where the word breaks up no thing can be) interpreted by Heidegger in *Unterwegs zur Sprache*.[31] We can distinguish three levels, three ways to read them. The first is to conceive of them as a paraphrase of the fundamental thesis of Gadamer's hermeneutics: being "is" only as understood, articulated in language; i.e., language forms the (historically mediated) transcendental horizon of the disclosure of being. However, as was pointed out by Gianni Vattimo,[32] what we get in Gadamer is an "urbanized" (domesticated, "gentrified") Heidegger, a Heidegger purified of disagreeable excesses which do not enter the frame of the academic circuit: he passes over in silence those features of Heidegger's thought which, although they may appear to belong to the mythological register of "blood and soil," actually announce the dimension of the *real*, of what cannot be reduced to the problematic of language *qua* transcendental horizon (*das Ding*, the opposition of sky and earth, etc.). It is precisely in this direction that Heidegger's reading of Trakl's verses points: true, things are only where there is a word, yet what really matters to Heidegger is the reverse of this thesis—the spoken word always revolves on the unspeakable, the ineffable kernel of the Thing which we experience as such when the word fails, when we confront silence. At the very point at which the word breaks up, at which there are no things (ontical objects), we encounter the Thing, the true "matter of thought" (*Sache des Denkens*).

There is, however, a third reading which, following Heidegger's steps, centers on the difference between a Thing and things *qua* inner-worldly, ontical objects. An ontical object is not the same as a Thing: a Thing is an "auratic" object, an object in which there is "something more than itself" (for that reason, man is a thing *par excellence*). This "something more," this sublime, indefinable X which cannot be located in any of the positive features of the object, yet the presence of which makes a Thing out of the object, is engendered by the word which names the object. In this precise sense, word is a *Vorstellungs-Repräsentanz*, a placeholder for the (lacking) representation, i.e., for the representation of that which is "unrepresentable" in the object and which, as such, makes a Thing out of it. This is how what Heidegger calls "word" differs from a mere sign: a sign designates positive properties of the object, whereas a word captures, encircles, precisely the elusive *je ne sais quoi* beyond positive properties. In this perspective, "Where the word breaks up no thing can be" means: it is only the word which opens up the sublime, "ineffable" dimension and thus makes a Thing out of an object. Bearing in mind Lacan's definition of the Sublime as "an object elevated to the dignity of the Thing," one is tempted to propose the following translation of Trakl's verse in Lacanese: *where the place-holder of the (missing) representation fails to intervene, no object can be elevated to the dignity of the Thing.*

And where, precisely, is *Verzicht*, renunciation, here? In the fact that the Thing remains forever unrepresentable: the *je ne sais quoi* which makes all the difference between the sublime and the ordinary can never be represented, every object is split into an ordinary ontical entity and the sublime X. The usual psychoanalytical name for this *Versagung*, for the loss of the Thing, of course, is "symbolic castration." Yet in order to avoid the misapprehensions which abound even with authors who proclaim themselves Lacanian, it is crucial to bear in mind the above-described "self-reflective" structure of the renunciation:

"castration" is always a "renunciation of renunciation," i.e., a reflection into itself of a renunciation, never a simple renunciation of something. The most succinct definition of castration is found in Lacan's Seminar on *Transference*, toward the end of his interpretation of Paul Claudel's Coufontaine trilogy: "castration is ultimately structured like this—we take away from somebody his desire, and in exchange for it we hand him over to somebody else—in this case, to the social order."[33] A couple of lines later, there is another formulation: "we deprive the subject of his desire, and in exchange for it we send him to the market where he becomes the object of general auction."[34] At the bottom of the same page, the third and more general formulation: "The effects on a human being of the fact that he becomes a subject of law are, in short, that he is deprived of what matters to him most, and in exchange for it, he is himself delivered to the texture which is woven between generations."[35]

The first thing which strikes the eye here is the asymmetry, i.e., as Lacan puts it, the "strange conjugation of a minus which is not redoubled by any plus."[36] That is to say, insofar as "castration" is defined as an act of exchange, one would expect the subject to obtain something in exchange for the renunciation (cultural progress, symbolic recognition, material goods, or the like); yet all that the second part of this strange act of exchange brings about is an additional loss—in thanks for handing over "everything," for sacrificing the very kernel of his being, the object in himself, i.e., that which is "in himself more than himself," *the subject himself is made into an object*, becomes an object of exchange. Such a formulation as qualifies the sacrificed object as *objet petit a*, the object in the subject, the hidden treasure, *agalma*, which confers dignity upon the subject, makes somewhat clearer the sense in which castration, after all, is an act of exchange: the exchange of an object for another—in exchange for the lost object-cause of desire, the subject himself becomes object.[37]

We can see, now, why castration is *symbolic*: by means of it, the subject exchanges his being (an object) for a place in the symbolic exchange, for a signifier which represents him. Conceived in this way, castration is strictly homologous to alienation—not only in the Lacanian sense of alienation in the signifier's order, but also in the Marxian sense of alienation which pertains to the status of a proletarian.

A proletarian is deprived of the very kernel of his being, of his productivity, of the surplus value brought about by it (Lacan modeled the term *plus de jouir*, surplus enjoyment, after the Marxian surplus value), and in exchange for it he gets what? He is himself reduced to labor force, an exchangeable object-commodity that can be bought on the market. To a connoisseur of structuralism, it is not difficult to discover the homology between this paradox of "castration" and the elementary formula of the transformation of myths proposed by Claude Lévi-Strauss:[38] the two subjects/agents not only exchange an object, one of them is himself exchanged, i.e., he passes from the status of subject to that of object. In the act of "castration," the subject donates all to the Other, and in exchange for it he is himself exchanged/donated: as if, in Hegelese, exchange, by a kind of "reflection into itself," would render exchangeable the very subject of exchange. This is what we encounter in the case of the proletarian: the proletarian designates the moment of "reflection into itself" of the exchange society, i.e., the moment when the subject of exchange offers on the market not only an object (his product/commodity), but *himself as a commodity*. Dialectical analysis conceives such a reflective inversion as a necessary consequence of the universalization of the exchange function: as soon as the exchange of commodities becomes universal and predominant, the labor force itself must appear on the market as a commodity. The crucial point not to be missed here, however, is that *this becoming an object of exchange coincides with the emergence of pure subjectivity*. That is to say, the whole point of Marx is that, in the opposition between the capitalist and the proletarian, it is the proletarian who stands for the pure subjectivity: it is precisely because he is reduced to pure, substanceless subjectivity (i.e., because he is devoid of all objective conditions of the productive process—all he owns is his labor power) that the proletarian has to exchange himself (his labor power) on the market. As a good Hegelian, Marx knew that pure subjectivity is strictly correlative to becoming an exchangeable object—in other words, the paradox is that what is alienated (the dimension of subjectivity) is literally constituted by way of the process of alienation.

An even more fundamental case of this inversion of the subject into the object of exchange, of course, is the status of women within the (patriarchal) symbolic order: according to Claude Lévi-Strauss, their reduction to an object of exchange between men (one of the three types of "objects" that are exchanged: women, words, material goods) pertains to the very notion of the symbolic order. If we bear in mind that, for a human being, "to become an object of exchange" implies the above-described structure of *Versagung* where, in exchange for the sacrifice of the kernel of his/her being, the subject is reduced to an object of exchange—in other words, if we bear in mind that this becoming an object of exchange is strictly correlative to the emergence of subjectivity—the Lacanian thesis according to which woman epitomizes castration appears in a new light: the reduction of the woman to an object of exchange means that *woman—not man—is the subject at its purest*, i.e., the Cartesian *cogito qua* void, emptied by way of *Versagung*. In other words, men possess and exchange objects, whereas it is only women who designate the point at which this exchange (i.e., the external relationship between the subject and object of exchange) is "reflected into itself," brought to the point of its self-reference, so that the subject of exchange so to speak "exchanges himself/herself" and becomes the object of exchange. In this precise sense, woman is "the symptom of man," of man *qua* Cartesian subject: she marks the "return" of his "repressed," i.e., she epitomizes what the Cartesian male subject, in his everyday self-understanding, is compelled to "repress," namely the *Versagung* which forms the hidden reverse of his freedom.

In order to specify this aspect of the feminine ethical attitude Hollywood, for the last time, can be of some help. What we have in mind, of course, is King Vidor's *Stella Dallas* (1937), a true counterpart to the male *Versagung* in *Rhapsody* by reference to which we opened this section: the story of a mother who deliberately assumes the role of a vulgar debauchee so that her daughter can leave her and marry her high-society fiancé with a clear conscience. When, at the very end of the film, the mother (Barbara Stanwyck) observes the marriage ceremony, anonymous in the crowd near the church fence, and then leaves with a blissful expression on her face, we find ourselves at the delicate turning point at which what appears to be the lowest level of patriarchal subordination of the woman turns into its opposite. That is to say, the first reading of the film which imposes itself is radically antifeminist: the mother finds the fulfillment of her feminine mission in the ultimate sacrifice for the sake of her child's (patriarchal-heterosexual) happiness. Yet the renunciation at work here is so radical that it is brought to the extreme of self-negation: the mother has to renounce the very effect of renunciation, the big Other (the public) does not perceive her gesture as a noble sacrifice, i.e., she is compelled to present her sacrifice as its opposite, as an act of loathsome corruption, so that she is deprived of the minimal narcissistic satisfaction. The void that the mother finds herself in at the end of the film is therefore simply the void of freedom: she is released from the burden of motherhood, the possibility of a new life opens up for her, of a new beginning from the zero point.[39]

What we encounter here, again, is the opposition between the hard-boiled detective's and the woman's renunciation: the first renunciation remains within the narcissistic economy, it always counts on a "deeper" recognition from the big Other, whereas only a woman is capable of renunciation, the result of which is that one is thrown upon oneself, absolutely. The Nietzschean subtitle of *Stella Dallas* could have been "the birth of the *cogito* from the spirit of melodramatic renunciation."

"Subjective destitution"

It should be clear, now, why this reference to *Versagung* does not entail any kind of "regression" to a pre-Enlightenment, quasi-ritual idolatry of a primordial sacrifice: *Versagung* designates "Enlightenment in becoming" in the precise Kierkegaardian sense, i.e., a founding gesture which disappears, becomes invisible, once the symbolic space of Enlightenment is established. We have already indicated how the purest realization of the paradox of *Versagung* is the victim in the Stalinist trials; no wonder, then, that in the domain of literature, one encounters the structure of *Versagung* in Bertolt Brecht's "learning plays" (*Lehrstücke*) from the late 1920s and early 1930s, a kind of literary counterpart to the Stalinist trials. Lacan takes as the third term that concludes the "trilogy of desire" in the Western drama, i.e., that comes after *Antigone* and *Hamlet*, the Coufontaine trilogy of Paul Claudel; *The Measure Taken*, the crucial "learning play," serves perhaps even better to exemplify the tragic dimension of modern subjectivity.

Brecht's "learning plays" were motivated by his encounter with the universe of Noh plays—what we encroach upon thereby is the relationship of the West with Japan *qua* fantasy object. That is to say, the history of the so-called cultural exchange between Europe and Japan is a long story of missed encounters epitomized by the fate of Kurosawa's *Rashomon*: in Europe it was celebrated as a discovery of Japan, whereas in Japan it failed, since it was perceived as all too European . . . In Europe, Japan functions as a kind of fantasy screen onto which one projects one's "repressed."[40] This fantasy image of Japan is ramified into two main branches: the "fanatic" Japan (kamikaze, samurai, the code of honor—Japan as the ethics of unconditional obedience) and the "semiotic" Japan (from Eisenstein to Barthes: kabuki, the Japanese art of painting—Japan as an empire of signs delivered from Western logocentrism). The first fantasy is usually appropriated by the political Right and the second by the Left—with one significant exception: Bertolt Brecht's "learning plays"; the play which starts the series, *Jasager* (*The One Who Says Yes*) (1929), is a revised translation of an old Noh play, and the paradox is here double. First, Brecht—a radical Leftist—appropriated a problematic which, usually, was the domain of the Right: since its theme is sacrifice, both the Left and the liberals attacked it as an unwelcome infusion of the authoritarian oriental attitude into the Western universe of democratic and rational openness. Yet, second point, things get complicated precisely apropos of this alleged import of the oriental attitude: upon a closer comparison of the Japanese original with Brecht's version, it is easy to ascertain that precisely the features which troubled liberal critics so much *were added by Brecht himself*—we look in vain for them in the Japanese original.[41]

Jasager is a story of a village boy who voluntarily joins an expedition bound for a city beyond the high mountains in order to fetch medicine against a disease which is raging in the village. Up in the mountains, the boy falls ill and thus prevents the further progress of the expedition; so the other members put him to death, yet only after the boy has accepted his death, i.e., has agreed with the custom which says that those who obstruct an expedition should be thrown over a precipice. *Die Massnahme* (*The Measure Taken*, 1930) transposes the same matrix into the communist revolution: a group of communist agitators bound for a Chinese city where they are to organize revolution is joined by a young zealot. At the crucial moment, the young comrade breaks down: overcome by compassion toward those who suffer, he takes off the mask and displays his face in public. The revolutionary conspiracy is thereby broken, a defeat ensues, and the group has to withdraw. On their escape, the young comrade is severely wounded; after obtaining his agreement, the group kills him and throws him into lime so that no trace of him will remain. The play is structured as a kind of flashback/ voiceover narrative: the four agitators describe their acts at a Party tribunal ("Control Chorus"); at the end, the tribunal declares them innocent since their "measure" was justified.

Brecht's learning plays were an exercise in what he called the "large pedagogics" (*die grosse Pädagogik*); later, he abandoned this approach and devised the "small pedagogics" of the "epic theatre," which for him was not a further step in a progressive development, but precisely a compromise formation: up to his death, Brecht insisted that the only part of his work which actualized the "theater of the future" was the learning plays. In the "large pedagogics," the partition that separates the actors from the public has to fall: those who "learn" are the actors themselves, not the public—how? It is here that we encounter the first Foucauldian element: apropos of *Lehrstücke*, Brecht spoke about "bodily semiotics" (*körperliche Semiotik*)—learning plays are to denounce and undermine the ruling ideology not on the level of its general theoretical propositions, but on the level of the "microphysics of power," of patterns of behavior, of the rituals which materialize ideological propositions. What we have here is the reverse of the Kantian freedom to argue—within the confines of the "public use of reason," argue as much as you want, but, insofar as you are a cog in the (social) machine, obey: Brecht's aim was to render visible this logic of "private" obedience.[42] Herefrom his request that the actors interchange parts, each of them successively assuming the role of the young comrade—does this request not bring to mind Foucault's fascination with the homosexual sado-masochist practices whose crucial feature is precisely the interchangeability of roles?

Yet—in a way Foucault would undoubtedly find cognate to his endeavor—what was truly at stake in this interchanging of roles was a certain ethical gesture that appealed to Brecht in that period, the gesture of renunciation, of self-sacrifice: of saying Yes to one's self-annihilation. This gesture is indicated by the very title of the first learning play, *Jasager*: there is a certain Yes which has to be *repeated*. The boy from *Jasager* says Yes twice: his first Yes is the Yes to the cause, to the mission he wants to join, while the second Yes affirms his agreement to his death, i.e., to the "valley-hurling." It is the same with *The Measure Taken*,[43] where the first Yes is:

> In the interests of communism, agreeing to the advance of the proletarian masses of all lands, saying Yes to the revolutionizing of the world. (82)

And the second Yes:

> FIRST AGITATOR: We must shoot you and throw you in the lime pit so the lime will burn you. And we ask you: do you agree to this?
> COMRADE: Yes. (106)

Two features have to be kept in mind here if one is to avoid totally missing the point by making out of this Yes an ordinary case of heroic sacrifice for the cause. The second Yes is of a strictly formal nature, an empty gesture, since (in *Jasager* as well as in *The Measure Taken*) the chorus in the background somewhat cynically emphasizes that the young man will be put to death irrespective of his answer:

> FIRST AGITATOR: We are going to ask him if he agrees, for he was a brave fighter.
> SECOND AGITATOR: But even if he does not agree, he must disappear, and totally. (106)

Furthermore, the requested sacrifice is not a simple case of the sacrifice for a cause, but far more radical: the subject must "disappear," die, yet his sacrifice will not become a myth, it will not be remembered, he will not be inscribed into the register of historical memory as a hero. He must disappear "totally"—although, in Brecht's text, "totally" refers to the destruction of the young comrade's body in the lime, it is not difficult to discern in the background what Jacques Lacan baptized "*l'entre-deuxmorts*," the difference between the two deaths, real and symbolic: "he must disappear," *and totally*, i.e., it is not enough for him to be put to death, the very trace of his existence in the symbolic order must be obliterated, he must become a "nonperson." This second "Yes," the Yes to one's own disappearance, the acceptance of one's "second death," designates the eruption of what Freud called *Todestrieb*, death drive;[44] it ultimately equals *die Versagung*.

It is precisely today, when the communist cause has failed, that one has to return to Brecht in order to delineate the gesture of *Versagung*, of renunciation, in its formal purity, as a subject position implied by his learning plays. In Kierkegaardian terms: the first Yes remains at the level of ethical mission, it designates the act of assuming an ethical mandate, whereas the second Yes points toward the "religious suspension of the ethical," of the latter's universal dimension.[45] The "Yes" to the ethical, brought to its extreme, sooner or later compels us to assume another, more radical Yes, a Yes which cuts the ground from under our feet, the Yes to the religious suspension of the ethical; the "Yes" to truth compels us to lie in the service of truth; the Yes to fight compels us to escape—in short, the Yes to a rule brings us to its founding exception, or, as Brecht himself puts it:

> Who fights for communism must be able to fight and not to fight; to speak the truth and not to speak the truth; to perform services and not to perform services, to keep promises and not to keep promises; to go into danger and to keep out of danger; to be recognizable and not to be recognizable. Who fights for communism has only one of all the virtues: that he fights for communism. (82)

The subject "is" only insofar as there is this "ply" of the universal which emerges not *against* the ethical obligation but as its ultimate *fulfillment*. In other words, what Brecht is aiming at is not the standard opportunist attitude which compels us to follow our interests, to tell the truth when it does not hurt, to tell a lie when the lie profits us, etc., but an inherent self-negation of ethics, i.e., an *ethical* injunction which suspends ethical universality. It is precisely because of this "suspension of the ethical," because of this split between honor and ethics (an ethical injunction to behave dishonorably), that *Versagung* is an eminently *modern* phenomenon. Consequently, when Brecht asserts that, in saying Yes to the Revolution, one must "blot out one's face," achieve the state in which "you are yourself no longer" (82), what we have here is not the usual ethics of self-obliteration for the sake of the cause: one must, so to speak, effectuate another turn of the screw and *obliterate the obliteration itself*, i.e., renounce the obliteration *qua* pathetic gesture of self-sacrifice—this supplementary renunciation is what Lacan called "destitution subjective." The young comrade runs to his ruin by capitulating to the logic of the pathetic sacrifice: he tears up the mask put on upon making a vow to the Revolution and begins to speak as "what he truly is," as a human being full of compassion:

"YOUNG COMRADE: I have seen too much.
I shall therefore go before them
As what I am
And state
What is.
. . .
FOUR AGITATORS: And we saw him in the twilight saw
His naked face, human, open, guileless.
He had torn up his mask. (102)

The fundamental lesson of it is that *there is more truth in the mask than in the face beneath it*: the young comrade is lost (politically and ethically) the moment he takes off the mask. Is not this very prevalence of the mask the lesson that we, Europeans, can get from Japan? In this sense, Japanese civilization, the civilization of the mask, of "keeping one's face," functions as the very contrast of, say, the American ethics of the 1970s—the latter is quick to denounce this obsession with "keeping one's face" as a "repressive" attitude that prevents us from giving free expression to our "true self," i.e., it compels us to bear every abasement only to attain the "true self's authentic expression."[46] Foucault was adamantly opposed to this ethics of true self-expression: he strictly delimited his ethics of the subject's self-construction from what he called the "Californian ethics" still subordinated to the truth regime—some expert or initiatic knowledge tells us "what we truly are" and thus impels us to realize our "true self."[47]

Which subject position, attitude, is therefore implied by this second

Yes, by this acceptance of one's disappearance? An identification with what psychoanalysis calls the "anal object," a remainder, an amorphous leftover of some harmonious Whole—Lacan quotes Luther's sermons: "You are the excrement which fell on the earth through the Devil's anus."[48] In *The Measure Taken*, this identification with excrement is carried to the extreme in the precise sense of identification with the paradoxical position of the legendary member of a cannibal tribe who ate the last cannibal so that there would be no cannibalism:

> Who are you?
> Stinking, be gone from
> The room that has been cleaned! Would that
> You were the last of the filth which
> You had to remove! (97)

This excrement—this "impossible" object, this exception by means of which universality is simultaneously established and suspended—is the objectal equivalent of the Lacanian subject: what we have here is the subjective position of a "vanishing mediator," of somebody who in advance takes into account that the process he initiated will ultimately sweep him away. And it is precisely this notion of the subject *qua* constitutive suspension of universality which enables us to approach in a new way the relationship between Foucault and Lacan.

Contemporary *doxa* conceives them as the two exemplary representatives of anti-Enlightenment "postmodernism" (Foucault: the mechanisms of discipline and control, Panopticon, etc., as the hidden reverse or the actual content of the Enlightenment's universal Reason; Lacan: the "*décentrement*" of the Cartesian subject). Yet both of them inscribed their theoretical activity within the confines of the Enlightenment project (Foucault in his last years; Lacan constantly—suffice it to mention the cover text of *Ecrits* which locates Lacan's endeavor in the continuation of *le débat des lumières*). In both cases, the crucial reference is Kant's transcendental turn as the apogee of the Enlightenment (Foucault elaborates it in his essay "What is Enlightenment?"; Lacan in his *écrit* "Kant avec Sade" in which Kant is explicitly conceived as the starting point of the process in the "history of ideas" which led to the emergence of psychoanalysis).[49] In both cases, this reference to Kant hinges upon the notion of the subject; yet the elaboration of this notion brings about two completely different, mutually exclusive results: with Foucault, we get a subject who shapes himself without guarantee in a heteronomous, superior universal Reason—implying an ethics of "proper measure," of self-masterhood, of the self *qua* harmonization of the antagonistic forces; with Lacan, we get $, a split/barred subject, subjected to an impossible imperative—implying an ethics of the incommensurate, of a constitutive imbalance, in short, of the real-impossible. Foucault quotes as one of the historical prototypes of his ethics of the "care for the self" the Renaissance ideal of the personality *qua* work of art; in this sense, one is tempted to conceive the opposition of Foucault and Lacan as the repetition of another opposition, that between Renaissance humanism and Protestantism, or, to fill in the names, between Erasmus of Rotterdam and Martin Luther. For that very reason, Lacan in his *Ethics of Psychoanalysis* refers to Luther who (as we have already seen) counters Erasmus's humanism with the identification of man to God's excrement—what we have here is the opposition between a harmonious work of art and the queer remainder which sticks out.

Our aim here, of course, is not to judge "who is right," i.e., simply to opt for one of the two possible readings of Kant, but rather to delineate *the feature, the characteristic, by way of which Kant's philosophy, viz. the Kantian ethical-philosophical attitude, opens up the field of both possibilities.*[50] This feature, of course, is the suspension of the universal: what Foucault and Lacan see in Kant is not an affirmation of the universal tribunal of Reason but, quite to the contrary, the affirmation of a certain fissure in the midst of this universality—in both cases, "subject" is a name for such a fissure. They both repudiate what Foucault succinctly baptized "the Enlightenment's blackmail" (if you refuse universal Reason and progress, you necessarily succumb to irrationalist obscurantism, etc.) by means of drawing a line of distinction between the "official" image of the Enlightenment—the ideology of universal Reason and the progress of humanity, etc.—and its reverse.

In the case of Foucault, this reverse of the Enlightenment to be asserted is the "ontology of the present": once support in the universal order of things is lost, once we are no longer able to rely on a preordained place in the all-embracing "chain of being," the subject is "left to his own self"—he has to concoct autonomously the universality he is to follow. The fatal enchainment of power and knowledge is thereby broken, i.e., the matrix, in force from the Christian practice of confession to psychoanalysis, which compels the subject to attain the truth in himself and of himself—ultimately the truth about sex—by way of its verbalization, of its translation into the language of an expert invested with power (theologian, psychoanalyst) who locates our proper place in the universal frame of knowledge and thereby tells us "what we really are." The very idea of such a truth is a kind of performative fiction at the service of power, i.e., legitimizing its exercise; the subject dwells in a void, he has so to speak to compose himself performatively, not just to arrive at his truth, not just to ascertain what he always already was. In this sense, one could say that Foucault's implicit model is Kant's critique of judgment, in which the subject confronts an object to which he cannot apply some preestablished rule or concept, but has himself to invent, to lay down, the universal rule under which this object falls—Foucault would probably endorse those new interpretations of Kant's philosophy which emphasize the paradigmatic status of the third critique as the key offering a model to conceive adequately the first two.

We can see, now, how Foucault is thoroughly justified in comparing his "esthetics of existence" to the Kantian turn: in his *Critique of Judgment*, Kant diagnoses esthetic judgments as a case of "universality without concept"—although without the guarantee in a previously established concept, they contain a claim to universal validity (when we say that something is beautiful, we do not know *why* it is beautiful, and yet we implicitly claim that *everybody* should find it beautiful). This is, then, the Foucauldian subject: a capacity of "self-relating," of shaping out of one's life an esthetic object, a "work of art," of instigating out of oneself the universal rule one is to follow—the aim is no longer to recognize one's place in the preordained structure of the cosmos, since every positing of a norm has its ground in the subject's self-constitution, it manifests a specific way the subject relates to himself. In other words, every ontology is ultimately an "ontology of the present": as universal and supratemporal as it may appear, it hinges upon the subject's incessant (re)construction of his own present, of the present historical moment. For that reason, the Olympian elevation and inner peace irradiated by the style of Foucault's last two books on antique ethical attitudes[51] should not lead us astray: their ultimate aim is to instigate us, *via* their exemplary value, to *repeat* today the antique gesture and thereby deliver ourselves of the Christian frame. There certainly is a deep link connecting Foucault's notion that Greek ethics strives toward a "universality without law" and Kant's notion of the esthetic judgment as a "universality without concept." In the case of Lacan, in contrast, this reverse of the Enlightenment is best epitomized by the title of one of his *écrits*: "Kant avec Sade"—as he says in the last page of *The Four Fundamental Concepts*, the truth of the Kantian moral law is

> desire in its pure state, that very desire that culminates in the sacrifice, strictly speaking, of everything that is the object of love in one's human tenderness—I would say, not only in the rejection of the pathological object, but also in its sacrifice and murder. That is why I wrote *Kant avec Sade*.[52]

Therein consists, according to Lacan, Kant's ultimate lesson: the subject "is" only insofar as the Thing (the Kantian Thing in itself as well as the Freudian impossible-incestuous object, *das Ding*) is sacrificed, "primordially repressed"—we are again at the motif of *Versagung*. This "primordial repression" introduces a fundamental imbalance in the universe: the symbolically structured universe we live in is organized around a void, an impossibility (the inaccessibility of the Thing in itself). The Lacanian notion of the split subject is to be conceived against this background: the subject can never fully "become himself," he can never fully realize himself, he only ex-sists as the void of a distance from the Thing. The split thus divides the subject in his positive (i.e., "pathological," empirical-contingent) features from the subject *qua* 0, the mark of the absent, "sacrificed" Thing. The Kantian overtones of this splitting are easy to recognize, since what we have here is the split between the subject *qua* the empty, substanceless "I think" of the transcendental apperception, and the subject *qua* fullness of "person," the pile of positive features of a phenomenal entity.

This way, the splitting of the Kantian ethical subject also appears in a new light. That is to say, in the standard version of Kant's philosophy, the ethical subject is torn between the universal moral law and particular "pathological" impulses; he appears condemned to a continuous inner struggle between complying with the law and succumbing to "pathological" temptations, dedicated to the unending task of obliterating the pathological. However, the moment we take into account the crucial fact that the "sacrifice of the Thing" restricts us to the form of law, to the law *qua* empty form (for Kant, the place of the supreme good is by definition empty), this standard version loses ground: the subject is split, yet the place of the split shifts, the split traverses the within of Law and of the domain of pleasures, imposing on each of them the loop-like structure of a Moebius band. Concerning the law: Enlightenment relies on the subject's maturity and autonomy, it demands that the subject renounce his unqualified obedience to heteronomous laws; yet at this very moment the subject encounters in his midst an incomparably more rigorous command which unconditionally claims its part, paying no regard to his actual abilities ("You can because you must!"). At the very moment of achieving autonomy, of suspending the hold of heteronomous, externally imposed laws, the subject is thus forced to confront a far more severe Master whose injunction decenters him from within.[53] A homologous inversion takes place in the domain of pleasures: the very renunciation to pleasures brings about a paradoxical surplus enjoyment, an "enjoyment in pain," in displeasure, baptized by Lacan *jouissance*, the "impossible"/traumatic/painful enjoyment beyond the pleasure principle. If we read these two theoretical gestures together, the conclusion which imposes itself, of course, is that Law, in its most radical dimension, is the "superego," i.e., an injunction to enjoyment with which it is impossible to comply. Foucault's implicit reproach to Lacan concerns the latter's allegedly negative conception of Law as the force of prohibition[54]—yet Lacan's concept of the superego designates precisely law in its positive, productive dimension.[55] The split, therefore, does not take place between moral law and pathological desires, but between enjoyment and pleasure: on the one hand, there is the mad-obscene law which is *incommensurate* with our well-being insofar as it derails the psychic equilibrium by way of ordering enjoyment; on the other hand, there is the tension between the pleasure principle and its externally imposed limitations, i.e., the dialectic of the pleasure and reality principles, the art of the "proper measure" of containing pleasure which assures its long-term preservation.

It may seem paradoxical to evoke a "crack in the universality" apropos of Kant: was Kant not obsessed by the Universal, was not his fundamental aim to establish the universal form (constitutive) of knowledge, does his ethics not propose the universal form of the rule which regulates our activity as the sole criterion of morality, etc.? Yet as soon as the Thing in itself is posited as unattainable, *every universality is potentially suspended*, it implies a point of exception at which its validity, its hold, is canceled, or, to put it in the language of contemporary physics, a point of singularity—this "singularity" is ultimately *the Kantian subject himself*, namely the empty subject of the transcendental apperception. The crack in the universality finds its clearest expression in the hypothesis of "radical evil," i.e., in the paradoxical possiblity, envisaged by Kant (later taken over and further elaborated by Schelling), of evilness *qua* ethical attitude, of our being evil on account of the principle, not because we succumbed to "pathological" impulses.[56] In his *Political Unconscious*, Fredric Jameson quotes Brecht's famous lines on the mask of the Japanese demon, its swollen veins and hideous grimace

> all betokening
> What an exhausting effort it takes
> To be evil.[57]

It is here, apropos of a Japanese mask, that Brecht and Kant unexpectedly meet: in this notion of evil as a pure spiritual attitude, far more "suprasensible" than good. Therein consists, ultimately, the secret of the Kantian sublime: if beauty is a symbol of morality (of the good), the sublime announces evilness *qua* ethical stance—this is the power discernible in what Kant calls the "dynamical sublime," the power that an image of terrifying unruly nature evokes by way of its very failure to represent it adequately: an ethical (principled, implacable), yet radically evil rage. It is easy to follow one's natural impulses of compassion and be good, help a neighbor in distress, etc.; how much more difficult it is to be truly evil! And is Foucault's image of antiquity ultimately not the mythical notion of an age in which we had a subject not yet caught in these annoying paradoxes of surplus enjoyment, a subject still capable of finding peace and harmony in the esthetic formation of his self?[58] That is to say, is not the fundamental paradox of the Christian logic of confession which Foucault wanted to get rid of that it extracts enjoyment out of the very renunciation/denunciation of the "pleasures of the flesh," is not this surplus enjoyment what drives a Christian believer into ever new renunciations?

Perhaps, these two notions of the subject, the Foucauldian and the Lacanian, are not after all so exclusive as it may appear: the construction of the self without a guarantee in the universality of Reason is possible only against the background of *Versagung*. If there was ever a theoretician sensitive to the latent *ascetic* dimension of the "esthetics of existence," it was Foucault: the Foucauldian "culture of the self" is ultimately nothing but a constant endeavor to *set measures* to the monstrous excess called "the Kantian subject," to introduce a semblance of harmonious design into it, i.e., to master, to contain, to reduce to a bearable level its incommensurability. The problem, of course, is that this endeavor is ultimately doomed to fail since the imbalance is constitutive: the Foucauldian subject is synonymous with the successful subjectivization, with the formation of the self *qua* an esthetic whole; the Lacanian subject is synonymous with its failure, i.e., it is correlative to the anal object, to the excrement which is the leftover of every subjectivization.

"Tarrying with the negative"

A crucial misunderstanding must be avoided here: thus conceived, *Versagung* is not something that arises in a second time, after a long period of our total imprisonment within the texture of symbolic destiny—it is, on the contrary, "originary," i.e., what we call "new-age subjectivity" actualized, brought to the light of the day, something that was contained *in potentia* in the most elementary relationship of the subject to the signifier. What we have here is an exemplary case of the difference between dialectical historicity proper and "historicism": in historicism, the paradox of historicity (the thing in question *becomes*—reveals itself, proves itself to be—what it *always already was*) is somehow "flattened," reduced to a linear succession of "epochs" (first the all-powerful fate whose puppets we are; then the subject capable of disengaging himself from it, of assuming distance from it, and so on). To elucidate this crucial distinction, let us recall two examples. According to the famous proposition from Marx's *Communist Manifesto*, all hitherto history is a history of class struggles; yet—in an apparently contradictory move—Marx never ceases to insist that the bourgeoisie is the first "class" *stricto sensu*: the antagonism between bourgeoisie and proletariat is the first class antagonism which "appears as such," not camouflaged by the rich texture of casts, guilds, etc.—thus, it enables us to decipher the preceding social antagonisms as concealed forms of class struggle. It is similar with Claude Lefort's famous definition of democracy as a system in which the locus of power is "empty," i.e., a system founded on an unsurpassable gap separating the symbolic locus of power from real political agents who, temporarily, occupy it ("exert power"): Lefort's point is not that it was only with democracy that the locus of power was evacuated—*it always already was empty*, anyone who purported to be its possessor always already *was* an impostor, yet this void became actual and visible only by the advent of democracy. This is, ultimately, what the Hegelian couple *in itself—for itself* is about, i.e., it is in this sense that the dialectical process forms a "closed circle" where a thing "becomes what it already was."

Consequently, our position here *is* radically "Eurocentric": the break of the Enlightenment is irreversible, the epoch of the Enlightenment *is* "an epoch to end all epochs," i.e., by means of the *Versagung* which constitutes the subject of the Enlightenment, an abyss becomes visible against the background of which all other epochs can be experienced in their epochal closure, as something ultimately contingent.[59] The point is simply that the Enlightenment, like a cancerous tissue, contaminates all preceding organic unity and changes it retroactively into an affected pose. In Hegelese: as soon as we enter the Enlightenment, every presupposition (of an organic ground) is suspected of being "posited." Suffice it to recall the returns to oriental wisdom, the rejections of the so-called "Western Protestant-Cartesian imperialist paradigm," which abound today. Apropos of them, one usually emphasizes the need to distinguish authentic cases of such "returns" from their commercialized distortions (newspaper ads for "transcendental meditation," e.g.). Yet perhaps such an opposition is all too naive; perhaps what appears as a commercialized distortion of the authentic oriental wisdom is today its *truth*; perhaps the very "return to the lost oriental wisdom" is already in service of the late-capitalist social machine, facilitating the untroubled run of its nuts and bolts—perhaps we betrayed "oriental wisdom" the moment we uprooted it from its pretechnological life world and transfunctionalized it into an individual therapeutic means. In other words, here, also, the dialectical maxim "the cleaner you are, the dirtier you are" is in force: the more "truly" you return to oriental wisdom, the more your effort contributes to the transformation of oriental wisdom into a cog in the Western social machine . . . The reverse of it is that those who preach "multicultural decenterment," "openness toward non-European cultures," etc., thereby unknowingly affirm their "Eurocentrism," since what they demand is imaginable only within the "European" horizon: the very idea of cultural pluralism relies on the Cartesian experience of the empty, substanceless subjectivity—it is only against the background of this experience that every determinate form of substantial unity can appear as something ultimately contingent.

All this has radical consequences for the problem which undoubtedly is *the* problem of our time: the ecological crisis. The most "natural" reaction to it—something akin to a "spontaneous philosophy of ecologists"—consists in the above-mentioned ideological gesture usually referred to as the "shift from the Protestant-Cartesian (mechanistic, anthropocentric) to a new post-Cartesian (holistic, organic) paradigm." According to it, the contemporary ecological crisis has its roots in modern-age subjectivism with its manipulative relationship to nature *qua* object of technological domination—so, to get out of the crisis, one has to commit oneself to a new attitude of assent, of complying with things instead of exerting control over them, to an attitude which conceives nature as a living organism (the earth as Gaia, a living body, etc.) and man as its subordinated part . . . What we have here is a desperate endeavor to return to the pre-Enlightenment, to a world in which the split between facts and meaning has not yet taken place, to a world where a deep sense inheres to nature itself, to a world animated by an invisible soul, to a world of a preestablished harmony between man, society, and cosmos, guaranteed by a set of metaphorical equivalences (society as a corporate body, e.g.)—an endeavor problematic not because of its utopian nature but due to the fact that, once the bacillus of Enlightenment has infected us, its very success corroborates subjectivism.[60] That is to say, the more we emphasize the break with anthropocentrism, man's subordination to the totality of nature, etc., *the more this totality of nature is perceived, in an implicit way, from the standpoint of the human interest*: there is no purely "natural" equilibrium, clean rivers and air, etc., are desirable only if, underhand, we observe nature *sub specie* man's survival. In other words, such an ecologically oriented "decenterment" already relies on a surreptitious *teleological* subordination of nature to man; if, consequently, we are to accept Heidegger's warning about "modern-age subjectivity" as the site of the ultimate "danger," we must add that this danger consists precisely in our unwillingness to confront the abyss of the subject, i.e., in our unquestioned acceptance of some self-posited ground authorizing us to exert power, be it nation or Earth as an organism. For that reason, the celebrated "postmodern" return to transsubjective roots (from discovering one's ethnic origins to identifying with the "space-ship Earth") remains thoroughly within the confines of the "modern age subjectivity"—the very remedy against ecological catastrophe regenerates its alleged cause.

The crucial point is to conceive the relationship between subject and subjectivization as an *antagonistic* one. By means of "subjectivization," the subject (presup)poses the existence of a symbolic network which enables him to experience the universe as a meaningful totality, as well as to locate his place in it, i.e., to identify himself with a place in the symbolic space: say, in the predominant ecological ideology, the gesture by means of which the subject assumes the "new holistic paradigm" and is interpellated as the one who should not disturb the natural balance . . . In other words, subjectivization designates what, in "deconstructionism," one calls assuming a determinate subject position, recognizing oneself as a socially defined "somebody"; in this way, the chaos of the encounter of the real is transformed into a meaningful narrative. The counterpoint to this process of subjectivization, the encounter of the real in its senselessness, however, is not a "process without the subject," but *the subject itself*: what the subjectivization renders invisible is *die Versagung*, its void—subjectivization is a way to elude the void which "is" the subject, it is ultimately a defense mechanism against the subject.[61]

Paradoxically, therefore, the only true step out of "modern-age subjectivism" is to acknowledge fully *die Versagung* constitutive of Cartesian subjectivity.

NOTES

1 The two exemplary cases of it are *Cahiers du Cinéma*'s extolling of *Under Capricorn* and Fredric Jameson's reaffirmation of *Stage Fright* as one of the crucial Hitchcock films.

2 One way to introduce a kind of order in this *bric-à-brac* of clichés on *noir* is to arrange them in four groups with reference to the four levels of interpretation theorized by medieval hermeneutics (a procedure reactualized by Fredric Jameson in his *Political Unconscious* (Princeton, N.J.: Princeton University Press, 1981)): (1) *literal* (the textual mechanisms: *chiaroscuro* photography, voiceover/flashback and other formal narrative devices, etc.); (2) *allegorical* (codes which regulate the diegetic reality of the *noir* universe: the figures of the hard-boiled detective, of the *femme fatale*, the corrupted social environs, etc.); (3) *anagogical* (the collective historical experience which forms the referential background of the *noir* universe: the corruption of the American megalopolis epitomized by Los Angeles, the disintegrative social impact of World War II, etc.); (4) *moral* (the existential *noir* vision: the dialectics of freedom and fate, etc.). What one has to do apropos of this tetrad, of course, is to subvert its underlying premise, the causal chain running from (4) to (1): in opposition to theology, level (1) is to be conceived as the "cause" of level (2)—i.e., the diegetic content depends upon formal procedures (the classical Jamesonian example: Hemingway arrived at the content of his stories by looking for themes which fit his type of sentences)—and level (3) as the "cause" of level (4)—i.e., the individual's existential vision depends upon the collective historical experience (which, in the case of *film noir*, coincides with the historical referent evoked by Deleuze as the background of the shift from the "movement image" to the "time image").

3 For a more detailed elaboration of this dialectic, see Slavoj Žižek, *Looking Awry: An Introduction to Lacan through Popular Culture* (Cambridge, MA.: MIT Press, 1991), pp. 71–73.

4 The usual quick sociologization explains the passage of the classical logic-and-deduction detective novel into the hard-boiled novel by reference to the passage of individualist capitalism with its Protestant ethic into corporate capitalism with its "heteronomous," "other-directed" individual (cf. John G. Cawelti, *Adventure, Mystery, and Romance* (Chicago: Chicago University Press, 1976)). However, it seems more productive to take as a starting point Fredric Jameson's hypothesis according to which the entire historiography, even when its "official" object is some distant, exotic civilization, actually varies one and only motif, the passage of precapitalist "organic" community into capitalist society—is not the transformation of the logic-and-deduction novel into the hard-boiled novel also one of the cases of it? The context of the logic-and-deduction novel is "capitalism which is not yet itself," a harmonious society with clearly defined hierarchy and order (it is by no means accidental that there

are two main locations which serve as the locus of murder in it: the mansion of a rich nobleman with the proverbial butler as the prime suspect; the idyllic small town—the two residues of the organic community within capitalism), whereas the hard-boiled novel marks the irruption of imbalance and corruption, the disintegration of the organic links (in its first page, Hammett's *Red Harvest* throws cards on the table as to how "Poisonville" became ruled by the gangsters: in order to crush the strike, the employers called out the mob who quickly broke the workers' resistance, yet on the way conquered power . . .). And, again, one should avoid the false problem of locating precisely the point of historical ("diachronic") demarcation—it is far more productive to conceive this opposition as a structural ("synchronous") antagonism inherent to capitalism as such: capitalism is never "pure," it is either caught in the illusion of organic unity or it perceives itself as a universe in disintegration.

5 Cf. Jacques Lacan, *Le Séminaire, livre VII: L'Ethique de la psychanalyse* (Paris: Editions du Seuil, 1986). In today's public opinion, this interspace is epitomized by the uncanny position of AIDS patients—still alive, yet already marked by death.

6 This logic was brought to the absurd utmost in Billy Wilder's *Sunset Boulevard* (1950) in which a corpse narrates the story that led to its death.

7 "What cinema must grasp is not the identity of a character, whether real or fictional, through his objective and subjective aspects. It is the becoming of the real character when he himself starts to 'make fictions', when he enters 'the flagrant offense of making up legends' " (Gilles Deleuze, *The Time-Image* (London: The Athlone Press, 1989), p. 150).

8 Herefrom the next characteristic which distinguishes the *noir* universe from the traditional detective novel: in the latter, the task with which the detective is charged can be taken at its face value (the problem is really the identity of the murderer, the novel does not cheat at this level), whereas in the hard-boiled novel, as a rule, it turns out that the client who hires the detective is part of a game which differs radically from what appears to be the case (e.g. say, the detective is hired to deliver ransom at an out-of-the-way location, yet the true aim of it is to assure his presence at this location at a time X in order to frame him with a murder . . .).

9 Cf. Pascal Bonitzer, *Décadrages* (Paris: Cahiers du Cinéma, 1985), pp. 67–68.

10 As for this shift, cf. Slavoj Žižek, *The Sublime Object of Ideology* (London: Verso Books, 1989), Chapter 2.

11 Cf. Otto Weininger, *Geschlecht und Character* (Vienna: 1903; Munich: Matthes und Seitz, 1980).

12 The parallel that imposes itself here, of course, is that between the *femme fatale* in the *noir* universe and the lady in the medieval tradition of "courtly love" (*amour courtois*): the *femme fatale* is the lady insofar as she is possible today, as the hard-boiled detective is the knight insofar as he is possible today. Yet why is *noir*'s *femme fatale* marked with overexposed sensuality and vulgarity, in contrast to the lady's sublime, unattainable stature? The answer is, again, the

changed status of the big Other, of the symbolic community, i.e., its deneutralization, its acquiring of paranoiac features. In the Middle Ages, evil was epitomized by the nameless Black Knight who, upon his defeat, pronounced his name and was thus reintegrated into the symbolic community; yet in the *noir* universe, it is the agent of good who is forced to operate in "*noir*," as fundamentally nameless and nonrecognized (in the stories and first novels of Hammett, the detective actually is a nameless "Continental Op"), since the space of the Other, the domain of public Names, is in itself evil. For that reason, the lady, the embodiment of social recognition, also turns evil.

13 As for the feminine nature of act, cf. chapter 2 of the present book.

14 Even in Poe's *The Purloined Letter* where the constellation of the three gazes is staged for the first time (the minister who steals the queen's letter; the queen who can only observe the act helplessly; the king who sees it all but does not recognize the meaning of it), the third gaze, that of the ignorant Other, is embodied in the king, the representative of symbolic authority.

15 Raymond Chandler, "The Simple Art of Murder," in *Pearls Are a Nuisance* (Harmondsworth: Penguin Books, 1977), p. 198.

16 In *Miller's Crossing* (Joel and Ethan Coen, 1989), a nonaccredited remake of *The Glass Key*, this opposition is rendered brilliantly by the contrast of the restrained Gabriel Byrne and the boastful Albert Finney.

17 LeCarré's *A Perfect Spy* is also centered on the relationship of the treacherous subject to the obscene paternal figure: its main character, Magnus Pym, the "perfect spy," took the way of perdition on account of his father, an obscene debauchee, a swindler, and an impostor, the very embodiment of boastful vulgarity. The key to the novel is offered by the formula "Love is whatever you can still betray," the quintessence of the obsessive economy: we can betray only those whom we truly love. In other words, the alternative "does he love me or did he betray me?" is wrong: betrayal is the ultimate confirmation of love.

18 The Name of the Father is therefore experienced as the "repressive" agency of prohibition which gives rise to the subject's desire for subversion, whereas the obscene "primordial father" drains the subject, hinders his desire. Instead of a son who endeavors to undermine the paternal authority and to "live fully," we get a son who, from shame at the father's obscene imposture, withdraws into ascetic purity.

19 Jacques Lacan, *The Four Fundamental Concepts of Psycho-Analysis* (Harmondsworth: Penguin Books, 1979), p. 276.

20 In the established hard-boiled universe, this triangle of the hero, the obscene paternal figure, and their shared woman undergoes a shift: the hero is torn between the *femme fatale* and the symbolic obligation, contract, which links him to "man's world"—yielding to the *femme fatale* is experienced as a betrayal of the symbolic obligation, i.e., the *femme fatale* seduces the hero into breaking the contract (even if it is only the contract with a gangster boss, as in *Criss-Cross*, *Out of the Past*, or *Killers*).

21 The constellation is here much clearer than in *The Maltese Falcon* which

remains the most popular among Hammett's novels, the only one still "alive," precisely because in it, *the Chandlerian gesture is already accomplished*: Sam Spade is already a standard hard-boiled detective whose integrity is threatened by a *femme fatale* (Brigid O'Shaughnessy), which is why the obscene paternal figure disappears from it—what we find in its place is a series of supplementary figures (Fatso Gutman, Joel Cairo, etc.).

22 Dashiell Hammett, *The Glass Key* (London: Pan Books Ltd, 1975), p. 220.

23 At the very end of Hitchcock's *Notorious*, Sebastian also disappears into the doors of his mansion and thereby falls into the hands of the Nazi butchers.

24 In this sense, *All the King's Men* (Robert Penn Warren's novel as well as Robert Rossen's film) is definitely to be counted as a *noir* work—we encounter in it all the crucial ingredients of the *noir* universe: the corrupted/charismatic paternal figure (Governor Stark); the ambiguous attitude of the main character (the journalist) toward him, centered upon the problem of fidelity and betrayal; the fact that they both share the love of the same woman; the main character's blackout in the crucial moment when he should elucidate his attitude toward Stark (upon learning that they share the same love, he withdraws into drunkenness); the flashback/voiceover narrative; the link connecting social depravity with the theme of the "ontological" corruption of the universe as such, etc.

25 Richard Rorty, *Contingency, Irony, and Solidarity* (Cambridge: Cambridge University Press, 1989), p. 179.

26 It is this shift into the "supernatural" which brings about the forceful rehabilitation of the "innocent" paternal figure (Major Briggs).

27 Chandler, "The Simple Art of Murder," op. cit., p. 195.

28 The untitled respondent paper by Etienne Balibar in *Lacan avec les philosophes* (Paris: Albin Michel, 1991), p. 92.

29 This is also what the "professional ethics" of the hard-boiled detective is about: on behalf of his commitment to his job, he casts off the woman precisely insofar as she "is everything to him" . . .

30 Cf. Jacques Lacan, *Le Seminaire, livre VIII: Le Transfert* (Paris: Editions du Seuil, 1991), pp. 353–55. Incidentally, Lacan articulates the concept of *Versagung* and the theme of the "father who knows" apropos of Paul Claudel's Coufontaine trilogy whose central constellation ressembles strangely the triangle constitutive of *The Glass Key*: a woman shared by the son and his obscene "humiliated father" (*le père humilié*, the title of the third part).

31 Cf. Martin Heidegger, "Das Wort," in *Unterwegs zur Sprache* (Pfullingen: Neske Verlag, 1959). This link connecting the *noir* hero with Heidegger is not so unusual as it may appear; attention to it was drawn already by Fredric Jameson in "The Synoptic Chandler," in *Shadows of Noir*, ed. Joan Copjec and Mike Davis (London and New York: Verso, 1992).

32 Cf. Gianni Vattimo, *The End of Modernity* (Baltimore: Johns Hopkins University Press, 1989).

33 Lacan, *Le Séminaire, livre VIII: Le Transfert*, p. 380.

34 Ibid., p. 380.

35 Ibid., pp. 380–81.

36 Ibid., p. 381.

37 Another way to determine this shift is *via* a distinction between the subjective and the objective genitive: as a shift from the desire of the Other in the sense of *what the Other desires*, to the desire of the Other in the sense of the desire for the Other, i.e., of *the Other as the object of desire*. (Ibid., pp. 314–15.) The enigma that pertains to the very status of the subject of desire is the famous "*Che vuoi*?"—what does the Other want of me, what does he see in me that causes his desire, which is that X, the object-treasure which makes me an object of the Other's desire? The only way to get out of this impasse is to offer myself to the Other as the object of his desire: as Lacan puts it, in love, the subject "gives what he does not possess," *objet petit a*, the hidden treasure which is what is "in him more tham himself." In this way, I simultaneously "return my love" to the Other, i.e., I determine my desire as the desire *for* the Other: I make him into the *object* of my desire in order to be able to avoid the abyss of *his* desire.

This, of course, is precisely what the psychoanalyst by definition must not do: his is to maintain open the abyss of "*Che vuoi*?" at any price, he must never return the (transferential) love to the analysand. For that reason, the ambiguity of the subjective and objective genitive enables us also to generate the antinomy of knowledge and being that pertains to the notion of transference: in transference, the analyst functions as the *sujet supposé savoir*, he is supposed to know the truth about the analysand's desire; yet he is simultaneously the object of the analysand's desire, the embodiment of *objet petit a*, possessing the mysterious *je ne sais quoi* which triggers transferential love. Although, in 1961, Lacan had not yet disposed of the notion of the "subject supposed to know," he was already able to explicate the terms of this antinomy: ". . . at the very place where we are supposed to know *[où nous sommes supposés savoir]*, we are expected to be, to be nothing more and nothing else than the real presence, precisely insofar as this presence is unconscious" (Ibid., p. 315). The only way for us, analysts, to attain the mystery of the desire of the Other (analysand) is—temporarily, for the time of the transference—to occupy ourselves the place of *objet petit a*, to incarnate the object-cause of his desire. In other words, the way to the *truth* about the Other's desire leads through the transferential *illusion* in which we incarnate the object of the Other's desire.

38 For an actualization of this formula with a view to the analysis of ideology, cf. Fredric Jameson, "The Vanishing Mediator; or, Max Weber as Story-teller," in *The Ideologies of Theory*, Vol. 2 (Minneapolis: University of Minnesota Press, 1988).

39 For a similar reading of the final scene of *Stella Dallas*, cf. William Rothman, "Pathos and Transfiguration in the Face of the Camera: A Reading of *Stella Dallas*," in *The "I" of the Camera* (Cambridge, MA.: Cambridge University Press, 1988).

40 The reverse of it is that reference to Japan becomes relevant in the most unexpected places. Is there anything more "European" than the Hegelian

notion of the state *qua* constitutional monarchy with well-defined estates, etc.? Yet those who are prone to dismiss quickly this model as outdated, as an expression of Hegel's political compromises and illusions, should first consider that modern Japan presents an almost verbatim realization of Hegel's vision: a monarchy with the emperor reduced to a symbolic role, with a corporate structure which checks the political dynamics, with a country estate kept alive to counterbalance the disintegrative impact of modern industry and to safeguard organic tradition, etc. Cf. David Colb, *The Critique of Pure Modernity* (Chicago: University of Chicago Press, 1988), p. 281.

41 Brecht relied on the German translation (Elizabeth Hauptmann) of the English version by Arthur Waley, *Taniko, The Valley-Hurling.*

42 Michel Foucault, in his interpretation of Kant's *What is Enlightenment?* (cf. "What is Enlightenment," in *The Foucault Reader*, ed. Paul Rabinow (Harmondsworth: Penguin Books, 1984)), draws attention to this paradoxical split between the "public" and "private" use of reason, yet, strangely, he does not establish the link between the required "private" obedience and his own motif of disciplinary mechanisms as the constitutive reverse of free subjectivity.

43 Numbers following the quotes from *The Measure Taken* refer to the pages in Bertolt Brecht, *The Jewish Wife and Other Short Plays* (New York: Grove Press, 1965).

44 As for the notion of the "between two deaths" and the "death drive," cf. chapter 4 of Žižek, *The Sublime Object of Ideology*.

45 As for these Kierkegaardian notions, cf. section 3.1 of the present book.

46 How far we are from the intersubjective relationships depicted in the great Henry James's masterpieces, where even the rudest refusal or betrayal is conveyed in the form of gentle, courteous conversation!

47 Cf. Michel Foucault, "On the Genealogy of Ethics: An Overview of Work in Progress," in *The Foucault Reader*.

48 Cf. Jacques Lacan, *Le séminaire, livre VII: L'Ethique de la psychanalyse*, p. 111.

49 Cf. Jacques Lacan, "Kant avec Sade," in *Ecrits* (Paris: Editions du Seuil, 1966), pp. 765–66. Furthermore, let us recall that the subtitle of one of Lacan's key *écrits*, "Instance of the Letter in the Unconscious," is "Reason after Freud."

50 We encounter a similar paradox of two opposite, mutually exclusive, yet uncannily close interpretations apropos of Spinoza, whose work served as a fundamental point of reference to Louis Althusser as well as to Gilles Deleuze: for Althusser, Spinoza was the first to elaborate the opposition between ideological imaginary and strict conceptual knowledge, whereas for Deleuze, Spinoza's philosophy articulates a polymorphous machinery of desire, its modalities and intensities, which excludes the possibility of an abstract-universal theoretical stance; one is even tempted to say that the opposition Lacan-Foucault repeats the opposition Althusser-Deleuze at another level, apropos of Kant.

51 Michel Foucault, *The Use of Pleasure* (New York: Vintage Books, 1986) and *The Care of the Self* (New York: Vintage Books, 1988).

52 Jacques Lacan, *The Four Fundamental Concepts of Psycho-Analysis*, pp. 275–76.

53 Cf. Mladen Dolar, "The Legacy of the Enlightenment: Foucault and Lacan," in *New Formations* 14 (Summer 1991).

54 This reproach is elaborated in Michel Foucault, *History of Sexuality, Volume I* (New York: Vintage, 1980).

55 "Nothing whatsoever presses us to enjoy except the superego. Superego is the imperative of enjoyment—*Enjoy!*" (Jacques Lacan, *Le séminaire, livre XX: Encore* (Paris: Editions du Seuil, 1975), p. 10).

56 Cf. Book One of Immanuel Kant, *Religion Within the Limits of Reason Alone* (New York: Harper, 1960).

57 Cf. Fredric Jameson, *The Political Unconscious* (Cornell: Cornell University Press, 1981), p. 269.

58 Cf. Jacques-Alain Miller, "Michel Foucault et la psychanalyse," in *Michel Foucault philosophe* (Paris: Editions du Seuil, 1989).

59 For a similar view, cf. Robert Pippin, *Modernism as a Philosophical Problem* (Cambridge, MA.: Basil Blackwell, 1991).

60 It is here that the difference between Freud and Jung is insurmountable: the fundamental premise of Freud's *Civilization and its Discontents* is that the universe is utterly meaningless—it is not structured in compliance with human desires, there is no harmony between microcosm and macrocosm—whereas Jung reinscribes a psychoanalytical problematic into the frame of "cosmic principles" which guarantee correspondences between human life and the universe at large (*yin* and *yang* as psychic *and* cosmic principles, etc.).

61 One could refer here to the Kantian opposition of the beautiful and the sublime: the chaos of wild nature is "sublime" insofar as, *per negationem*, it recalls the dimension of the suprasensible Idea. It is the same with the encounter of the senseless real: the subject is never simply absent from it—the very absence, the lack that the brute presence of the real recalls *is* the subject.

6

WHY IS REALITY ALWAYS MULTIPLE?

6.1 IS THERE A PROPER WAY TO REMAKE A HITCHCOCK FILM?

In any large American bookstore, it is possible to purchase some volumes of the unique series *Shakespeare Made Easy*,[1] a "bilingual" edition of Shakespeare's plays, with the original archaic English on the left page and the translation into common contemporary English on the right page. The obscene satisfaction provided by reading these volumes resides in how what purports to be a mere translation into contemporary English turns out to be much more: as a rule, Durband tries to formulate directly, in everyday locution, what he considers to be the thought expressed in Shakespeare's metaphoric idiom; "To be or not to be, that is the question" becomes something like, "What's bothering me now is: Shall I kill myself or not?" And my idea is, of course, that the standard remakes of Alfred Hitchcock's films are precisely something like "Hitchcock Made Easy": although the narrative is the same, the "substance," the flair that accounts for Hitchcock's uniqueness, evaporates. Here, however, one should avoid the jargon-laden talk on Hitchcock's unique touch, and approach the difficult task of specifying what gives Hitchcock's films their unique flair.

Or, what if this uniqueness is a myth, the result of our (spectators) transference, elevation of Hitchcock into the Subject Supposed to Know? What I have in mind is the attitude of overinterpretation: everything in a Hitchcock film has to have a meaning—there are no contingencies—so that when something doesn't fit, it's not his fault, but ours—we didn't really get it. While watching *Psycho* for the twentieth time, I noticed a strange detail during the final psychiatrist's explanation: Lilah (Vera Miles) listens to him, rapt, and nods two times with a deep satisfaction, instead of being shaken by the final confirmation of her sister's meaningless death. Was this a pure contingency, or did Hitchcock want to suggest a strange libidinal ambiguity and rivalry between the two sisters? Or the scene of Marion driving in the night on her escape from Phoenix: just before reaching the Bates motel, when she listens to the imagined voices of her boss and the millionaire who bought the house, furious at her deception, her expression is no longer anguished; what we perceive is a strange manic smile of a deeply perverse satisfaction, an expression that uncannily resembles the very last shot of Norman-mother, just before it dissolves into the skull and then the car appearing out of the swamp. So, in a way, even before actually meeting him, Marion already becomes Norman: a further feature that confirms this point is that her expression emerges when she is listening to the voices in her head, exactly like Norman in his final appearance. Or—the supreme example—the scene in which Marion checks in at the Bates Motel: while Norman has his back turned to her, inspecting the row of keys to the rooms, she furtively looks around to get an idea which city to put down as her residence, sees the words "Los Angeles" as part of a newspaper headline and writes them down. Here two hesitations coincide: while Marion hesitates as to which town to write (which lie to tell), Norman hesitates as to which unit to put her in (if it's number 1, this means that he will be able to observe her secretly through a peephole). When, after some hesitation, she tells him "Los Angeles," Norman picks up and gives her the key of the number 1 unit. Is his hesitation a simple sign that he was considering her sexual attraction and then finally opted to pursue her, or is it that, at a more refined level, he detected in her hesitation that she is about to tell him a lie, and then countered her lie with an illegal act of his own, finding in her small crime the justification for his own? (Or is it rather that, upon hearing that she is from Los Angeles, he thinks that the girl from such a decadent town can be an easy pick?) Although Joseph Stefano, who wrote the scenario, claims[2] the creators had in mind only the growing sexual attraction that Norman felt for Marion, there remains the shadow of a doubt that the coincidence of two hesitations cannot be purely contingent . . . This is called "true love" in theory. So, out of this true love, I claim that there is a unique Hitchcockian dimension.

The Hitchcockian sinthom

My first thesis is that this unique dimension is not to be sought primarily at the level of the narrative content; its original locus is elsewhere, but where? Let me begin by contrasting two scenes from two non-Hitchcockian films. There is one memorable scene in the otherwise dull and pretentious Robert Redford's *A River Runs through It*. Of the two preacher's sons, we are all the time aware that the younger one (Brad Pitt) is on a path to self-destruction, approaching catastrophe because of his compulsive gambling, drinking, and womanizing. The thing that keeps the two sons together with their father is fly fishing in the wild Montana rivers—these Sunday fishing expeditions are a kind of sacred family ritual, a time when the threats of the life outside family are temporarily suspended. So when they go fishing for the last time, Pitt achieves perfection: he adroitly catches the biggest fish ever; however, the way he proceeds is presented with a shadow of constant threat: will the dark river bend where he spots the great trout swallow him, will he reappear after he slips into the fast water? It is as if this potential threat announces the final tragedy that occurs shortly afterward (Pitt is found dead, with his fingers broken, a result of his gambling debts).

What renders this scene from *A River Runs through It* rather ordinary is that the underlying threatening dimension is directly reinscribed into the main narrative line, as an index pointing toward the final catastrophe. In contrast to it, Peter Yates' outstanding *Breaking Away* (1979), a gentle comedy/drama about the coming of age of four high school kids in Bloomington, Indiana, in the final summer before they face the inexorable choices of jobs or college or the Army, resisted this temptation. In one of the memorable small sequences, Dave, one of the kids, on a racing bicycle engages in a high-speed highway duel with a semitrailer truck. The uneasy effect is here the same as in a couple of scenes involving swimming in an abandoned quarry, in which kids jump into deep dark water with bits of sharp stones hidden beneath the surface: Yates suggests the constant possibility of sudden catastrophe. We wait for the terrible accident to happen, for Dave to be hit and crushed by the truck, for one of the kids to drown in the dark water or to hit some sharp stone when jumping into it. None does, but the hints of one (its threatening shadow evoked just by the general atmosphere of the way the scene is shot, not by any direct psychological references, like the uneasiness felt by the kids) make the characters seem strangely vulnerable. It is as if these hints lay the ground for the very end of the film, when we learn, from the legend on the screen, that, afterwards, one of these kids died in Vietnam, another had a different accident. This tension between the two levels is what I want to focus on: the gap that separates the explicit narrative line from the diffused threatening message delivered between the lines of the story.

Let me introduce here a parallel with Richard Wagner (is not the ring from Wagner's *Nibelungen* the greatest MacGuffin of all times?). In his last two operas, the same gesture is performed: toward the end of *Götterdämmerung*, the dead Siegfried, when Hagen approaches him in order to snatch the ring from his hand, threateningly raises his hand; toward the end of *Parsifal*, in the midst of Amfortas's lament and refusal to perform the ritualistic unveiling of the Grail, his dead father Titurel also miraculously lifts his hand. Features like this attest to the fact that Wagner was a Hitchcockian *avant la lettre*: in Hitchcock's films, we also find the same visual or other motif that insists, imposing itself through an uncanny compulsion and repeating itself from one film to another, in totally different narrative contexts. Best known is the motif of what Sigmund Freud called *Niederkommenlassen*, "letting oneself fall down," with all the undertones of melancholic suicidal fall:[3] a person desperately clinging by his hand onto another person's hand, as in the Nazi *saboteur* clinging from the good American hero's hand from the torch of the Statue of Liberty in *Saboteur*; the final confrontation of *Rear Window*, the crippled James Stewart hanging from the window, trying to grab the hand of his pursuer who, instead of helping him, tries to make him fall; in *The Man Who Knew Too Much* (remake, 1955), at the sunny Casablanca market, the dying Western agent, dressed as an Arab, stretches his hand to the innocent American tourist (James Stewart), pulling him down toward himself; the finally unmasked thief clinging from Cary Grant's hand in *To Catch a Thief*; James Stewart clinging from the roof funnel and desperately trying to grasp the policeman's hand stretching toward him at the very beginning of *Vertigo*; Eva Marie-Saint clinging from Cary Grant's hand at the edge of the precipice (with the immediate jump to her clinging to his hand in the sleeping car's berth) at the end of *North by Northwest*. Upon a closer look, we become aware that Hitchcock's films are full of such motifs. There is the motif of a car on the border of a precipice in *Suspicion* and in *North by Northwest*—in each of the two films, there is a scene with the same actor (Cary Grant) driving a car and dangerously approaching a precipice; although the films are separated by almost twenty years, the scene is shot in the same way, including a subjective shot of the actor casting a glance into the precipice. (In Hitchcock's last film, *Family Plot*, this motif explodes in a long sequence of the car that rushes down the hill, since its brakes were meddled with by the villains.) There is the motif of the "woman who knows too much," intelligent and perceptive, but sexually unattractive, with spectacles, and—significantly—resembling or even directly played by Hitchcock's own daughter Patricia: Ruth Roman's sister in *Strangers On a Train*, Barbara del Geddes in *Vertigo*, Patricia Hitchcock in *Psycho*, and even Ingrid Bergman prior to her sexual awakening in *Spellbound*. There is the motif of the mummified skull that first appears in *Under Capricorn* and finally in *Psycho*—both times, it terrifies the young woman (Ingrid Bergman, Vera Miles) in the final confrontation. There is the motif of a Gothic house with big stairs, with the hero walking up the stairs where, in the room, there is nothing, although he previously saw a feminine silhouette on the first-floor window: in *Vertigo*, it is the enigmatic episode of Madeleine seen by Scottie as a shade in the window and then inexplicably disappearing from the house; in *Psycho*, it is the appearance of the mother's shadow in the window—again, bodies that appear out of nowhere and disappear back into the void. Furthermore, the fact that in *Vertigo* this episode remains unexplained opens up the temptation to read it in a kind of *futur antérieur*, as already pointing toward *Psycho*. Is the old lady who is the hotel clerk of the house not a kind of strange condensation of Norman Bates and his mother—the clerk (Norman) who is at the same time the old lady (mother)—thus giving in advance the clue to their identity, which is the big mystery of *Psycho? Vertigo* is of a special interest, insofar as in it the same sinthom of the spiral that draws us into its abyssal depth repeats itself and resonates at a multitude of levels: first as a purely formal motif of the abstract form emerging out of the close-up of the eye in the credits sequence; then as the curl of Carlotta Valdes' hair in her portrait, repeated in Madeleine's haircut; then as the abyssal circle of the staircase of the church tower; and, finally, in the famous 360 degrees shot around Scottie and Judy/Madeleine who are passionately embracing in the decrepit hotel room, and during which the background changes to the stable of the Juan Batista Mission and then back to the hotel room; perhaps, this last shot offers the key to the temporal dimension of "vertigo"—the self-enclosed temporal loop in which past and present are condensed into the two aspects of the same endlessly repeated circular movement. It is this multiple resonance of surfaces that generates the specific density, the "depth" of the film's texture.

Here we have a set of (visual, formal, material) motives that "remain the same" across different contexts of meaning. How are we to read such persisting gestures or motifs? One should resist the temptation to treat them as Jungian archetypes with a deep meaning—the raised hand in Wagner expressing threat of the dead person to the living; or the person clinging by another's hand expressing the tension between spiritual fall and salvation. We are dealing here with the level of material signs that resists meaning and establishes connections not grounded in narrative symbolic structures: they just relate in a kind of presymbolic cross-resonance. They are not signifiers, neither the famous Hitchcockian stains, but elements of what, a decade or two ago, one would have called cinematic writing, *écriture*. In the last years of his teaching, Jacques Lacan established the difference between symptom, and sinthom: in contrast to symptom which is a cipher of some repressed meaning, sinthom has no determinate meaning; it just gives body, in its repetitive pattern, to some elementary matrix of jouissance, of excessive enjoyment. Although sinthoms do not have sense, they do radiate *jouis*-sense, enjoy-meant.[4] According to Svetlana Alliluyeva, Joseph Stalin's daughter, the last gesture of the dying Stalin, significantly preceded by the cast of the evil gaze, was the same gesture as in Wagner's last operas, the gesture of threateningly raising the left hand:

> At what seemed like the very last moment [Stalin] suddenly opened his eyes and cast a glance over everyone in the room. It was a terrible glance, insane or perhaps angry and full of fear of death and the unfamiliar faces of the doctors bent over him. The glance swept over everyone in a second. Then something incomprehensible and terrible happened that to this day I can't forget and don't understand. He suddenly lifted his left hand as though he were pointing to something up above and bringing down a curse on us all. The gesture was incomprehensible and full of menace, and no one could say to whom or what it might be directed. The next moment, after a final effort, the spirit wrenched itself free of the flesh.[5]

What, then, did this gesture mean? The Hitchcockian answer is *nothing*—yet this nothing was not an empty nothing, but the fullness of libidinal investment, a tic that gave body to a cipher of enjoyment. Perhaps, the closest equivalent in painting are the protracted stains that "are" the yellow sky in van Gogh, or the water or grass in Munch: this uncanny "massiveness" pertains neither to the direct materiality of the color stains nor to the materiality of the depicted objects; it dwells in a kind of intermediate spectral domain of what Friedrich Schelling called *geistige Körperlichkeit*, the spiritual corporeality. From the Lacanian perspective, it is easy to identify this spiritual corporeality as materialized jouissance, "jouissance which turned into flesh." Hitchcock's sinthoms are thus not mere formal patterns: they already condense a certain libidinal investment. As such, they determined his creative process: Hitchcock did not proceed from the plot to its translation in cinematic audio-visual terms. He rather started with a set of (usually visual) motifs that haunted his imagination, that imposed themselves as his sinthoms; he then constructed a narrative that served as the pretext for their use. These sinthoms provide the specific flair, the substantial density of the cinematic texture of Hitchcock's films: without them we would have a lifeless formal narrative. So all the talk about Hitchcock as the "master of suspense," about his unique twisted plots, and so forth, misses the key dimension. Fredric Jameson said of Hemingway that he selected his narratives in order to be able to write certain kinds of (tense, masculine) phrases. The same goes for Hitchcock: he invented stories in order to be able to shoot a certain kind of scene. And, while the narratives of his films provide a funny and often perceptive comment of our times, it is in his sinthoms that Hitchcock lives forever. They are the true cause of why his films continue to function as objects of our desire.

The case of the missing gaze

Our next concern is with the status of the gaze. The so-called posttheorists (cognitivist critics of psychoanalytic cinema theory) like to vary the motif of how writers of the theory refer to mythical entities like the (capitalized) Gaze, entities to which no empirical, observable facts (like the actual cinema viewers and their behavior) correspond. The title of one of the essays in David Bordwell and Noel Carroll's *Post-Theory* is "The Case of the Missing Spectator."[6] Posttheory relies here on the commonsense notion of the spectator (the subject who perceives cinematic reality on the screen, equipped with his emotional and cognitive predispositions, etc.) and within this simple opposition between subject and object of cinematic perception, there is, of course, no place for the gaze as the point from which the viewed object itself returns the gaze and regards us, the spectators. That is to say, crucial for the Lacanian notion of the gaze is that it involves the reversal of the relationship between subject and object: as Lacan puts it in volume 11 of his *Seminar* series, there is an antinomy between the eye and the gaze—that is, the gaze is on the side of the object, it stands for the blind spot in the field of the visible from which the picture itself photographs the spectator; or, as he puts it in volume 1 of his *Seminar* series, in a passage which uncannily evokes the central scene of *Rear Window*, the film shot in the same year that Lacan's *Seminar* was held (1954):

> I can feel myself under the gaze of someone whose eyes I do not see, not even discern. All that is necessary is for something to signify to me that there may be others there. This window, if it gets a bit dark, and if I have reasons for thinking that there is someone behind it, is straight-away a gaze.[7]

Is this notion of the gaze not perfectly rendered by the exemplary Hitchcockian scene in which the subject is approaching some uncanny threatening object, usually a house? There we encounter the antinomy between the eye and the gaze at its purest: the subject's eye sees the house, but the house—the object—seems somehow to return the gaze. No wonder, then, that the posttheorists speak of the "missing gaze," complaining that the Freudo-Lacanian gaze is a mythical entity nowhere found in the actuality of the spectator's experience: this gaze effectively is missing, its status is purely fantasmatic. At a more fundamental level, what we are dealing with here is the positivization of an impossibility that gives rise to the fetish object. For example, how does the object/gaze become a fetish? Through the Hegelian reversal from the impossibility to see the object, into an object that gives body to this very impossibility: since the subject cannot directly see that, the true object of fascination, he accomplishes a kind of reflection-into-self by means of which the object that fascinates him becomes the gaze itself. In this sense (although not in an entirely symmetrical way), gaze and voice are "reflective" objects, objects that give body to an impossibility (in Lacanian "mathems": = ø/a).

In this precise sense, fantasy proper is not the scene itself that attracts our fascination, but the imagined/inexistent gaze observing it, like the impossible gaze from above for which old Aztecs created gigantic figures of birds and animals on the ground, or the impossible gaze for which details of the sculptures on the old aqueduct to Rome were formed, although they were essentially unobservable from the ground. In short, the most elementary fantasmatic scene is not that of a fascinating scene to be looked at, but the notion that "there is someone out there looking at us"; it is not a dream, but the notion that "we are the objects in someone else's dream." Milan Kundera, in *La Lenteur*, presents as the ultimate sign of today's false aseptic pseudovoluptuous sex the couple feigning to have anal sex at the side of a hotel pool, in view of the guests in the rooms above, faking pleasurable cries but effectively not even accomplishing the penetration; to this he opposes the slow galant intimate erotic games of eighteenth-century France. Did not something similar to the scene from *La Lenteur* effectively take place in Khmer Rouge Cambodia where, after too many people died from purges and starvations, the regime, eager to multiply the population, proclaimed the first, tenth and twentieth day of each month the day for copulation: in the evening, the married couples (who otherwise had to sleep in separate barracks) were allowed to sleep together and compelled to make love. Their private space was a small cubicle isolated by a half-transparent bamboo curtain; in front of the row of such cubicles, Khmer Rouge guards walked, verifying that couples were effectively copulating. Since the couples knew that not making love was considered an act of sabotage to be severely punished, and since, on the other hand, after a fourteen-hour workday they were as a rule too tired to effectively have sex, they pretended to make love in order to dupe the guardian's attention: they made false movements and faked sounds. Is this not the exact inverse of the experience from the prepermissive youth of some of us, when one had to sneak into the bedroom with the partner and do it as silently as possible, so that parents, if they were still awake, would not suspect that sex was going on? What if, then, such a spectacle for the Other's gaze is part of the sexual act—what if, since there is no sexual relationship, it can only be staged for the Other's gaze?

Does not the recent trend of "web cam" sites that realize the logic of *The Truman Show* (in these sites, we are able to follow continuously some event or place: the life of a person in her apartment, the view on a street, etc.) display this same urgent need for the fantasmatic Other's gaze serving as the guarantee of the subject's being? "I exist only insofar as I am looked at all the time." (Similar to this is the phenomenon, noted by Claude Lefort, of the TV set that is left on all the time, even when no one effectively watches it, serving as the minimum guarantee of the existence of social link.) The situation is here thus the tragicomic reversal of the Bentham-Orwellian notion of panopticon society in which we are (potentially) "observed all the time" and have no place to hide from the omnipresent gaze of the power: here, anxiety arises from the prospect of *not* being exposed to the Other's gaze all the time, so that the subject needs the camera's gaze as a kind of ontological guarantee of his being . . .

As to this paradox of the omnipresent gaze, a funny thing happened not long ago to a friend of mine in Slovenia: he returned to his office late in the night to finish some work; before he put the light on, he observed in the office across the courtyard a senior (married) manager and his secretary copulating on his table. In the midst of their passion, they had forgotten that there is a building across the courtyard, from which they could be clearly seen since their office was brightly lit and there were no curtains on the large windows. My friend phoned this particular office, and when the manager, interrupting his sexual activity for a brief intermission picked up the phone, he whispered ominously into the receiver: "God is observing you!" The poor manager collapsed and almost had a heart attack. The intervention of such a traumatic voice that cannot be directly located in reality is perhaps the closest we can come to the experience of the sublime.

And Hitchcock is at its most uncanny and disturbing when he engages us directly with the point of view of this external fantasmatic gaze. One of the standard horror-movie procedures is the "resignification" of the objective into the subjective shot (what the spectator first perceives as an objective shot—say, of a house with a family at dinner—is all of a sudden, by means of such codified markers as the slight trembling of the camera or the "subjectivized" soundtrack, revealed as the subjective shot of a murderer stalking his potential victims). However, this procedure is to be supplemented with its opposite, the unexpected reversal of subjective into objective shot: in the midst of a long shot unambiguously marked as subjective, the spectator is all of a sudden compelled to acknowledge that there is no possible subject within the space of diegetic reality who can occupy the point of view of this shot. So we are not dealing here with the simple reversal of objective into subjective, but in constructing a place of impossible subjectivity, a subjectivity that taints the very objectivity with a flavor of unspeakable, monstrous evil. An entire heretic theology is discernible here, secretly identifying creator himself as the devil (which was already the thesis of the Cathar heresy in twentieth-century France). The exemplary cases of this impossible subjectivity are the "subjective" shot from the standpoint of the murderous thing itself upon the tranfixed face of the dying detective Arbogast in *Psycho*, or, in *The Birds*, the famous God's view shot of the burning Bodega Bay, which is then, with the entry into the frame of the birds, resignified, subjectivized into the point of view of the evil aggressors themselves.

Multiple endings

There is yet another, third, aspect that adds a specific density to Hitchcock's films: the implicit resonance of multiple endings. The most obvious and well-documented case is, of course, that of *Topaz*: before deciding on the ending that we all know, Hitchcock shot two alternative endings, and my point is that it is not sufficient to say that he simply chose the most appropriate ending—the ending we have now in a way presupposes the two other, with the three endings forming a kind of syllogism, that is Granville, the Russian spy, (Michel Piccoli) telling himself, "They cannot prove anything to me, I can simply leave for Russia" (the first discarded ending); "But the Russians themselves now do not want me, I am now even dangerous to them, so they will probably kill me" (the second discarded meaning); "What can I do then if in France I am outcast as a Russian spy and Russia itself no longer wants me? I can only kill myself" (the ending that was effectively chosen). There are, however, much more refined versions of this implicit presence of alternative endings. I think that *Notorious* owes at least a part of its powerful impact to the fact that its denouement should be perceived against the background of at least two other possible outcomes that resonate in it as a kind of alternative history.[8] In the first outline of the story, Alicia wins redemption by the film's end, but loses Devlin, who is killed rescuing her from the Nazis. The idea was that this sacrificial act should solve the tension between Devlin, who is unable to admit to Alicia his love for her, and Alicia, who is unable to perceive herself as worthy of love: Devlin admits his love for her without words, by dying in order to save her life. In the final scene, we find Alicia back in Miami with her group of drinking friends: although she is more "notorious" than ever, she has in her heart the memory of a man who loved her and died for her, and, as Hitchcock put it in a memo to the producer David. O. Selznick, "to her this is the same as if she had achieved a life of marriage and happiness." In the second version, the outcome is the opposite; here, we already have the idea of a slow poisoning of Alicia by Sebastian and his mother. Devlin confronts the Nazis and flees with Alicia, but Alicia dies in the process. In the epilogue, Devlin sits alone in the café in Rio, where he used to meet Alicia, and overhears people discussing the death of Sebastian's wanton and treacherous wife. However, the letter in his hands is a commendation from President Harry Truman citing Alicia's bravery. Devlin pockets the letter and finishes his drink. Finally, the version we know was arrived at, with a finale that implies that Devlin and Alicia are now married. Hitchcock then left this finale out, to end on a more tragic note, with Sebastian, who truly loved Alicia, left to face the Nazi's deadly wrath. The point is that both alternative endings are incorporated into the film, as a kind of fantasmatic background of the action we see on the screen: if they are to constitute a couple, both Devlin and Alicia have to undergo the "symbolic death," so that the happy ending emerges from the combination of two unhappy endings—that is, these two alternative fantasmatic scenarios sustain the denouement we actually see.

This feature allows us to insert Hitchcock into the series of artists whose work forecasts today's digital universe. That is to say, art historians often noted the phenomenon of the old artistic forms pushing against their own boundaries and using procedures that, at least from our retroactive view, seem to point toward a new technology that will be able to serve as a more "natural" and appropriate "objective correlative" to the life experience the old forms endeavored to render by means of their "excessive" experimentations. A whole series of narrative procedures in nineteenth-century novels announce not only the standard narrative cinema (the intricate use of "flashback" in Emily Brontë or of "cross-cutting" and "close-ups" in Charles Dickens), but sometimes even the modernist cinema (the use of "off space" in *Madame Bovary*)—as if a new perception of life was already here but still struggling to find its proper means of articulation until it finally found it in cinema. What we have here is thus the historicity of a kind of *futur antérieur*: it is only once cinema had come about and developed its standard procedures that we could really grasp the narrative logic of Dickens's great novels or of *Madame Bovary*.

And is it not that today we are approaching a homologous threshold? A new "life experience" is in the air, a perception of life that explodes the form of the linear, centered narrative and renders life as a multiform flow—even and up to the domain of "hard" sciences (quantum physics and its multiple reality interpretation, or the utter contingency that provided the spin to the actual evolution of life on Earth—as Stephen Jay Gould demonstrated in his *Wonderful Life*,[9] the fossils of Burgess Shale bear witness to how evolution may have taken a wholly different turn) we seem to be haunted by the chanciness of life and the alternate versions of reality. Either life is experienced as a series of multiple parallel destinies that interact and are crucially affected by meaningless contingent encounters, the points at which one series intersects with and intervenes into another (see Robert Altman's *Short Cuts*), or different versions/outcomes of the same plot are repeatedly enacted (the "parallel universes" or "alternative possible worlds" scenarios—see Krzysztof Kieslowski's *Chance*, *Veronique*, and *Red*; even "serious" historians themselves recently produced a volume, *Virtual History*,[10] a reading of crucial modern age events from Oliver Cromwell's victory over the Stuarts to the American Revolutionary War to the disintegration of Communism as hinging on unpredictable and sometimes even improbable chances). This perception of our reality as one of the possible—often even not the most probable—outcomes of an "open" situation, this notion that other possible outcomes are not simply cancelled out but continue to haunt our "true" reality as a specter of what might have happened, conferring on our reality the status of extreme fragility and contingency, implicitly clashes with the predominant "linear" narrative forms of our literature and cinema, they seem to call for a new artistic medium in which they would not be an eccentric excess, but its "proper" mode of functioning. The notion of creation also changes with this new experience of the world: it no longer designates the positive act of imposing a new order, but rather the negative gesture of choice, of limiting the possibilities, of privileging one option at the expense of all others. One can argue that the cyberspace hypertext is the new medium in which this life experience will find its "natural," more appropriate objective correlative, so that, again, it is only with the advent of cyberspace hypertext that we can effectively grasp what Altman and Kieslowski—and, implicitly, also Hitchcock—were effectively aiming at.

The Ideal Remake

This, perhaps, also points towards what a proper remake of a Hitchcock film would be. To try and imitate Hitchcockian sinthoms is an exercise condemned in advance to failure; to remake the same narrative results in a Shakespeare Made Easy output. So there are only two ways left. One is indicated by Gus van Sant's remake of *Psycho* which, paradoxically, I am inclined to consider a failed masterpiece, rather than a simple failure. The idea of the exact frame-by-frame remake is an ingenious idea, and, in my view, the problem was rather that the film did not go far enough in this direction. Ideally, what the film should strive for is to achieve the uncanny effect of the double: in shooting formally the same film, the difference would have become all the more palpable. Everything would have been the same—same shots, angles, and dialogue—but nonetheless, on account of this very sameness we would all the more powerfully experience that we are dealing with a totally different film. This gap should have been signaled by barely perceptible nuances in the way of acting, in the choice of actors, in the use of color, and so on. Some elements in van Sant's film already point in this direction: the roles of Norman, Lilah (portrayed as a lesbian) and Marion (a nonmaternal, withdrawn, cold bitch in contrast to the big-breasted and maternal Janet Leigh), even Arbogast and Sam, nicely indicate the shift from the late 1950s to the present. While some added shots are acceptable (like the enigmatic subjective shots of cloudy sky during the two murders), problems resurface with the more brutal changes (like Norman's masturbating while he spies on Marion before killing her, one is tempted to make the rather obvious point that if he were to be able to arrive at this kind of sexual satisfaction there would have been no need for him to accomplish the violent *passage à l'acte* of slaughtering her!); worse yet, some scenes are completely ruined, their impact completely lost, by changing Hitchcock's precise framing (say, the key scene in which, after leaving her office with the money, Marion, now at home, prepares to escape). Hitchcock's own remakes (the two versions of *The Man Who Knew Too Much*, as well as *Saboteur* and *North by Northwest*) point in this direction: although the narrative is very similar, the underlying libidinal economy is wholly different in each of the subsequent remakes, as if sameness serves the purpose of marking difference.[11]

The second way would be to stage, in a well-calculated strategic move, one of the alternative scenarios that underlie the one actualized by Hitchcock, like the remake of *Notorious* in which Ingrid Bergman survives alone. This would be a proper way to honor Hitchcock as an artist who belongs to our era. Perhaps, more than Brian de Palma's and others' direct homages to Hitchcock, the scenes that announce such a proper remake are to be found in unexpected places, like a scene in the film *The Conversation* by Francis Ford Coppola, who certainly is not a

Hitchcockian director. In it, the investigator inspects a hotel room, the scene of a crime, with a Hitchcockian gaze, like Lilah and Sam do in Marion's motel room in *Psycho*, moving from the main bedroom to the bathroom and focusing there on the toilet and the shower. This shift from the shower (where there are no traces of the crime, everything is clean) to the toilet, elevating it into the Hitchcockian object that attracts our gaze, fascinating us with its premonition of some unspeakable horror, is crucial here (recall Hitchcock's battle with censorship to allow the inside view of the toilet, from where Sam picks up a torn piece of paper with Marion's writing of the amounts of spent money, the proof that she was there). After a series of obvious references to *Psycho* apropos the bathroom (quickly pulling open the curtain, inspecting its drain), the investigator focuses on the (allegedly clean) toilet, flushes it, and then the stain appears as if out of nowhere, blood and other traces of the crime overflowing the edge of the toilet bowl. This scene, a kind of *Psycho* reread through *Marnie* (with its red stain blurring the screen) contains the main elements of the Hitchcockian universe: it has the Hitchcockian object that materializes some unspecified threat, functioning as the hole of passage into another abyssal dimension (is flushing the toilet in this scene not like pushing the wrong button that dissolves the entire universe in science fiction novels?); this object, which simultaneously attracts and repels the subject, can be said to be the point from which the inspected setting returns the gaze (is it not that the hero is somehow regarded by the toilet sink?); and, finally, Coppola realizes the alternative scenario of the toilet itself as the ultimate locus of mystery. What makes this mini-remake of a scene so effective is that Coppola suspends the prohibition operative in *Psycho*: the threat *does* explode, the camera *does* show the danger hanging in the air in *Psycho*, the chaotic bloody mess erupting from the toilet.[12] (And is not the swamp behind the house in which Norman sinks the car with the body of his victim a kind of gigantic pool of excremental mud, so that one can say that he has in a way flushed the car down the toilet? The famous moment, earlier in the film, with the worried expression on Norman's face as Marion's car stops its descent into the swamp for a couple of seconds effectively signals the worry that the toilet did not swallow the traces of the crime. The very last shot of *Psycho*, in which we see Marion's car being pulled out of the swamp, is thus a kind of

Hitchcockian equivalent to the blood reemerging out of the toilet sink—in short, this swamp is another in the series of the entrance points to the preontological netherworld.)

And is not the same reference to the preontological underworld operative also in the final scene of *Vertigo*? In predigital times, when I was in my teens, I remember seeing a bad copy of *Vertigo*. Its last seconds were simply missing, so that the movie appeared to have a happy ending: Scottie reconciled with Judy, forgiving her and accepting her as a partner, the two of them passionately embracing. My point is that such an ending is not as artificial as it may seem: it is rather, in the actual ending, that the sudden appearance of the Mother Superior from the staircase below functions as a kind of negative deus ex machina, a sudden intrusion in no way properly grounded in the narrative logic, that prevents the happy ending.[13] Where does the nun appear from? From the same preontological realm of shadows from which Scottie himself secretly observes Madeleine in the florist's shop.[14] It is the reference to this preontological realm that allows us to approach the quintessential Hitchcockian scene that was never shot, precisely because it renders the basic matrix of his work directly, its actual filming undoubtedly would have produced a vulgar, tasteless effect. Here is this scene that Hitchcock wanted to insert in *North by Northwest*, as reported in Truffauts' conversations with the Master:

> I wanted to have a long dialogue between Cary Grant and one of the factory workers [at a Ford automobile plant] as they walk along the assembly line. Behind them a car is being assembled, piece by piece. Finally, the car they've seen being put together from a simple nut and bolt is complete, with gas and oil, and all ready to drive off the line. The two men look at each other and say, "Isn't it wonderful!" Then they open the door of the car and out drops a corpse.[15]

Where did this corpse emerge—fall—from? Again, from the very void from which Scottie observes Madeleine in the florist's shop, or from the void from which blood emerges in *The Conversation*. (One should also bear in mind that what we would have seen in this long shot is the elementary unity of the production process; is then the corpse that mysteriously drops out from nowhere not the perfect stand-in for the surplus value that is generated "out of nowhere" through the production process?) This shocking elevation of the ridiculously lowest (the "beyond" to where excrement disappears) into the metaphysical sublime is perhaps one of the mysteries of Hitchcock's art. Is not the sublime sometimes part of our most common everyday experience? When, in the midst of accomplishing a simple task (say, climbing the long line of stairs), we are overwhelmed by an unexpected fatigue, it all of a sudden appears as if the simple goal we want to reach (the top of the stairs) is separated from us by an unfathomable barrier and thus changed into a metaphysical object forever out of our reach, as if there is something that forever prevents us from accomplishing it. And the domain to where excrement vanishes after we flush the toilet is effectively one of the metaphors for the horrifyingly sublime "beyond" of the primordial, preontological chaos into which things disappear. Although we rationally know what goes on with the excrement, the imaginary mystery nonetheless persists: shit remains an excess that does not fit our daily reality, and Lacan was right in claiming that we pass from animals to humans the moment an animal has problems with what to do with its excrement, the moment that waste turns into an excess that annoys the animal. What is "Real" in the scene from *The Conversation* is thus not primarily the horrifying and disgusting stuff reemerging from the toilet sink, but rather the toilet's drain itself, the hole that serves as the passage to a different ontological order. The similarity between the empty toilet sink before the remainders of the murder reemerge from it and Kasimir Malevich's *The Black Square on the White Surface* is significant here: does the look from above into the toilet sink not reproduce almost the same minimalist visual scheme, a black (or, at least, darker) square of water framed by the white surface of the sink itself? Again, we of course know that the excrement that disappears is somewhere in the sewage network; what is here "real" is the topological hole or torsion that bends the space of our reality so that we perceive/imagine excrement as disappearing into an alternative dimension that is not part of our everyday reality.

Hitchcock's obsession with cleansing the bathroom or the toilet after its use is well-known, and it is significant that when, after Marion's murder, he wants to shift our point of identification to Norman, he does this with a long rendering of the careful process of cleaning the bathroom. This is perhaps the key scene of the film, a scene that provides an uncanny profound satisfaction of the job properly done, of things returning back to normal, of situation being again under control, of the traces of the horrifying netherworld being erased. One is tempted to read this scene against the background of the well-known proposition of Saint Thomas Aquinas according to which a virtue (defined as a proper way to accomplish an act) can also serve evil purposes: one can also be a perfect thief, murderer, extortioner, that is accomplish an evil act in a "virtuous" way. What this scene of cleansing the bathroom in *Psycho* demonstrates is how the "lower" perfection can imperceptibly affect the "higher" goal: Norman's virtuous perfection in cleaning the bathroom, of course, serves the evil purpose of erasing the traces of the crime; however, this very perfection, the dedication and the thoroughness of his act, seduces us, into assuming that, if someone acts in such a "perfect" way, he should be in his entirety a good and sympathetic person. In short, someone who cleans the bathroom so thoroughly cannot be really bad, in spite of his other minor peculiarities. (Or, to put it even more pointedly, in a country governed by Norman, trains would certainly run on time!) While watching this scene recently, I caught myself nervously noticing that the bathroom was not properly cleaned—two small stains on the side of the bathtub remained! I almost wanted to shout, Hey, it's not yet over, finish the job properly! Is it not that *Psycho* points here towards today's ideological perception in which work itself (manual labor as opposed to "symbolic" activity), and not sex, becomes the site of obscene indecency to be concealed from the public eye? The tradition, going back to Richard Wagner's *Rheingold* and Fritz Lang's *Metropolis*, in which the working process takes place underground, in dark caves, today culminates in the millions of anonymous workers sweating in third world factories, from Chinese gulags to Indonesian or Brazilian assembly lines; in their invisibility, the West can itself afford to babble on about the "disappearing working class." Yet what is crucial in this tradition is the equation of labor with crime, the idea that labor—hard work—is originally an indecent criminal activity to be hidden from the public eye. The only place in Hollywood films where we see the production process in all its intensity are when the action hero penetrates the master criminal's secret domain and locates there the site of intense labor (the manufacture and packaging of drugs, the construction of a rocket that will destroy New York). When, in a James Bond movie, the master criminal, after capturing Bond, usually takes him on a tour of his illegal factory, is this not the closest Hollywood comes to the socialist-realist proud presentation of the production in a factory?[17] And the function of Bond's intervention, of course, is to blow up this site of production, allowing us to return to the daily semblance of our existence in a world with a "disappearing working class."

And, incidentally, is the same attitude of forceful identification against one's will not clearly discernible in those leftist cinema theorists who are in a similar way forced to love Hitchcock, to libidinally identify with him, although they are well aware that, measured by the standards of "political correctness," his work reads as a catalog of sins (obsession with cleanliness and control, women created upon the male image, etc.)? I never found convincing the standard explanation from leftist theorists who cannot help but love Hitchcock: Yes, his universe is a male chauvinist one, but at the same time he renders visible its cracks and as it were subverts it from within. I think the socio-political dimension of Hitchcock's films is to be sought elsewhere. Let us take the two closures at the end of *Psycho*—first the psychiatrist wraps up the story, then Norman-Mother herself delivers the final monologue, "I wouldn't even hurt a fly!" This split between the two closures tells more about the deadlock of contemporary subjectivity than a dozen essays in cultural criticism. That is to say, it may appear that we are dealing with the well-known split between expert knowledge and our private solipsistic universes, deplored by many social critics today: common sense, a shared set of ethically engaged presuppositions, is slowly disintegrating, and what we get is, on the one hand, the objectivized language of experts and scientists that can no longer be translated into the common language accessible to everyone but is present in it in the mode of fetishized formulas that no one really understands, but which shape our artistic and popular imaginary (black holes, the big bang theory, superstrings, quantum oscillation . . .); and, on the other hand, the multitude of life styles that one cannot translate into each other: all we can do is secure the conditions for their tolerant coexistence in a multicultural society. The icon of today's subject is perhaps the Indian computer programmer who, during the day, excels in his expertise, while in the evening, upon returning home, lights a candle to a Hindu divinity and respects the sacredness of the cow.

However, on a closer look, it soon becomes apparent how this opposition is displaced at the end of *Psycho*: it is the psychiatrist, the representative of cold objective knowledge, who speaks in an engaged, almost warmly human way—his explanation is full of personal tics, sympathetic gestures—while Norman, withdrawn into his private world, is precisely no longer himself, but totally possessed by another psychic entity, the mother's ghost. This final image of Norman reminds me of the way they are shooting soap operas in Mexico: because of the extremely tight schedule (the studio has to produce each day a half-hour installment of the series), actors do not have time to learn their lines in advance, so they simply have hidden in their ears a tiny voice receiver, and a man in the cabin behind the set simply reads to them the instructions on what they are to do (what words they are to say, what acts they are to accomplish). Actors are trained to enact immediately, with no delay, these instructions. This is Norman at the end of *Psycho*, and this is also a good lesson to those New Agers who claim that we should drop the social masks and set free our "innermost true selves." We see the final result in Norman who, at the end of *Psycho*, effectively realizes his true self and follows Arthur Rimbaud's motto from his letter to Demeny ("Car je est un autre. Si le cuivre s'éveille clairon, il n'y a rien de sa faute"): If Norman starts to talk with the strange voice of his mother, it's not his fault. The price he has to pay in order to become "really himself," undivided subject, is total alienation, becoming an Other with regard to himself: the obstacle to full self-identity is the very condition of selfhood.

Another aspect of this same antagonism concerns architecture: one can also consider Norman as a subject split between two buildings, the modern horizontal motel and the vertical Gothic mother's house, forever running between the two, never finding a proper place of his own. In this sense, the *unheimlich* character of the film's end means that, in his full identification with the mother, he has finally found his *heim*, his home. In modernist works like *Psycho*, this split is still visible, while the main goal of today's postmodern architecture is to obfuscate it. Suffice it to recall "new urbanism," with its return to small family houses in small towns, with front porches, recreating the cozy atmosphere of the local community; clearly this is the case of architecture as ideology at its purest, providing an imaginary (although "real," materialized in the actual disposition of houses) solution to a real social deadlock that has nothing to do with architecture and all to do with late capitalist dynamics. A more ambiguous case of the same antagonism is the work of Frank Gehry. Why is he so popular, a true cult figure? He takes as the basis one of the two poles of the antagonism, either the old-fashioned family house or a modernist concrete-and-glass building, and then either submits it to a kind of cubist anamorphic distortion (curved angles of walls and windows, etc.) or combines the old family home with a modernist supplement, in which case, as Fredric Jameson has pointed out, the focal point is the place (the room) at the intersection of the two spaces. In short, is Gehry not doing in architecture what the Caduveo Indians (in Claude Levi-Strauss's magnificent description from his *Les Tristes Tropiques*) were trying to achieve with their tatooed faces: to resolve through a symbolic act the "real" of social antagonism by constructing a utopian solution, a mediation between opposites? So here is my final hypothesis: if the Bates Motel were to be built by Gehry, directly combining the old mother's house and the flat modern motel into a new hybrid entity, there would have been no need for Norman to kill his victims, since he would have been relieved of the unbearable tension that compels him to run between the two places—he would have a place of mediation between the two extremes.

6.2 THE MATRIX, OR THE TWO SIDES OF PERVERSION

If, then, Hitchcock's *Psycho* confronts us with the antagonisms of modernity, how are these antagonisms displaced in our postmodern era? Andy and Larry Wachowski's *The Matrix* unwittingly provides the answer. When I saw this film at a local theater in Slovenia, I had the unique opportunity of sitting close to the ideal spectator of the film—namely, an idiot. A man in his late twenties seated to my right was so immersed in the film that he all the time disturbed other spectators with loud exclamations, like "My God, wow, so there is no reality!" I definitely prefer such naive immersion to the pseudosophisticated intellectualist readings that project into the film the refined philosophical or psychoanalytic conceptual distinctions.[18]

It is nonetheless easy to understand this intellectual attraction to *The Matrix*. Is it not that *The Matrix* is one of the films that function as a kind of Rorschach test, setting in motion the universalized process of recognition (like the proverbial painting of God that seems always to stare directly at you, from whichever angle you view it), that practically every orientation seems to recognize itself in it? My Lacanian friends are telling me that the authors must have read Lacan; the Frankfurt School partisans see in *The Matrix* the extrapolated embodiment of Kulturindustrie, the alienated-reified social substance (of capital) directly taking over, colonizing our inner life itself, using us as the source of energy; New Agers see it in the source of speculations on how our world is just a mirage generated by a global Mind embodied in the World Wide Web. This series goes back to Plato's *Republic*: does *The Matrix* not repeat exactly Plato's *dispositif* of the cave (ordinary humans as prisoners, tied firmly to their seats and compelled to watch the shadowy performance of what is falsely considered to be reality)? The important difference, of course, is that when some individuals escape their cave predicament and step out to the surface of the Earth, what they find there is no longer the bright surface illuminated by the rays of the sun, the supreme good, but the desolate "desert of the real." The key opposition is here the one between the Frankfurt school and Lacan: should we historicize *The Matrix* into the metaphor of the capital that colonized culture and subjectivity, or is it the reification of the symbolic order as such? What if, however, this very alternative is false? What if the virtual character of the symbolic order *as such* is the very condition of historicity?

Reaching the end of the world

The idea of the hero living in a totally manipulated and controlled artificial universe is hardly original: *The Matrix* just radicalizes it by bringing in virtual reality (VR). The point here is the radical ambiguity of VR with regard to the problematic of iconoclasm. On the one hand, VR marks the radical reduction of the wealth of our sensory experience to not even letters, but the minimal digital series of 0 and 1, of the passing and not-passing of the electrical signal. On the other hand, this very digital machine generates the "simulated" experience of reality that tends to become indiscernable from the "real" reality, with the consequence of undermining the very notion of "real" reality—VR is thus, at the same time, the most radical assertion of the seductive power of images.

Is not the ultimate American paranoiac fantasy that of an individual living in a small idyllic Florida city, a consummerist paradise, who suddenly starts to suspect that the world he lives in is a fake, a spectacle staged to convince him that he lives in a real world, while all people around him are effectively actors and extras in a gigantic show? The most recent example of this is Peter Weir's *The Truman Show* (1998), with Jim Carrey playing the small town clerk who gradually discovers that he is the protagonist of a twenty-four-hour TV series: his hometown is constructed on a gigantic studio set, with cameras following him constantly. Peter Sloterdijk's "sphere" is here literally realized as the gigantic metal sphere that envelopes and isolates Truman's entire city. This final shot of *The Truman Show* may seem to enact the liberating experience of breaking out from the ideological suture of the enclosed universe into its outside, invisible from the ideological inside. However, what if it is precisely this "happy" denouement of the film (let us not forget: applauded by the millions around the world watching the last minutes of the show), with the hero breaking out and, as we are led to believe, soon to join his true love (so that we have again the formula of the production of the couple!), that is ideology at its purest? What if ideology resides in the very belief that, outside the closure of the finite universe, there is some "true reality" to be entered?[19]

Among the predecessors of this notion, it is worth mentioning Philip K. Dick's *Time Out of Joint* (1959), in which a hero living a modest daily life in a small idyllic California city of the late 1950s gradually discovers that the whole town is a fake staged to keep him satisfied. The underlying experience of *Time Out of Joint* and of *The Truman Show* is that the late capitalist consummerist paradise is in its very hyperreality irreal, substanceless, and deprived of material inertia. So it is not only that Hollywood stages a semblance of real life deprived of the weight and inertia of materiality; in the late capitalist consummerist society, "real social life" itself somehow acquires the features of a staged fake, with our neighbors behaving in "real" life as stage actors and extras. The ultimate truth of the capitalist utilitarian despiritualized universe is the dematerialization of the "real life" itself, its reversal into a spectral show.

In the realm of science fiction, one should mention also Brian Aldiss's *Starship*, in which members of a tribe live in a closed world of a tunnel in a giant starship, isolated from the rest of the ship by thick vegetation, unaware that there is a universe beyond; finally, some children penetrate the bushes and reach the world beyond, populated by other tribes. Among the older, more "naive" forerunners, one should mention George Seaton's *36 Hours*, a film from the early 1960s about an American officer (James Garner) who knows all the plans for the D-Day invasion of Normandy and is accidentally taken prisoner by Germans just days before the invasion. Since he is unconscious from an explosion when taken prisoner, the Germans quickly construct for him a replica of a small American military hospital resort, trying to convince him that he now lives in 1950, that America won the war and that he has lost memory for the last six years—the idea being that he can now safely tell all about the invasion plans, in order for the Germans to prepare themselves. Cracks soon appear in this carefully constructed edifice. (Did not Vladimir Lenin himself, in the last two years of his life, live in a similarly controlled environment, in which, as we now know, Stalin had printed for him a specially prepared single copy of *Pravda*, censored of all news that would tell Lenin about the political struggles going on, with the justification that Comrade Lenin should take a rest and not be excited by unnecessary provocations?)

What lurks in the background is, of course, the premodern notion of "arriving at the end of the universe": in the well-known engravings, the surprised wanderers approach the screen/curtain of heaven, a flat surface with painted stars on it, pierce it and reach beyond—it is exactly this that happens at the end of *The Truman Show*. No wonder that the last scene of the film, in which Truman steps up the stairs attached to the wall on which the blue sky horizon is painted and there opens up a door, has a distinct Magrittean touch; is it not that, today, this same sensitivity is returning with a vengeance? Do works like Hans Jürgen Syberberg's *Parsifal*, in which the infinite horizon is also blocked by obviously "artificial" rear projections, not signal that the time of the Cartesian infinite perspective is running out, and that we are returning to a kind of renewed medieval pre-perspective universe? Fredric Jameson has perspicuously drawn attention to the same phenomenon in some of Raymond Chandler's novels and Hitchcock's films: the shore of the Pacific Ocean in *Farewell, My Lovely* functions as a kind of end/limit of the world, beyond which there is an unknown abyss; and it is similar with the vast open valley that stretches out in front of Mount Rushmore's heads when, on the run from their pursuers Eva-Marie Saint and Cary Grant reach the peak of the monument (and into which Saint almost falls before being pulled up by Cary Grant); and one is tempted to add to this series the famous battle scene at a bridge on the Vietnamese/Cambodian frontier in *Apocalypse Now*, where the space beyond the bridge is experienced as the "beyond of our known universe." And how not to recall that the idea that our Earth is not the planet floating in the infinite space, but a circular opening, a hole, within the endless compact mass of eternal ice, with the sun in its center, was one of the favorite Nazi pseudoscientific fantasies (according to some reports, they even considered putting some telescopes on the Sylt Islands in order to observe America)?

The "really existing" big Other

What, then, is *The Matrix*? Simply the Lacanian "big Other," the virtual symbolic order, the network that structures reality for us. This dimension of the "big Other" is that of the constitutive alienation of the subject in the symbolic order: the big Other pulls the strings, the subject doesn't speak, he "is spoken" by the symbolic structure. In short, this "big Other" is the name for the social substance, for all that on account of which the subject never fully dominates the effects of his acts, that is on account of which the final outcome of his activity is always something else with regard to what he aimed at or anticipated. However, it is here crucial to note that, in the key chapters of volume 11 of his *Seminar*, Lacan struggles to delineate the operation that follows alienation and is in a sense its counterpoint, that of separation: alienation *in* the big Other is followed by the separation *from* the big Other. Separation takes place when the subject takes note of how the big Other is in itself inconsistent, purely virtual, "barred," deprived of the thing—and fantasy is an attempt to fill out this lack of the Other, not of the subject (i.e. to (re)constitute the consistency of the big Other). For that reason, fantasy and paranoia are inherently linked: paranoia is at its most elementary a belief into an "Other of the Other", into another Other who, hidden behind the Other of the explicit social texture, programs what appears to us as the unforeseen effects of social life and thus guarantees its consistency: beneath the chaos of market, the degradation of morals, and so on, there is the purposeful strategy of the Jewish plot. This paranoiac stance acquired a further boost with today's digitalization of our daily lives: when our entire (social) existence is progressively externalized/materialized in the big Other of the computer network, it is easy to imagine an evil programmer erasing our digital identity and thus depriving us of our social existence, turning us into non-persons.

Following the same paranoiac twist, the thesis of *The Matrix* is that this big Other is externalized in the really existing megacomputer. There is—there *has* to be—a matrix because "things are not right, opportunities are missed, something goes wrong all the time"; that is, the film's idea is that it is so because there is the matrix that obfuscates the "true" reality that is behind it all. Consequently, the problem with the film is that it is *not* "crazy" enough because it supposes another "real" reality behind our everyday reality sustained by the matrix. However, to avoid the fatal misunderstanding: the inverse notion that "all there is is generated by the matrix," that there is *no* ultimate reality just an infinite series of virtual realities mirroring themselves in each other, is no less ideological. (In the sequels to *The Matrix*, we shall probably learn that the very "desert of the real" is generated by another matrix.) Much more subversive than this multiplication of virtual universes would have been the multiplication of realities themselves—something that would reproduce the paradoxical danger that some physicians see in recent high accelerator experiments. As is well known, scientists are now trying to construct the accelerator capable of smashing together the nuclei of very heavy atoms at nearly the speed of light. The idea is that such a collision will not only shatter the atom's nuclei into their constituent protons and neutrons, but will pulverize the protons and neutrons themselves, leaving a "plasma," a kind of energy soup consisting of loose quark and gluon particles, the building blocks of matter that have never before been studied in such a state, since such a state only existed briefly after the big bang. However, this prospect has given rise to a nightmarish scenario: What if the success of this experiment will create a doomsday machine, a kind of world-devouring monster that will with inexorable necessity annihilate the ordinary matter around itself and thus abolish the world as we know it? The irony of it is that this end of the world, this disintegration of the universe, would be the ultimate irrefutable proof that the tested theory is true, since it would suck all matter into a black hole and then bring about a new universe, to perfectly recreate the big bang scenario.

The paradox is thus that both versions—(1) a subject freely floating from one to another VR, a pure ghost aware that every reality is a fake; and (2) the paranoiac supposition of the real reality beneath the Matrix—are false: they both miss the real. The film is not wrong in insisting that there *is* a real beneath the VR simulation; as Morpheus puts to Neo when he shows him the ruined Chicago landscape, "Welcome to the desert of the real." However, the real is not the "true reality" behind the virtual simulation, but the void that makes reality incomplete/inconsistent, and the function of every symbolic matrix is to conceal this inconsistency—one of the ways to effect this concealment is precisely to claim that, behind the incomplete/inconsistent reality we know, there is another reality with no deadlock of impossibility structuring it.

The big Other doesn't exist

"Big Other" also stands for the field of common sense at which one can arrive after free deliberation; philosophically, its last great version is Jürgen Habermas's communicative community with its regulative ideal of agreement. And it is this big Other that progressively disintegrates today. The expert jargon is presented as an objective insight with which one cannot really argue, and which is simultaneously untranslatable into our common experience. In short, the gap between scientific insight and common sense is unbridgeable, and it is this very gap that elevates scientists into the popular cult-figures of the "subjects supposed to know" (the Stephen Hawking phenomenon). The strict obverse of this objectivity is the way in which, in the cultural matters, we are confronted with the multitude of lifestyles that one cannot translate into each other. This split is perfectly rendered in the phenomenon of cyberspace. Cyberspace was supposed to bring us all together in a global village; however, what effectively happens is that we are bombarded with the multitude of messages belonging to inconsistent and incompatible universes; instead of the global village, the big Other, we get the multitude of "small others," of tribal particular identifications at our choice. To avoid a misunderstanding: Lacan is here far from relativizing science into just one of the arbitrary narratives, ultimately on equal footing with "politically correct" myths and the like: science *does* "touch the real," its knowledge *is* "knowledge in the real"; the deadlock resides simply in the fact that scientific knowledge cannot serve as the *symbolic* "big Other." The gap between modern science and the Aristotelian commonsense philosophical ontology is here insurmountable: it emerges already with Galileo, and is brought to the extreme in quantum physics, where we are dealing with the rules/laws that function, although they cannot ever be retranslated into our experience of representable reality.

The theory of risk society and its global reflexivization is right in its emphasis on how, today, we are at the opposite end of the classical Enlightenment universalist ideology that presupposed that, in the long run, fundamental questions can be resolved by way of the reference to the "objective knowledge" of the experts: when we are confronted with the conflicting opinions about the environmental consequences of a certain new product (say, of genetically modified vegetables), we search in vain for the ultimate expert opinion. And the point is not simply that the real issues are blurred because science is corrupted through financial dependence on large corporations and state agencies; even in themselves, sciences cannot provide the answer. Ecologists predicted fifteen years ago the death of our forests—the problem is now a too-large increase of wood. Where this theory of risk society is too short is in emphasizing the irrational predicament into which this puts us, the common subjects: we are again and again compelled to decide, although we are well aware that we are in no position to decide that our decision will be arbitrary. Ulrich Beck and his followers refer here to the democratic discussion of all options and consensus building. However, this does not resolve the immobilizing dilemma: Why should the democratic discussion in which the majority participates lead to better result, when, cognitively, the ignorance of the majority remains? The political frustration of the majority is thus understandable: they are called to decide, while, at the same time, receiving the message that they are in no position effectively to decide, to objectively weigh the pros and cons. The recourse to "conspiracy theories" is a desperate way out of this deadlock, an attempt to regain a minimum of what Fredric Jameson calls "cognitive mapping."

Jodi Dean[20] drew attention to a curious phenomenon clearly observable in the "dialogue of the mutes" between the official ("serious," academically institutionalized) science and the vast domain of so-called pseudo-sciences, from ufology to those who want to decipher the secrets of the pyramids: one cannot but be struck by how it is the oficial scientists who proceed in a dogmatic dismissive way, while the pseudoscientists refer to facts and argumentation deprived of the common prejudices. Of course, the answer will be here that established scientists speak with the authority of the big Other of the scientific institution; but the problem is that, precisely, this scientific big Other is again and again revealed as a consensual symbolic fiction. So when we are confronted with conspiracy theories, we should proceed in a strict homology to the proper reading of Henry James' *The Turn of the Screw*: we should neither accept the existence of ghosts as part of the (narrative) reality nor reduce them, in a pseudo-Freudian way, to the "projection" of the heroine's hysterical sexual frustrations. Conspiracy theories, of course, are not to be accepted as "fact." However, one should also not reduce them to the phenomenon of modern mass hysteria. Such a notion still relies on the "big Other," on the model of "normal" perception of shared social reality, and thus does not take into account how it is precisely this notion of reality that is undermined today. The problem is not that ufologists and conspiracy theorists regress to a paranoiac attitude unable to accept (social) reality; the problem is that this reality itself is becoming paranoiac. Contemporary experience again and again confronts us with situations in which we are compelled to take note of how our sense of reality and normal attitude toward it is grounded in a symbolic fiction, that is how the big Other that determines what counts as normal and accepted truth—what is the horizon of meaning in a given society—is in no way directly grounded in "facts" as rendered by the scientific "knowledge in the real." Let us take a traditional society in which modern science is not yet elevated into the master discourse: if, in its symbolic space, an individual advocates propositions of modern science, he will be dismissed as "madman." The key point is that it is not enough to say that he is not "really mad," that it is merely the narrow ignorant society that puts him in this position—in a certain way, being treated as a madman, being excluded from the social big Other effectively *equals* being mad. "Madness" is not the designation that can be grounded in a direct reference to "facts" (in the sense that a madman is unable to perceive things the way they really are, since he is caught in his hallucinatory projections), but only with regard to the way an individual relates to the "big Other." Lacan usually emphasizes the opposite aspect of this paradox in that "the madman is not only a beggar who thinks he is a king, but also a king who thinks he is a king," that madness designates the collapse of the distance between the symbolic and the real, an immediate identification with the symbolic mandate; or, to take his other exemplary statement, when a husband is pathologically jealous, obsessed by the idea that his wife sleeps with other men, his obsession remains a pathological feature even if it is proven that he is right and that his wife effectively *does* sleep with other men. The lesson of such paradoxes is clear: pathological jealousy is not a matter of getting the facts false, but of the way these facts are integrated into the subject's libidinal economy. However, what one should assert here is that the same paradox should also be performed as it were in the opposite direction: the society (its socio-symbolic field, the big Other) is "sane" and "normal" even when it is proven factually wrong. (Maybe it was in this sense that Lacan designated himself as "psychotic": he effectively was psychotic insofar as it was not possible to integrate his discourse into the field of the big Other.)

One is tempted to claim, in the Kantian mode, that the mistake of the conspiracy theory is somehow homologous to the "paralogism of the pure reason," to the confusion between the two levels: the suspicion (of the received scientific, social, etc. common sense) as the formal methodological stance, and the positivation of this suspicion in another all-explaining global paratheory.

Screening the real

From another standpoint, *The Matrix* also functions as the "screen" that separates us from the real, that makes the "desert of the real" bearable. However, it is here that we should not forget the radical ambiguity of the Lacanian real: it is not the ultimate referent to be covered/gentrified/domesticated by the screen of fantasy; the real is also and primarily the screen itself as the obstacle that always already distorts our perception of the referent, of the reality "out there." In philosophical terms, therein resides the difference between Immanuel Kant and G. W. F. Hegel: for Kant, the real is the noumenal domain that we perceive "schematized" through the screen of transcendental categories; for Hegel, on the contrary, if we subtract from the thing the distortion of the screen, we lose the thing itself (in religious terms, the death of Christ is the death of the God in himself, not only of his human embodiment)—which is why, for Lacan, who here follows Hegel, the thing in itself is ultimately the gaze, not the perceived object. So, back to *The Matrix:* the matrix itself is the real that distorts our perception of reality.

A reference to Levi-Strauss's exemplary analysis, from his *Structural Anthropology*, of the spatial disposition of buildings in the Winnebago, one of the Great Lake's tribes, might be of some help here. The tribe is divided into two subgroups (*moieties*), "those who are from above" and "those who are from below"; when we ask an individual to draw on a piece of paper, or on sand, the plan of his village (the spatial disposition of cottages), we obtain two quite different answers, depending on his belonging to one or the other subgroup. Both perceive the village as a circle; but for one subgroup, there is within this circle another circle of central houses, so that we have two concentric circles, while for the other subgroup, the circle is split into two by a clear dividing line. In other words, a member of the first subgroup (let us call it "conservative corporatist") perceives the plan of the village as a ring of houses more or less symmetrically disposed around the central temple, whereas a member of the second ("revolutionary antagonistic") subgroup perceives his village as two distinct heaps of houses separated by an invisible frontier.[21] The central point of Levi-Strauss is that this example should in no way entice us into cultural relativism, according to which the perception of social space depends on the observer's group membership: the very splitting into the two "relative" perceptions implies a hidden reference to a constant—not the objective, "actual" disposition of buildings but a traumatic kernel, a fundamental antagonism that inhabitants of the village were unable to symbolize, to account for, to "internalize," to come to terms with; an imbalance in social relations that prevented the community from stabilizing itself into a harmonious whole. The two perceptions of the village's-plan are simply two mutually exclusive endeavors to cope with this traumatic antagonism, to heal its wound via the imposition of a balanced symbolic structure. Is it necessary to add that things stand exactly the same with respect to sexual difference: "masculine" and "feminine" are like the two configurations of houses in the Levi-Straussian village? And in order to dispel the illusion that our "developed" universe is not dominated by the same logic, suffice it to recall the splitting of our political space into left and right: a leftist and a rightist behave exactly like members of the opposite subgroups of the Levi-Straussian village. They not only occupy different places within the political space; each of them perceives differently the very disposition of that space, a leftist as the field that is inherently split by some fundamental antagonism, a rightist as the organic unity of a community disturbed only by foreign intruders.

However, Levi-Strauss makes here a further crucial point: since the two subgroups nonetheless form one and the same tribe, living in the same village, this identity somehow has to be symbolically inscribed, but how, if the entire symbolic articulation, all social institutions, of the tribe are not neutral, but are overdetermined by the fundamental and constitutive antagonistic split? Levi-Strauss's answer is what he ingeniously calls the "zero-institution," a kind of institutional counterpart to the famous mana, the empty signifier with no determinate meaning, since it signifies only the presence of meaning as such in opposition to its absence: a specific institution that has no positive, determinate function. Its only function is the purely negative one of signaling the presence and actuality of social institution as such, in opposition to its absence, to presocial chaos. It is the reference to such a zero-institution that enables all members of the tribe to experience themselves as such, as members of the same tribe. Is, then, this zero-institution not ideology at its purest, that is the direct embodiment of the ideological function of providing a neutral all-encompassing space in which social antagonism is obliterated, in which all members of society can recognize themselves? And is the struggle for hegemony not precisely the struggle for how this zero-institution will be overdetermined, colored by some particular signification? To provide a concrete example: Is not the modern notion of nation such a zero-institution that emerged with the dissolution of social links grounded in direct family or traditional symbolic matrixes, that is, when with the onslaught of modernization, social institutions were less and less grounded in naturalized tradition and more and more experienced as a matter of "contract"?[22] Of special importance is here the fact that national identity is experienced as at least minimally "natural," as a belonging grounded in "blood and soil," and as such opposed to the "artificial" belonging to social institutions proper (state, profession, etc.) premodern institutions functioned as "naturalized" symbolic entities (as institutions grounded in unquestionable traditions), and the moment institutions were conceived as social artifacts the need arose for a "naturalized" zero-institution that would serve as their neutral common ground.

And, back to sexual difference, I am tempted to risk the hypothesis that, perhaps, the same logic of zero-institution should be applied not only to the unity of a society, but also to its antagonistic split: what if sexual difference is ultimately a kind of zero-institution of the social split of humankind, the naturalized minimal zero-difference—a split that, prior to signaling any determinate social difference, signals this difference as such? The struggle for hegemony is then, again, the struggle for how this zero-difference will be overdetermined by other particular social differences. It is against this background that one should read an important, although usually overlooked, feature of Lacan's schema of the signifier: Lacan replaces the standard Saussurean scheme—above the bar the word *arbre*, and beneath it the drawing of a tree)—with two words above the bar, *homme* and *femme*, and, beneath the bar, two identical drawings of a door. In order to emphasize the differential character of the signifier, Lacan first replaces Saussure's single scheme with a signifier's couple, with the opposition man/woman, with the sexual difference; but the true surprise resides in the fact that, at the level of the imaginary referent, *there is no reference*; we do not get some graphic index of the sexual difference, the simplified drawing of a man and a woman, as is usually the case in most of today's restrooms, but *the same* door reproduced twice). Is it possible to state in clearer terms that sexual difference does not designate any biological opposition grounded in "real" properties, but a purely symbolic opposition to which nothing corresponds in the designated objects—nothing but the real of some undefined X that cannot ever be captured by the image of the signified?

Back to Levi-Strauss's example of the two drawings of the village. It is here that one can see in what precise sense the real intervenes through anamorphosis. We have first the "actual," "objective" arrangement of the houses, and then two different symbolizations that both distort in an amamorphic way the actual arrangement. However, the "real" is here not the actual arrangement, but the traumatic core of the social antagonism that distorts the tribe members' view of the actual antagonism. The real is thus the disavowed X on account of which our vision of reality is anamorphically distorted. (And, incidentally, this three-level *dispositif* is strictly homologous to Freud's three-level *dispositif* of the interpretation of dreams: the real kernel of the dream is not the dream's latent thought, which is displaced/translated into the explicit texture of the dream, but the unconscious desire that inscribes itself through the very distortion of the latent thought into the explicit texture.)

And the same goes for today's art scene: in it, the real does *not* return primarily in the guise of the shocking brutal intrusion of excremental objects, mutilated corpses, shit, and so on. These objects are, for sure, out of place, but in order for them to be out of place, the (empty) place must already be here, and this place is rendered by "minimalist" art, starting from Malevich. Therein resides the complicity between the two opposed icons of high modernism, Malevich's *The Black Square on the White Surface* and Marcel Duchamp's display of ready-made objects as works of art. The underlying notion of Duchamp's elevation of an everyday common object into the work of art is that being a work of art is not an inherent property of the object; it is the artist himself who, by preempting the (or, rather, *any*) object and locating it at a certain place, makes it the work of art—being a work of art is not a question of why but where. And what Malevich's minimalist disposition does is simply to render—to *isolate*—this place as such, the empty place (or frame) with the protomagic property of transforming any object that finds itself within its scope into the work of art. In short, there is no Duchamp without Malevich: only after the art practice isolates the frame/place as such, emptied of all its content, can one indulge in the ready-made procedure. Before Malevich, a urinal would have remained just a urinal, even if it were to be displayed in the most distinguished gallery.

The emergence of excremental objects that are out of place is thus strictly correlative to the emergence of the place without any object in it, of the empty frame as such. Consequently, the real in contemporary art has three dimensions, which somehow repeat within the real the triad of imaginary/symbolic/real. The real is first here as the anamorphotic stain, the anamorphotic distortion of the direct image of reality—as a distorted image, as a pure semblance that "subjectivizes" objective reality. Then, the real is here as the empty place, as a structure, a construction that is never here, experiences as such, but can only be retroactively constructed and has to be presupposed as such—the real as symbolic construction. Finally, the real is the obscene excremental object out of place, the real "itself." This last real, if isolated, is a mere fetish whose fascinating/captivating presence masks the structural real—in the same way that in Nazi anti-Semitism, the Jew as excremental object is the real that masks the unbearable "structural" real of the social antagonism. These three dimensions of the real result from the three modes to acquire a distance toward "ordinary" reality: one submits this reality to anamorphic distortion; one introduces an object that has no place in it; one subtracts/erases all content (objects) of reality, so that all that remains is the very empty place these objects were filling in.

The Freudian touch

The falsity of *The Matrix* is perhaps most directly discernible in its designation of Neo as "the One." Who is "the One"? He who is able to see that our everyday reality is not real, but just a codified virtual universe, and who therefore is able to unplug from it, to manipulate and suspend its rules (fly in the air, stop bullets). Crucial for the function of *this* One is his virtualization of reality: reality is an artificial construct whose rules can be suspended or at least rewritten; therein resides the properly paranoiac notion that the One can suspend the resistance of the real ("I can walk through a thick wall, if I really decide it," i.e., that the impossibility for most of us in doing this is reduced to the failure of the subject's will). However, it is here that, again, the film does not go far enough: in the memorable scene in the waiting room of the prophetess who will decide if Neo is the One, a child who is seen twisting a spoon with his mere thoughts tells the surprised Neo that the way to do it is not to convince oneself that one can twist the spoon, but to convince myself that *there is no spoon*. However, what about oneself? Is it not that the further step should have been to accept the Buddhist proposition that oneself, the subject, does not exist?

In order to further specify what is false in *The Matrix*, one should distinguish simple technological impossibility from fantasmatic falsity: time travel is (probably) impossible, but fantasmatic scenarios about it are nonetheless "true" in the way they render libidinal deadlocks. The most improbable narrative twists are usually those which are most strongly libidinally invested. Billy Wilder's underrated *Fedora* tells the story of an elderly Hollywood star who mysteriously retains the beauty of her youthful appearance; a young actor who falls in love with her finally discovers the secret of her eternal youth: the woman who appeared as Fedora is actually her own look-alike daughter who replaced her at a certain point, while the true Fedora lives a secluded life in a lone villa. Fedora organized this replacement (which condemned her daughter to the total identification with the maternal image) so that her stardom will outlive her and continue to shine even after her physical decline. Both the mother and the daughter are thus thoroughly alienated: the mother is excluded from the public space, since her public self is embodied in her daughter; the daughter is allowed to appear in the public space, but deprived of her symbolic identity. Is the very unpalatable, disturbing, taste of the film not due to the fact that it comes all too close to the fantasy? Do we not get here the distilled fantasmatic scenario that underlies Mike Nichols' much more successful *The Graduate*, whose hero is also libidinally split between a mother (Mrs. Robinson) and her daughter?[23]

Consequently, the problem with *The Matrix* is not the scientific naïveté of its tricks: the idea of passing from reality to VR through the phone makes sense, since all we need is a gap/hole through which one can escape. (Perhaps, an even better solution would have been the toilet, as discussed earlier.) The problem is a more radical fantasmatic inconsistency, which erupts most explicitly when Morpheus (the African-American leader of the resistance group who believes that Neo is the One) tries to explain to the still-perplexed Neo what the matrix is, he quite consequently links it to a failure in the structure of the universe:

> MORPHEUS: It's that feeling you have had all your life. That feeling that something was wrong with the world. You don't know what it is but it's there, like a splinter in your mind, driving you mad. . . . The matrix is everywhere, it's all around us, here even in this room. . . . It is the world that has been pulled over your eyes to blind you from the truth.
>
> NEO: What truth?
>
> MORPHEUS: That you are a slave, Neo. That you, like everyone else, was born into bondage . . . kept inside a prison that you cannot smell, taste, or touch. A prison of your mind.

Here the film encounters its ultimate inconsistency: the experience of the lack/inconsistency/obstacle is supposed to bear witness of the fact that what we experience as reality is a fake. However, toward the end of the film, Smith, the agent of the matrix, gives a different, much more Freudian explanation:

> Did you know that the first Matrix was designed to be a perfect human world? Where none suffered, where everyone would be happy? It was a disaster. No one would accept the program. Entire crops [of humans serving as batteries] were lost. Some believed we lacked the programming language to describe your perfect world. But I believe that, as a species, human beings define their reality through suffering and misery. The perfect world was a dream that your primitive cerebrum kept trying to wake up from. Which is why the matrix was redesigned to this, the peak of your civilization.

The imperfection of our world is thus at the same time the sign of its virtuality *and* the sign of its reality. One could effectively claim that the agent Smith (let us not forget: not a human being as other, but the direct virtual embodiment of the Matrix—the big Other—itself) is the stand-in for the figure of the analyst within the universe of the film: his lesson is that the experience of an insurmountable obstacle is the positive condition for us, as humans, to perceive something as reality. Reality is ultimately that which resists.

Staging the Fundamental Fantasy

The further inconsistency concerns death: Why does one "really" die when one dies only in the VR regulated by the matrix? The film provides the obscurantist answer:

> NEO: If you are killed in the Matrix, you die here [i.e., not only in the VR, but also in real life]?
> MORPHEUS: The body cannot live without the mind.

The logic of this solution is that your "real" body can only stay alive (function) in conjunction to the mind, that is, to the mental universe into which you are immersed: so if you are in VR and killed there, this death affects also your real body. The obvious opposite solution (you only really die when you are killed in reality) is also too short. The catch is: is the subject *wholly* immersed into the Matrix-dominated VR or does he know or at least *suspect* the actual state of things? If the answer is yes, then a simple withdrawal into a prelapsarian Adamic state of distance would render us immortal *in VR* and, consequently, Neo who is already liberated from the full immersion in the VR should *survive* the struggle with the agent Smith that takes place *within* the VR controlled by the matrix (in the same way he is able to stop bullets, he should also have been able to derealize blows that wound his body).

It is a well-known fact that the "close door" button in most elevators is a totally disfunctional placebo, placed there just to give the individuals the impression that they are somehow participating, contributing to the speed of the elevator journey. When we push this button, the door closes in exactly the same time as when we just pressed the floor button without "speeding up" the process by pressing also the "close door" button. This extreme and clear case of fake participation is an appropriate metaphor of the participation of individuals in our "postmodern" political process. So we are all the time pressing such buttons, and it is the matrix's incessant activity that coordinates between them and the event that follows (the door closing), while we think the event results from our pushing the button.

The final inconsistency concerns the ambiguous status of the liberation of humanity anounced by Neo in the last scene. As the result of Neo's intervention, there is a "*system failure*" in the matrix; at the same time, Neo addresses people still caught in the matrix as if he is the savior who will teach them how to liberate themselves from the constraints of the matrix—they will be able to break the physical laws, bend metals, fly in the air. However, the problem is that all these "miracles" are possible only if we remain within the VR sustained by the Matrix and merely bend or change its rules. Our "real" status is still that of slaves of the matrix; we, as it were, are merely gaining additional power to change our mental prison rules. So what about exiting from the Matrix altogether and entering the "real reality" in which we are miserable creatures living on the destroyed earth surface?

In an Adornian way, one should claim that these inconsistencies[24] are the film's moment of truth: they signal the antagonisms of our late-capitalist social experience, antagonisms concerning basic ontological pairings like *reality and pain* (reality as that which disturbs the reign of the pleasure principle), *freedom and system* (freedom is only possible within the system that hinders its full deployment). However, the ultimate strength of the film is nonetheless to be located at a different level. Years ago, a series of science fiction films like *Zardoz* and *Logan's Run* forecast today's postmodern predicament: the isolated group living an aseptic life in a secluded area longs for the experience of the real world of material decay. Till postmodernism, utopia was an endeavor to break out of the real of historical time into a timeless otherness. With postmodern overlapping of the "end of history" with full disposability of the past in digitalized memory, in this time where we live the atemporal utopia as everyday ideological experience, utopia becomes the longing for the real of history itself, for memory, for the traces of the real past, the attempt to break out of the closed dome into smell and decay of the raw reality. *The Matrix* gives the final twist to this reversal, combining utopia with dystopia: the very reality we live in, the atemporal utopia staged here is in place so that we can be effectively reduced to a passive state of living batteries providing the matrix with the energy.

The unique impact of the film thus resides not so much in its central thesis (what we experience as reality is an artificial virtual reality generated by the matrix, the megacomputer directly attached to all our minds), but in its central image of the millions of human beings leading claustrophobic lives in water-filled cradles, kept alive in order to generate the energy (electricity) for the matrix. So when (some of the) people "awaken" from their immersion into Matrix-controlled virtual reality, this awakening is not the opening into the wide space of the external reality, but first the horrible realization of this enclosure, where each of us is effectively just a foetus-like organism, immersed in the prenatal fluid. The first association that imposes itself here, of course, is the miserable position of human as the self-reflective allegory of the very position of the cinema viewer: Are we all not, when we sit in the cinema, in the position of humans in *The Matrix*, tied to chairs, immersed in the spectacle run by a machine? However, a more appropriate allegory is that of the viewer himself: beneath the illusion that we "just look" at the perceived objects from a safe distance, freely sliding along them, there is the reality of the innumerable ties that bind us to what we perceive. While just looking, we are always hunting among objects, looking for what we desire or fear, endeavoring to recognize some pattern; on the other hand, objects themselves always "stare back," vie for our attention, throw at us their lures and endeavor to entrap us. As James Elkins explains,

> There is also something quietly hypnotic about just looking, something less like hunting and more like dreaming. It is as if the looker were Gulliver, tied to the beach by the Lilliputians but still dreaming he's in England having a nice time, perhaps out for a stroll, but beginning to notice in some dull way that it's hard to move—it's inexplicably difficult to just walk down that street in London, to reach out and turn that doorknob—and then waking up and discovering himself in a much worse nightmare. But unlike Gulliver, I never really wake up. Just looking is like dreaming, but dreaming fitfully, tossing and turning and not knowing quite what's happening."[25]

Does this phenomenological description of the stance of "just looking" not uncannily echo the dispositif of humans in *The Matrix*?

However, one is tempted to reverse the relationship between "illusion" and "reality" implied by this description and to claim that the utter passivity of humans in *The Matrix* stages the foreclosed fantasy that sustains our conscious experience as active, self-positing subjects—it renders the ultimate perverse fantasy, the notion that we are ultimately instruments of the Other's (the matrix's) jouissance, sucked of our life substance like batteries. Therein resides the true libidinal enigma of this *dispositif*: Why does the matrix need human energy? The purely energetic solution is, of course, meaningless: the matrix could have easily found another, more reliable, source of energy that would not have demanded the extremely complex arrangement of the virtual reality coordinated for millions of human units. (Another inconsistency is discernible here: Why does the matrix not immerse each individual into her own solipsistic artificial universe? Why complicate matters with coordinating the programs so that the entire humanity inhabits one and the same virtual universe?) The only consistent answer is: the matrix feeds on the human's jouissance—so we are here back at the fundamental Lacanian thesis that the big Other itself, far from being an anonymous machine, needs the constant influx of jouissance.

The intimate connection between perversion and cyberspace is today a commonplace. According to the standard view, the perverse scenario stages the "disavowal of castration": perversion can be seen as a defense against the motif of death and sexuality, against the threat of mortality as well as the contingent imposition of sexual difference. What the pervert enacts is a universe in which, as in cartoons, a human being can survive any catastrophe; in which adult sexuality is reduced to a childish game; in which one is not forced to die or to choose one of the two sexes. As such, the pervert's universe is the universe of pure symbolic order, of the signifier's game running its course, unencumbered by the real of human finitude. In a first approach, it may seem that our experience of cyberspace fits perfectly this universe: Isn't cyberspace also a universe unencumbered by the inertia of the real, constrained only by its self-imposed rules? And is it not the same with virtual reality in *The Matrix*? The "reality" in which we live loses its inexorable character, becomes a domain of arbitrary rules (imposed by the matrix) that one can violate if one's will is strong enough. However, according to Lacan, what this standard notion leaves out of consideration is the unique relationship between the Other and the jouissance in perversion. What, exactly, does this mean?

In "Le prix du progres," one of the fragments that conclude *The Dialectic of Enlightenment*, Theodor Adorno and Max Horkheimer quote the argumentation of the nineteenth century French physiologist Pierre Flourens against medical anesthesia with chloroform: Flourens claims that it can be proven that the anaesthetic works only on our memory's neuronal network. In short, while we are butchered alive on the operating table, we fully feel the terrible pain, but later, after awakening, we do not remember it. For Adorno and Horkheimer, this, of course, is the perfect metaphor of the fate of reason based on the repression of nature in itself: his body, the part of nature in the subject, fully feels the pain; it is only that, due to repression, the subject does not remember it. Therein resides the perfect revenge of nature for our domination over it: unknowingly, we are our own greatest victims, butchering ourselves alive. Isn't it also possible to read this as the perfect fantasy scenario of interpassivity, of the Other scene in which we pay the price for our active intervention into the world? There is no active free agent without this fantasmatic support, without this Other scene in which one is totally manipulated by the Other.[26] A sadomasochist willingly assumes this suffering as the access to being.

Perhaps, it is along these lines that one can also explain the obsession of Adolf Hilter's biographers with his relationship to his niece Geli Raubal who was found dead in Hitler's Munich appartment in 1931, as if Hitler's alleged sexual perversion will provide the "hidden variable," the intimate missing link, the fantasmatic support that would account for his public personality. Here is this scenario as reported by Otto Strasser:

> Hitler made her undress [while] he would lie down on the floor. Then she would have to squat down over his face where he could examine her at close range, and this made him very excited. When the excitement reached its peak, he demanded that she urinate on him, and that gave him his pleasure."[27]

Crucial is here the utter passivity of Hitler's role in this scenario as the fantasmatic support that pushed him into his frenetically destructive public political activity; no wonder Geli was desperate and disgusted at these rituals.

Therein resides the correct insight of *The Matrix*: in its juxtaposition of the two aspects of perversion—on the one hand, reduction of reality to a virtual domain regulated by arbitrary rules that can be suspended, and on the other the concealed truth of this freedom, the reduction of the subject to an utter instrumentalized passivity. In other words, *The Matrix* gets it right, but in a wrong (inverted) way. That is, we just have to turn around the terms in order to get at the true state of things: what the film renders as the scene of our awakening into our true situation is effectively its exact opposition, the very fundamental fantasy that sustains our being. We are not dreaming in VR that we are free agents in our everyday common reality, while we are actually passive prisoners in the prenatal fluid exploited by the matrix; it is rather that our reality *is* that of the free agents in the social world we know, but in order to sustain this situation, we have to supplement it with the disavowed, terrible, impending fantasy of being passive prisoners in the prenatal fluid exploited by the matrix. The mystery of the human condition, of course, is *why* the subject needs this obscene fantasmatic support of his existence.

NOTES

1 The *Shakespeare Made Easy*, series is edited by Alan Durband and published by Barrons Educational Series publishers.
2 During the public discussion at the Hitchcock Centenary Conference organized by NYU, October 12–17, 1999.
3 See Sigmund Freud, "The Psychogenesis of a Case of Homosexuality in a Woman," *The Pelican Freud Library*, vo. 9: *Case Histories II* (Harmondsworth, U.K.: Penguin, 1979), 389.
4 For a more detailed account of this Hitchcockian sinthom, see Slavoj Žižek, ed., *Everything You Always Wanted to Know About Lacan (But Were Afraid to Ask Hitchcock)* (London: Verso, 1993).
5 Svetlana Alliluyeva, *Twenty Letters To a Friend* (New York: Simon and Schuster, 1967), 183.
6 David Bordwell and Noel Carroll, eds., *Post-Theory*, Madison: University of Wisconsin Press, 1996).

7 Jacques Lacan, *The Seminar*, book 1: *Freud's Papers* and *Technique* (New York: Norton 1988), 215. I rely here on Miran Bozovic, "The Man Behind His Own Retina," in Slavoj Žižek, ed., *Everything You Always Wanted to Know About Lacan (But Were Afraid to Ask Hitchcock).*

8 See the fascinating report in Thomas Schatz, *The Genius of the System* (New York: Henry Holt, 1996), 393–403.

9 See Stephen Jay Gould, *Wonderful Life: The Burgess Shale and the Nature of History* (New York: Norton 1989).

10 See Niall Ferguson, ed., Virtual History (London: Macmillan 1997).

11 Perhaps the greatest achievement of van Sant's remake is the scene during the final credits, which follows the shot that ends Hitchcock's film and goes on for many minutes—a continuous crane shot showing what goes on around the car being dragged out of the swamp, the bored policemen around the towing truck, all accompanied by a soft guitar repeating in an improvised way the main motif of Bernard Herrmann's score. This feature supplements the film with the unique touch of the 1990s.

12 In an interview Hitchcock once boasted that he always left the restroom so clean that no one would have guessed, upon inspecting it, that he had been there. This obsession also accounts for the obvious pleasure-in-disgust Hitchcock finds in the small filthy details that characterize the Cuban mission in Harlem in *Topaz*, like the official diplomatic document stained by the grease from a sandwich.

13 Is this sudden appearance not similar to Wagner's Tristan? Toward the very end of *Tristan und Isolde*, after Tristan's death, Isolde's arrival and plunging into the death trance, the break occurs with the arrival of another, second, ship, when the slow progress all of a sudden accelerates in an almost comic way. In five minutes, more events happen than in all the opera that has preceded. This is similar to Giuseppe Verdi's *Il Trovatore*, in which, in the last two minutes a whole package of things happen. Such unexpected intrusions just before the ending are crucial for the reading of the underlying tensions of a narrative.

14 When Lesley Brill claims that in *Under Capricorn* is a kind of underworld creature trying to drag Ingrid Bergman back into hell, one is tempted to say that the nun who appears at the very end of *Vertigo* belongs to the same evil netherworld—the paradox being, of course, that is a *nun*, a woman of God, who embodies the force of evil that drags the subject down and prevents her salvation.

15 François Truffaut, *Hitchcock* (New York: Simon and Schuster 1985), 257.

16 It's similar with the saliva: as we all know, although we can without problem swallow our own saliva, we find it extremely repulsuve to swallow again a saliva that has been spit out of our body—again a case of violating the inside/outside frontier.

17 I owe this observation to Boris Groys.

18 If one compares the original script (available on the Internet) with the film

itself, one can see that the directors (the Wachowski brothers, who also authored the script) were intelligent enough to throw out too-direct pseudointellectual references, as in the following exchange: "Look at 'em. Automatons. Don't think about what they're doing or why. Computer tells 'em what to do and they do it." "The banality of evil." This pretentious reference to Hannah Arendt totally misses the point: people immersed in the VR of the matrix are in an entirely different, almost opposite, position in comparison with the executioners of the holocaust. Another similar wise move was to drop the all-too-obvious references to the Eastern techniques of emptying one's mind as the way to escape the control of the matrix: "You have to learn to let go of that anger. You must let go of everything. You must empty yourself to free your mind." 19It is also crucial that what enables the hero of *The Truman Show* to see through and exit his manipulated world is the unforeseen intervention of his father. There are two paternal figures in the film, the actual symbolic-biological father and the paranoiac "real" father, the director of the TV show (played by Ed Harris), who totally manipulates Truman's life and protects him in the closed environment, played by Ed Harris.

20 On whom I rely extensively here: see Jodi Dean, *Aliens in America: Conspiracy Cultures from Outerspace to Cyberspace* (Ithaca, NY: Cornell University Press, 1998).

21 Claude Levi-Strauss, "Do Dual Organizations Exist?" in *Structural Anthropology* (New York: Basic Books 1963), 131–63; the drawings are on pages 133–34.

22 See Rastko Močnik, "Das 'Subjekt, dem unterstellt wird zu glauben' und die Nation als eine Null-Institution," in *Denk-Prozesse nach Althusser*, edited by H. Boke (Hamburg: Argument Verlag 1994).

23 The final scene of *The Graduate*, with Ben and Elaine (Mrs. Robinson's daughter) disturbing the marriage ceremony and eloping, is thus far from being transgressive with regard to the common bourgeois morality. On the contrary, it stands for the constitution of the normal heterosexual couple, while the true transgressive sexual link is that between Ben and Mrs. Robinson.

24 A further pertinent inconsistency also concerns the status of intersubjectivity in the universe run by the matrix: do all individuals share the *same* virtual reality? *why*? Why not to each her preferred own?

25 James Elkins, *The Object Stares Back* (New York: Harvest 1996), 20.

26 What Hegel does is to "traverse" this fantasy by demonstrating its function of filling in the preontological abyss of freedom, i.e. of reconstituting the positive scene in which the subject is inserted into a positive noumenal order. In other words, for Hegel, Kant's vision is meaningless and inconsistent, since it secretly reintroduces the ontologically fully constituted divine totality, i.e. a world conceived only as substance, not also as subject.

27 Quoted in Ron Rosenbaum, *Explaining Hitler* (New York: HarperCollins 1999), 134.

INDEX

Page references to footnotes will be illustrated by the letter 'n' and note number following the page reference.

For Product Safety Concerns and Information please contact our EU representative GPSR@taylorandfrancis.com Taylor & Francis Verlag GmbH, Kaufingerstraße 24, 80331 München, Germany

Batch number: 10725863

Printed by Printforce, the Netherlands